W9-AUI-930

Explore Your World!

Focus on case studies to understand your world.

To learn about **Latin America**, you will take a close look at specific countries. In each case study, the story of that country will be told through an important world theme—such as the relationship between people and their environment or a nation's quest for independence. After studying each country, you can apply what you've learned to understand other parts of the world.

Interact with exciting online activities.

Journey to different parts of the world by using dynamic online activities on geography, history and culture. Use the web codes listed in the Go Online boxes and in the chart below to tour this region.

Latin America Activities

Web Code	Activity
	History Interactive
lfd-1700	Tour a Maya City
lfp-1701	Learn More About Maya Achievements
lfp-1702	Tour the Panama Canal
lfp-1704	Travel Along the Inca Roads
lfp-1711	Explore Templo Mayor
	MapMaster
lfp-1703	Aztec Empire
lfd-1705	Maya Cities
lfp-1706	Inca Empire
lfp-1707	Geography of South America
lfp-1708	Geography of Mexico
lfp-1709	Geography of Mesoamerica
lfp-1710	New Nations of Latin America
lfp-1712	Maya Cities
lfp-1713	The Seasons

Go Online
PHSchool.com

For: An activity on South American culture
Visit: PHSchool.com
Web Code: lfd-1303

Get hands-on with the Geographer's Apprentice Activity Pack.

Explore the geography, history and culture of the world's regions through hands-on activities. Each activity pack includes maps, data and primary sources to make learning geography fun!

PRENTICE HALL
WORLD STUDIES
LATIN AMERICA

Geography • History • Culture

In association with DK

Discovery CHANNEL SCHOOL

PEARSON
Prentice Hall

Boston, Massachusetts
Upper Saddle River, New Jersey

Program Consultants

Heidi Hayes Jacobs

Heidi Hayes Jacobs, Ed.D., has served as an education consultant to more than 1,000 schools across the nation and abroad. Dr. Jacobs serves as an adjunct professor in the Department of Curriculum on Teaching at Teachers College, Columbia University. She has written two best-selling books and numerous articles on curriculum reform. She received an M.A. from the University of Massachusetts, Amherst, and completed her doctoral work at Columbia University's Teachers College in 1981. The core of Dr. Jacobs' experience comes from her years teaching high school, middle school, and elementary school students. As an educational consultant, she works with K–12 schools and districts on curriculum reform and strategic planning.

Michal L. LeVasseur

Michal LeVasseur is the Executive Director of the National Council for Geographic Education. She is an instructor in the College of Education at Jacksonville State University and works with the Alabama Geographic Alliance. Her undergraduate and graduate work were in the fields of anthropology (B.A.), geography (M.A.), and science education (Ph.D.). Dr. LeVasseur's specialization has moved increasingly into the area of geography education. Since 1996 she has served as the Director of the National Geographic Society's Summer Geography Workshops. As an educational consultant, she has worked with the National Geographic Society as well as with schools and organizations to develop programs and curricula for geography.

Senior Reading Consultants

Kate Kinsella

Kate Kinsella, Ed.D., is a faculty member in the Department of Secondary Education at San Francisco State University. A specialist in second-language acquisition and content area literacy, she consults nationally on school-wide practices that support adolescent English learners and striving readers to make academic gains. Dr. Kinsella earned her M.A. in TESOL from San Francisco State University, and her Ed.D. in Second Language Acquisition from the University of San Francisco.

Kevin Feldman

Kevin Feldman, Ed.D., is the Director of Reading and Early Intervention with the Sonoma County Office of Education (SCOE) and an independent educational consultant. At the SCOE, he develops, organizes, and monitors programs related to K–12 literacy. Dr. Feldman has an M.A. from the University of California, Riverside in Special Education, Learning Disabilities and Instructional Design. He earned his Ed.D. in Curriculum and Instruction from the University of San Francisco.

Acknowledgments appear on pages 233–234, which constitutes an extension of this copyright page.

Copyright © 2008 by Pearson Education, Inc., publishing as Pearson Prentice Hall, Boston, Massachusetts 02116. All rights reserved. Printed in the United States of America. This publication is protected by copyright, and permission should be obtained from the publisher prior to any prohibited reproduction, storage in a retrieval system, or transmission in any form or by any means, electronic, mechanical, photocopying, recording, or likewise. For information regarding permission(s), write to: Rights and Permissions Department, One Lake Street, Upper Saddle River, New Jersey 07458.

MapMaster™ is a trademark of Pearson Education, Inc.
Pearson Prentice Hall™ is a trademark of Pearson Education, Inc.
Pearson® is a registered trademark of Pearson plc.
Prentice Hall® is a registered trademark of Pearson Education, Inc.
Discovery Channel School® is a registered trademark of Discovery Communications, Inc.

DK is a registered trademark of Dorling Kindersley Limited.
Prentice Hall World Studies is published in collaboration with DK Designs, Dorling Kindersley Limited, 80 Strand, London WC2R 0RL. A Penguin Company.

ISBN 0-13-204148-0
345678910   12 11 10 09 08

Cartography Consultant
DK Andrew Heritage

Andrew Heritage has been publishing atlases and maps for more than 25 years. In 1991, he joined the leading illustrated nonfiction publisher Dorling Kindersley (DK) with the task of building an international atlas list from scratch. The DK atlas list now includes some 10 titles, which are constantly updated and appear in new editions either annually or every other year.

Academic Reviewers

Africa
Barbara B. Brown, Ph.D.
African Studies Center
Boston University
Boston, Massachusetts

Ancient World
Evelyn DeLong Mangie, Ph.D.
Department of History
University of South Florida
Tampa, Florida

Central Asia and the Middle East
Pamela G. Sayre
History Department,
    Social Sciences Division
Henry Ford Community College
Dearborn, Michigan

East Asia
Huping Ling, Ph.D.
History Department
Truman State University
Kirksville, Missouri

Eastern Europe
Robert M. Jenkins, Ph.D.
Center for Slavic, Eurasian and
    East European Studies
University of North Carolina
Chapel Hill, North Carolina

Latin America
Dan La Botz
Professor, History Department
Miami University
Oxford, Ohio

Medieval Times
James M. Murray
History Department
University of Cincinnati
Cincinnati, Ohio

North Africa
Barbara E. Petzen
Center for Middle Eastern Studies
Harvard University
Cambridge, Massachusetts

Religion
Charles H. Lippy, Ph.D.
Department of Philosophy
    and Religion
University of Tennessee
    at Chattanooga
Chattanooga, Tennessee

Russia
Janet Vaillant
Davis Center for Russian
    and Eurasian Studies
Harvard University
Cambridge, Massachusetts

United States and Canada
Victoria Randlett
Geography Department
University of Nevada, Reno
Reno, Nevada

Western Europe
Ruth Mitchell-Pitts
Center for European Studies
University of North Carolina
    at Chapel Hill
Chapel Hill, North Carolina

Reviewers

Sean Brennan
Brecksville-Broadview Heights
    City School District
Broadview Heights, Ohio

Stephen Bullick
Mt. Lebanon School District
Pittsburgh, Pennsylvania

Louis P. De Angelo, Ed.D.
Archdiocese of Philadelphia
Philadelphia, Pennsylvania

Paul Francis Durietz
Social Studies
    Curriculum Coordinator
Woodland District #50
Gurnee, Illinois

Gail Dwyer
Dickerson Middle School,
    Cobb County
Marietta, Georgia

Michal Howden
Social Studies Consultant
Zionsville, Indiana

Rosemary Kalloch
Springfield Public Schools
Springfield, Massachusetts

Deborah J. Miller
Office of Social Studies,
    Detroit Public Schools
Detroit, Michigan

Steven P. Missal
Plainfield Public Schools
Plainfield, New Jersey

Catherine Fish Petersen
Social Studies Consultant
Saint James, Long Island, New York

Joe Wieczorek
Social Studies Consultant
Baltimore, Maryland

Table of Contents

LATIN AMERICA

▊ Develop Skills

Use these pages to develop your reading, writing, and geography skills.

Build a Regional Background

Learn about the geography, history, and culture of the region.

v

Focus on Countries

Create an understanding of the region by focusing
on specific countries.

MAP MASTER	**DK**	**DISCOVERY CHANNEL SCHOOL** Video/DVD	**Interactive Textbook**
• Learn map skills with the MapMaster Skills Handbook. • Practice your skills with every map in this book. • Interact with every map online and on CD-ROM.	Maps and illustrations created by DK help build your understanding of the world. The DK World Desk Reference Online keeps you up to date.	The *World Studies* Video Program takes you on field trips to study countries around the world.	The *World Studies* Interactive Textbook online and on CD-ROM uses interactive maps and other activities to help you learn.

Special Features

COUNTRY DATABANK

Read about all the countries that make up Latin America.

Literature

A selection by a Latin American author brings social studies to life.

COUNTRY PROFILES

Theme-based maps and charts provide a closer look at countries, regions, and provinces.

Links

See the fascinating links between social studies and other disciplines.

Skills for Life

Learn skills that you will use throughout your life.

Target Reading Skills

Chapter-by-chapter reading skills help you read and understand social studies concepts.

Citizen Heroes

Meet people who have made a difference in their country.

DK Eyewitness Technology

Detailed drawings show how technology shapes places and societies.

Discovery Channel School Video/DVD

Explore the geography, history, and cultures of the countries of Latin America.

Maps and Charts

MAP★MASTER™

MAP★MASTER™ Interactive

Go online to find an interactive version of every MapMaster map in this book. Use the Web Code provided to gain direct access to these maps.

How to Use Web Codes:

1. Go to **www.PHSchool.com**.
2. Enter the Web Code.
3. Click Go!

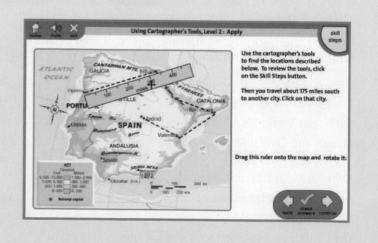

Building Geographic Literacy

Learning about a country often starts with finding it on a map. The MapMaster™ system in *World Studies* helps you develop map skills you will use throughout your life. These three steps can help you become a MapMaster!

The MAP★MASTER™ System

1 Learn

You need to learn geography tools and concepts before you explore the world. Get started by using the MapMaster Skills Handbook to learn the skills you need for success.

MAP★MASTER™ Skills Activity

Location The Equator runs through parts of Latin America, but it is far from other parts of the region.

Locate Find the Equator on the map. Which climates are most common in Latin America, and how far is each climate region from the Equator?

Draw Conclusions How do climates change as you move away from the Equator?

Go Online
PHSchool.com Use Web Code lfp-1142 for step-by-step map skills practice.

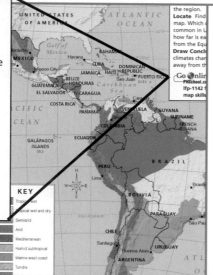

2 Practice

You need to practice and apply your geography skills frequently to be a MapMaster. The maps in *World Studies* give you the practice you need to develop geographic literacy.

3 Interact

Using maps is more than just finding places. Maps can teach you many things about a region, such as its climate, its vegetation, and the languages that the people who live there speak. Every MapMaster map is online at **PHSchool.com,** with interactive activities to help you learn the most from every map.

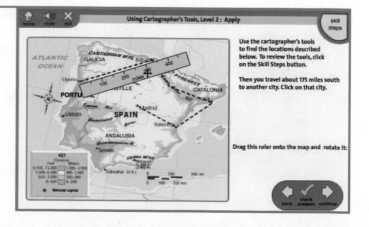

Learning With Technology

You will be making many exciting journeys across time and place in *World Studies*. Technology will help make what you learn come alive.

Go Online
PHSchool.com

For: An activity on South American culture
Visit: PHSchool.com
Web Code: lfd-1303

For a complete list of features for this book, use Web Code lfk-1000.

Go Online at PHSchool.com

Use the Web Codes listed below and in each Go Online box to access exciting information or activities.

How to Use the Web Code:
1. Go to **www.PHSchool.com**.
2. Enter the Web Code.
3. Click Go!

Latin America Activities

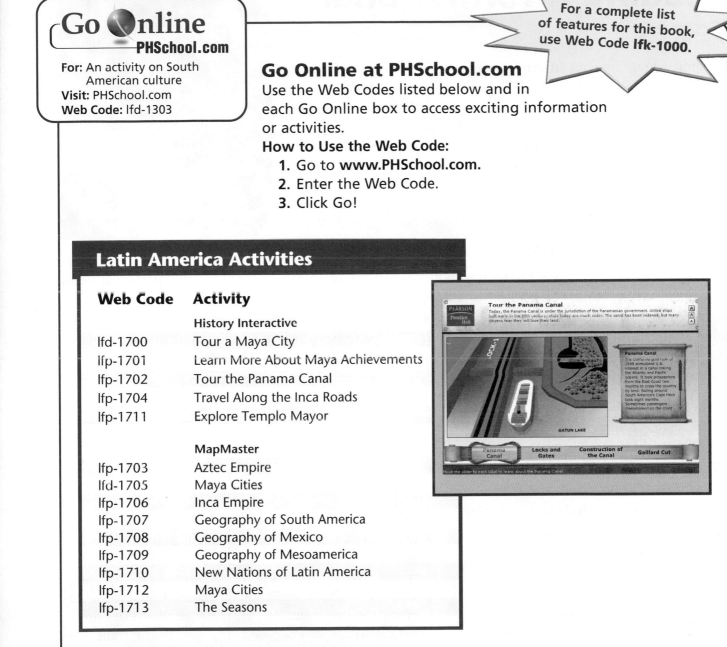

Tour the Panama Canal
Today, the Panama Canal is under the jurisdiction of the Panamanian government. Unlike ships built early in the 20th century, ships today are much wider. The canal has been widened, but many citizens fear they will lose their land.

Panama Canal
The California gold rush of 1849 stimulated U.S. interest in a canal linking the Atlantic and Pacific oceans. It took prospectors from the East Coast two months to cross the country by land. Sailing around South America's Cape Horn took eight months. Sometimes passengers disembarked on the coast.

GATUN LAKE

Panama Canal | Locks and Gates | Construction of the Canal | Gaillard Cut

Web Code	Activity
	History Interactive
lfd-1700	Tour a Maya City
lfp-1701	Learn More About Maya Achievements
lfp-1702	Tour the Panama Canal
lfp-1704	Travel Along the Inca Roads
lfp-1711	Explore Templo Mayor
	MapMaster
lfp-1703	Aztec Empire
lfd-1705	Maya Cities
lfp-1706	Inca Empire
lfp-1707	Geography of South America
lfp-1708	Geography of Mexico
lfp-1709	Geography of Mesoamerica
lfp-1710	New Nations of Latin America
lfp-1712	Maya Cities
lfp-1713	The Seasons

 ## World Desk Reference Online

There are more than 190 countries in the world. To learn about them, you need the most up-to-date information and statistics.
The **DK World Desk Reference Online** gives you instant access to the information you need to explore each country.

Reading Informational Texts

Reading a magazine, an Internet page, or a textbook is not the same as reading a novel. The purpose of reading nonfiction texts is to acquire new information. On page M18 you'll read about some  Target Reading Skills that you'll have a chance to practice as you read this textbook. Here we'll focus on a few skills that will help you read nonfiction with a more critical eye.

Analyze the Author's Purpose

Different types of materials are written with different purposes in mind. For example, a textbook is written to teach students information about a subject. The purpose of a technical manual is to teach someone how to use something, such as a computer. A newspaper editorial might be written to persuade the reader to accept a particular point of view. A writer's purpose influences how the material is presented. Sometimes an author states his or her purpose directly. More often, the purpose is only suggested, and you must use clues to identify the author's purpose.

Distinguish Between Facts and Opinions

It's important when reading informational texts to read actively and to distinguish between fact and opinion. A fact can be proven or disproven. An opinion cannot—it is someone's personal viewpoint or evaluation.

For example, the editorial pages in a newspaper offer opinions on topics that are currently in the news. You need to read newspaper editorials with an eye for bias and faulty logic. For example, the newspaper editorial at the right shows factual statements in blue and opinion statements in red. The underlined words are examples of highly charged words. They reveal bias on the part of the writer.

> More than 5,000 people voted last week in favor of building a new shopping center, but the opposition won out. The margin of victory is irrelevant. Those <u>radical</u> voters who opposed the center are obviously <u>self-serving elitists</u> who do not care about anyone but themselves.
>
> This month's unemployment figure for our area is 10 percent, which represents an increase of about 5 percent over the figure for this time last year. These figures mean unemployment is getting worse. But the people who voted against the mall probably do not care about creating new jobs.

Identify Evidence

Before you accept an author's conclusion, you need to make sure that the author has based the conclusion on enough evidence and on the right kind of evidence. An author may present a series of facts to support a claim, but the facts may not tell the whole story. For example, what evidence does the author of the newspaper editorial on the previous page provide to support his claim that the new shopping center would create more jobs? Is it possible that the shopping center might have put many small local businesses out of business, thus increasing unemployment rather than decreasing it?

Evaluate Credibility

Whenever you read informational texts, you need to assess the credibility of the author. This is especially true of sites you may visit on the Internet. All Internet sources are not equally reliable. Here are some questions to ask yourself when evaluating the credibility of a Web site.

☐ Is the Web site created by a respected organization, a discussion group, or an individual?

☐ Does the Web site creator include his or her name as well as credentials and the sources he or she used to write the material?

☐ Is the information on the site balanced or biased?

☐ Can you verify the information using two other sources?

☐ Is there a date telling when the Web site was created or last updated?

Writing for Social Studies

Writing is one of the most powerful communication tools you will ever use. You will use it to share your thoughts and ideas with others. Research shows that writing about what you read actually helps you learn new information and ideas. A systematic approach to writing—including prewriting, drafting, revising, and proofing—can help you write better, whether you're writing an essay or a research report.

Narrative Essays

Writing that tells a story about a personal experience

1 Select and Narrow Your Topic

A narrative is a story. In social studies, it might be a narrative essay about how an event affected you or your family.

2 Gather Details

Brainstorm a list of details you'd like to include in your narrative.

3 Write a First Draft

Start by writing a simple opening sentence that conveys the main idea of your essay. Continue by writing a colorful story that has interesting details. Write a conclusion that sums up the significance of the event or situation described in your essay.

4 Revise and Proofread

Check to make sure you have not begun too many sentences with the word *I*. Replace general words with more colorful ones.

Main idea →
Details →
Significance of narrative →

In my last year of college, I volunteered for an organization called Amigos De Las Americas (Friends of the Americas). I was sent to a remote village in Brazil and worked with villagers to improve the community's water supply and sanitation systems. The experience made me realize I wanted to work in the field of public health. When I went to Brazil, I never imagined what an incredible sense of purpose it would add to my life.

Persuasive Essays

Writing that supports an opinion or position

① Select and Narrow Your Topic

Choose a topic that provokes an argument and has at least two sides. Choose a side. Decide which argument will appeal most to your audience and persuade them to understand your point of view.

② Gather Evidence

Create a chart that states your position at the top and then lists the pros and cons for your position below, in two columns. Predict and address the strongest arguments against your stand.

③ Write a First Draft

Write a strong thesis statement that clearly states your position. Continue by presenting the strongest arguments in favor of your position and acknowledging and refuting opposing arguments.

④ Revise and Proofread

Check to make sure you have made a logical argument and that you have not oversimplified the argument.

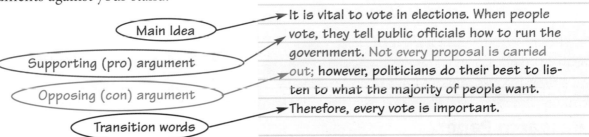

Main Idea

Supporting (pro) argument

Opposing (con) argument

Transition words

It is vital to vote in elections. When people vote, they tell public officials how to run the government. Not every proposal is carried out; however, politicians do their best to listen to what the majority of people want. Therefore, every vote is important.

Expository Essays

Writing that explains a process, compares and contrasts, explains causes and effects, or explores solutions to a problem

1 Identify and Narrow Your Topic

Expository writing is writing that explains something in detail. It might explain the similarities and differences between two or more subjects (compare and contrast). It might explain how one event causes another (cause and effect). Or it might explain a problem and describe a solution.

2 Gather Evidence

Create a graphic organizer that identifies details to include in your essay.

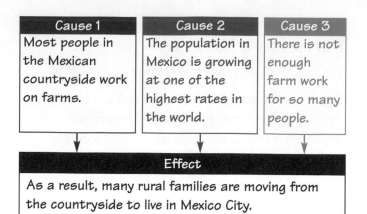

Cause 1	Cause 2	Cause 3
Most people in the Mexican countryside work on farms.	The population in Mexico is growing at one of the highest rates in the world.	There is not enough farm work for so many people.

Effect

As a result, many rural families are moving from the countryside to live in Mexico City.

3 Write Your First Draft

Write a topic sentence and then organize the essay around your similarities and differences, causes and effects, or problem and solutions. Be sure to include convincing details, facts, and examples.

4 Revise and Proofread

Research Papers

Writing that presents research about a topic

1 Narrow Your Topic

Choose a topic you're interested in and make sure that it is not too broad. For example, instead of writing a report on Panama, write about the construction of the Panama Canal.

2 Acquire Information

Locate several sources of information about the topic from the library or the Internet. For each resource, create a source index card like the one at the right. Then take notes using an index card for each detail or subtopic. On the card, note which source the information was taken from. Use quotation marks when you copy the exact words from a source.

Source #1
McCullough, David. *The Path Between the Seas: The Creation of the Panama Canal, 1870-1914*. N.Y., Simon and Schuster, 1977.

3 Make an Outline

Use an outline to decide how to organize your report. Sort your index cards into the same order.

Outline
I. Introduction
II. Why the canal was built
III. How the canal was built
    A. Physical challenges
    B. Medical challenges
IV. Conclusion

Introduction
Building the Panama Canal
Ever since Christopher Columbus first explored
the Isthmus of Panama, the Spanish had been
looking for a water route through it. They wanted
to be able to sail west from Spain to Asia without
sailing around South America. However, it was not
until 1914 that the dream became a reality.

Conclusion
It took eight years and more than 70,000
workers to build the Panama Canal. It
remains one of the greatest engineering
feats of modern times.

4 Write a First Draft

Write an introduction, a body, and a conclusion.
Leave plenty of space between lines so you can go
back and add details that you may have left out.

5 Revise and Proofread

Be sure to include transition words between sentences and paragraphs. Here are some examples:

To show a contrast—*however, although, despite.*

To point out a reason—*since, because, if.*

To signal a conclusion—*therefore, consequently, so, then.*

Evaluating Your Writing

Use this table to help you evaluate your writing.

	Excellent	Good	Acceptable	Unacceptable
Purpose	Achieves purpose—to inform, persuade, or provide historical interpretation—very well	Informs, persuades, or provides historical interpretation reasonably well	Reader cannot easily tell if the purpose is to inform, persuade, or provide historical interpretation	Purpose is not clear
Organization	Develops ideas in a very clear and logical way	Presents ideas in a reasonably well-organized way	Reader has difficulty following the organization	Lacks organization
Elaboration	Explains all ideas with facts and details	Explains most ideas with facts and details	Includes some supporting facts and details	Lacks supporting details
Use of Language	Uses excellent vocabulary and sentence structure with no errors in spelling, grammar, or punctuation	Uses good vocabulary and sentence structure with very few errors in spelling, grammar, or punctuation	Includes some errors in grammar, punctuation, and spelling	Includes many errors in grammar, punctuation, and spelling

CONTENTS

Use Web Code lap-0000 for all of the maps in this handbook.

Five Themes of Geography

Studying the geography of the entire world is a huge task. You can make that task easier by using the five themes of geography: location, regions, place, movement, and human-environment interaction. The themes are tools you can use to organize information and to answer the where, why, and how of geography.

LOCATION

1 Location answers the question, "Where is it?" You can think of the location of a continent or a country as its address. You might give an absolute location such as 22 South Lake Street or 40° N and 80° W. You might also use a relative address, telling where one place is by referring to another place. *Between school and the mall* and *eight miles east of Pleasant City* are examples of relative locations.

▲ **Location**
This museum in England has a line running through it. The line marks its location at 0° longitude.

REGIONS

2 Regions are areas that share at least one common feature. Geographers divide the world into many types of regions. For example, countries, states, and cities are political regions. The people in any one of these places live under the same government. Other features, such as climate and culture, can be used to define regions. Therefore the same place can be found in more than one region. For example, the state of Hawaii is in the political region of the United States. Because it has a tropical climate, Hawaii is also part of a tropical climate region.

MOVEMENT

4 Movement answers the question, "How do people, goods, and ideas move from place to place?" Remember that what happens in one place often affects what happens in another. Use the theme of movement to help you trace the spread of goods, people, and ideas from one location to another.

PLACE

3 Place identifies the natural and human features that make one place different from every other place. You can identify a specific place by its landforms, climate, plants, animals, people, language, or culture. You might even think of place as a geographic signature. Use the signature to help you understand the natural and human features that make one place different from every other place.

INTERACTION

5 Human-environment interaction focuses on the relationship between people and the environment. As people live in an area, they often begin to make changes to it, usually to make their lives easier. For example, they might build a dam to control flooding during rainy seasons. Also, the environment can affect how people live, work, dress, travel, and communicate.

◀ **Interaction**
These Congolese women interact with their environment by gathering wood for cooking.

PRACTICE YOUR GEOGRAPHY SKILLS

1 Describe your town or city, using each of the five themes of geography.

2 Name at least one thing that comes into your town or city and one that goes out. How is each moved? Where does it come from? Where does it go?

Understanding Movements of Earth

The planet Earth is part of our solar system. Earth revolves around the sun in a nearly circular path called an orbit. A revolution, or one complete orbit around the sun, takes 365¼ days, or one year. As Earth orbits the sun, it also spins on its axis, an invisible line through the center of Earth from the North Pole to the South Pole. This movement is called a rotation.

▼ **Spring begins**
On March 20 or 21, the sun is directly overhead at the Equator. The Northern and Southern Hemispheres receive almost equal hours of sunlight and darkness.

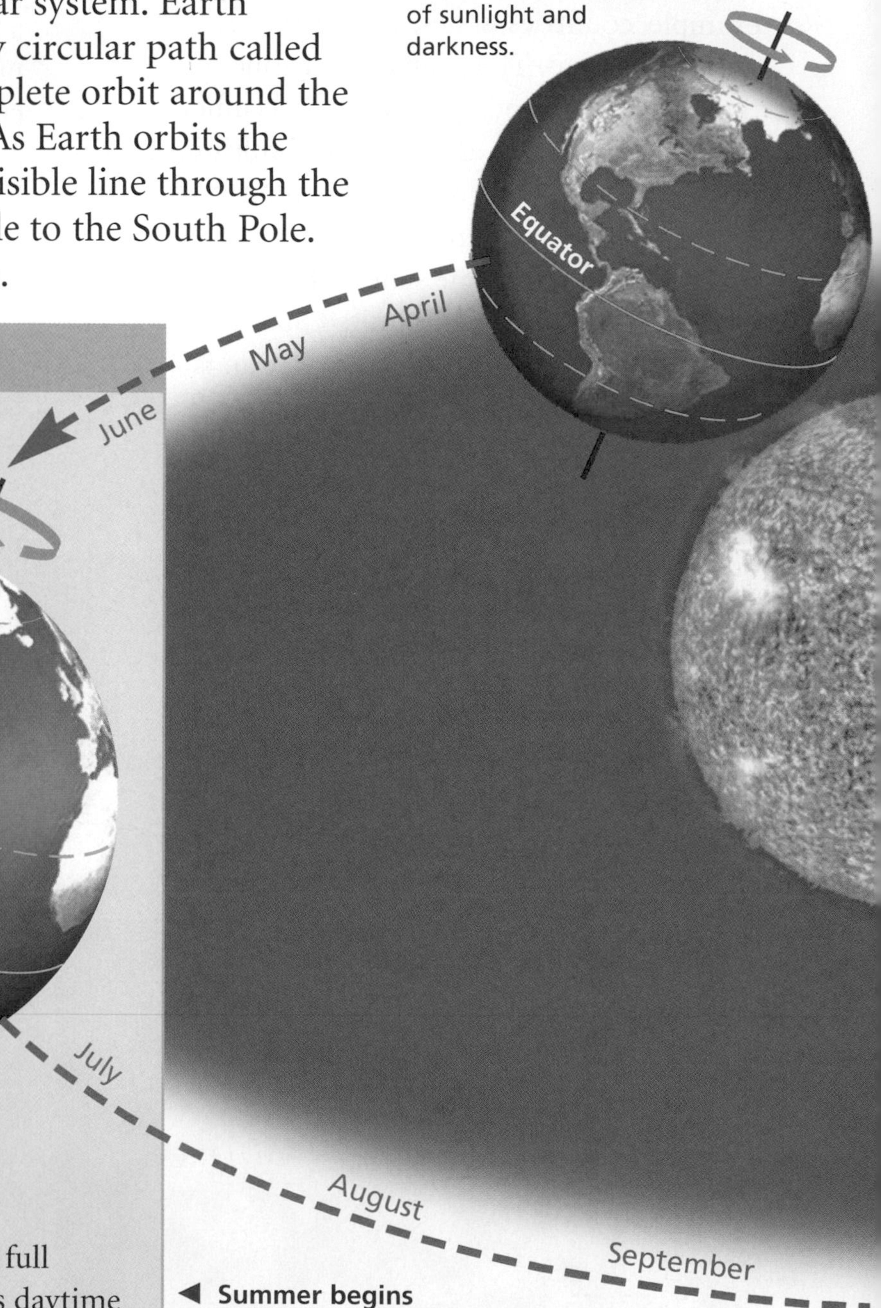

Equator

How Night Changes Into Day

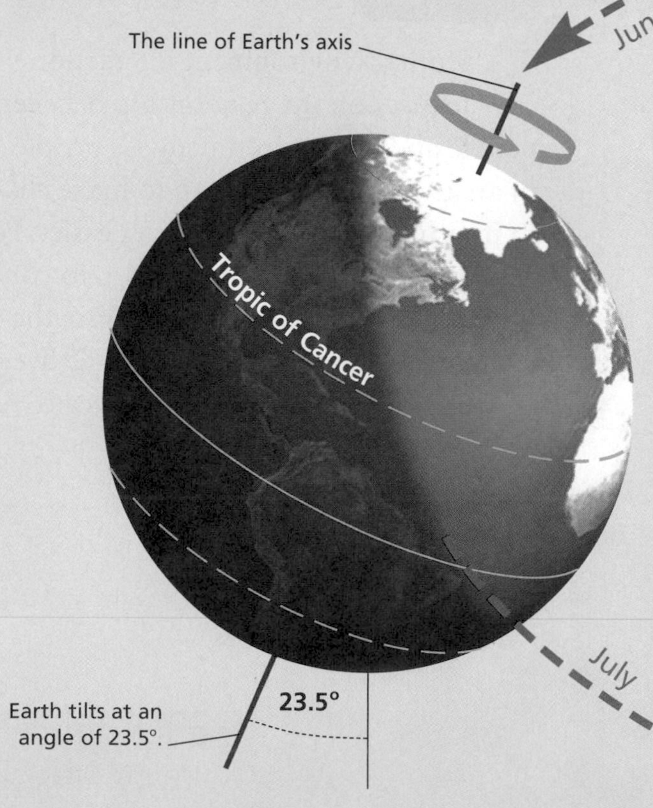

The line of Earth's axis

June
May
April

Tropic of Cancer

July

23.5°

Earth tilts at an angle of 23.5°.

August

September

Earth takes about 24 hours to make one full rotation on its axis. As Earth rotates, it is daytime on the side facing the sun. It is night on the side away from the sun.

◄ **Summer begins**
On June 21 or 22, the sun is directly overhead at the Tropic of Cancer. The Northern Hemisphere receives the greatest number of sunlight hours.

The Seasons

Earth's axis is tilted at an angle. Because of this tilt, sunlight strikes different parts of Earth at different times in the year, creating seasons. The illustration below shows how the seasons are created in the Northern Hemisphere. In the Southern Hemisphere, the seasons are reversed.

PRACTICE YOUR GEOGRAPHY SKILLS

1 What causes the seasons in the Northern Hemisphere to be the opposite of those in the Southern Hemisphere?

2 During which two days of the year do the Northern Hemisphere and Southern Hemisphere have equal hours of daylight and darkness?

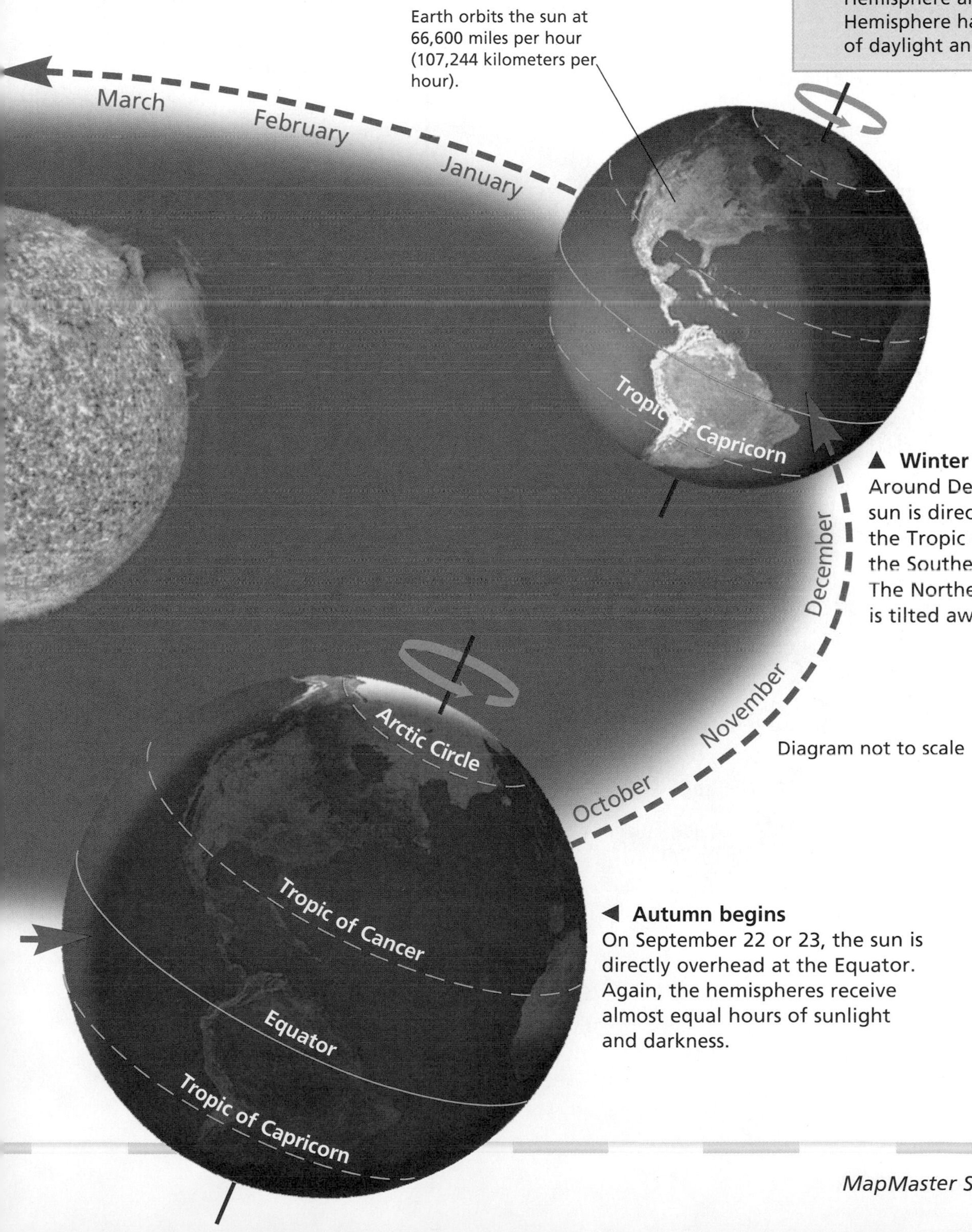

Earth orbits the sun at 66,600 miles per hour (107,244 kilometers per hour).

March
February
January

Tropic of Capricorn

December
November
October

Arctic Circle

Tropic of Cancer

Equator

Tropic of Capricorn

▲ **Winter begins**
Around December 21, the sun is directly overhead at the Tropic of Capricorn in the Southern Hemisphere. The Northern Hemisphere is tilted away from the sun.

Diagram not to scale

◄ **Autumn begins**
On September 22 or 23, the sun is directly overhead at the Equator. Again, the hemispheres receive almost equal hours of sunlight and darkness.

Understanding Globes

A globe is a scale model of Earth. It shows the actual shapes, sizes, and locations of all Earth's landmasses and bodies of water. Features on the surface of Earth are drawn to scale on a globe. This means that a small unit of measure on the globe stands for a large unit of measure on Earth.

Northern Hemisphere

NORTH LATITUDE

Equator (0° latitude)

SOUTH LATITUDE

Southern Hemisphere

Parallels of Latitude

Geographers divide the globe along imaginary horizontal lines called parallels of latitude. One of these latitude lines is the Equator, located halfway between the North and South Poles. Parallels of latitude are measured in degrees (°). One degree of latitude represents a distance of about 69 miles (111 kilometers).

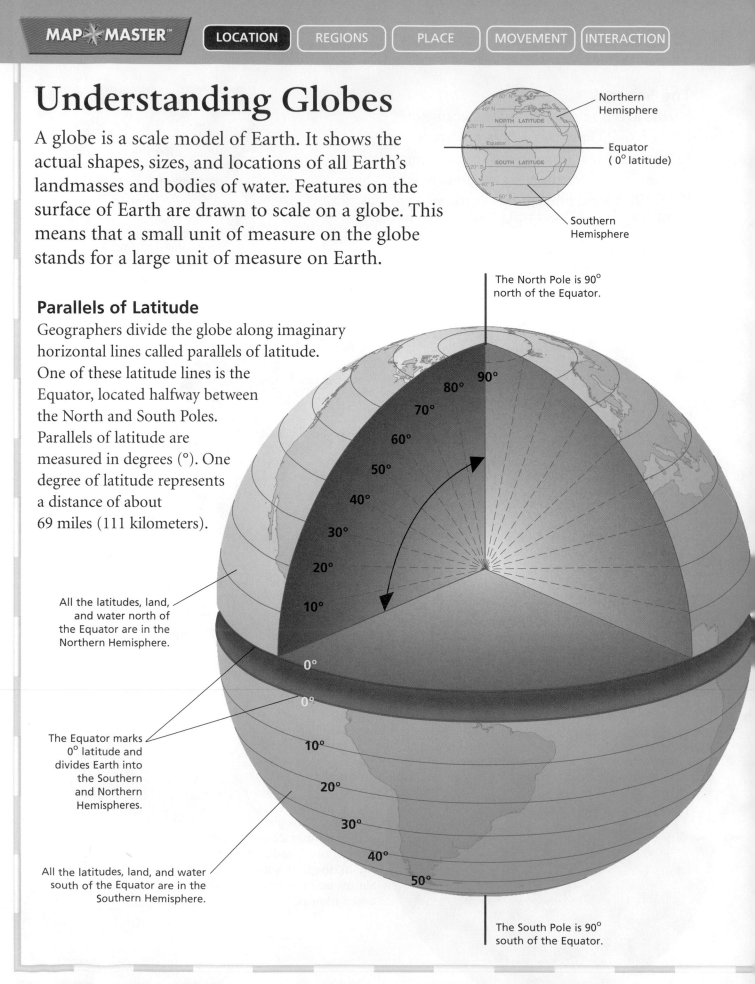

The North Pole is 90° north of the Equator.

90°
80°
70°
60°
50°
40°
30°
20°
10°
0°
0°
10°
20°
30°
40°
50°

All the latitudes, land, and water north of the Equator are in the Northern Hemisphere.

The Equator marks 0° latitude and divides Earth into the Southern and Northern Hemispheres.

All the latitudes, land, and water south of the Equator are in the Southern Hemisphere.

The South Pole is 90° south of the Equator.

Meridians of Longitude

Geographers also divide the globe along imaginary vertical lines called meridians of longitude, which are measured in degrees (°). The longitude line called the Prime Meridian runs from pole to pole through Greenwich, England. All meridians of longitude come together at the North and South Poles.

PRACTICE YOUR GEOGRAPHY SKILLS

1 Which continents lie completely in the Northern Hemisphere? In the Western Hemisphere?

2 Is there land or water at 20° S latitude and the Prime Meridian? At the Equator and 60° W longitude?

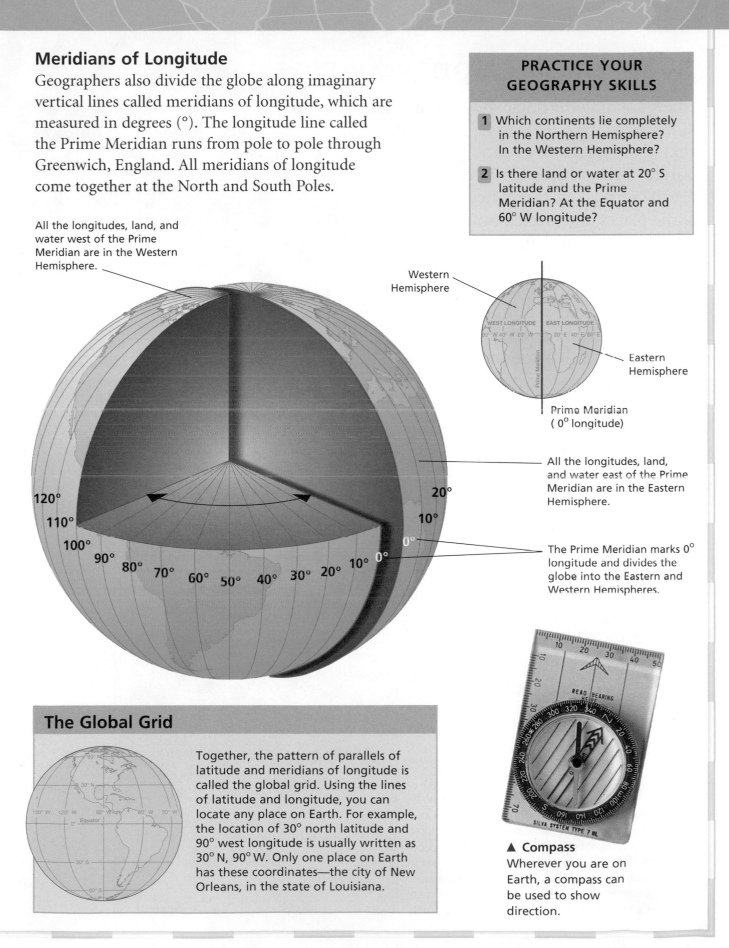

All the longitudes, land, and water west of the Prime Meridian are in the Western Hemisphere.

Western Hemisphere

Eastern Hemisphere

WEST LONGITUDE   EAST LONGITUDE
60° W 40° W 20° W   20° E 40° E 60° E

Prime Meridian (0° longitude)

120° 110° 100° 90° 80° 70° 60° 50° 40° 30° 20° 10° 0° 0° 10° 20°

All the longitudes, land, and water east of the Prime Meridian are in the Eastern Hemisphere.

The Prime Meridian marks 0° longitude and divides the globe into the Eastern and Western Hemispheres.

The Global Grid

60° N

30° N

150° W   120° W   90° W   60° W   30° W

0° Equator

30° S

60° S

Together, the pattern of parallels of latitude and meridians of longitude is called the global grid. Using the lines of latitude and longitude, you can locate any place on Earth. For example, the location of 30° north latitude and 90° west longitude is usually written as 30° N, 90° W. Only one place on Earth has these coordinates—the city of New Orleans, in the state of Louisiana.

▲ **Compass**
Wherever you are on Earth, a compass can be used to show direction.

Map Projections

Maps are drawings that show regions on flat surfaces. Maps are easier to use and carry than globes, but they cannot show the correct size and shape of every feature on Earth's curved surface. They must shrink some places and stretch others. To make up for this distortion, mapmakers use different map projections. No one projection can accurately show the correct area, shape, distance, and direction for all of Earth's surface. Mapmakers use the projection that has the least distortion for the information they are presenting.

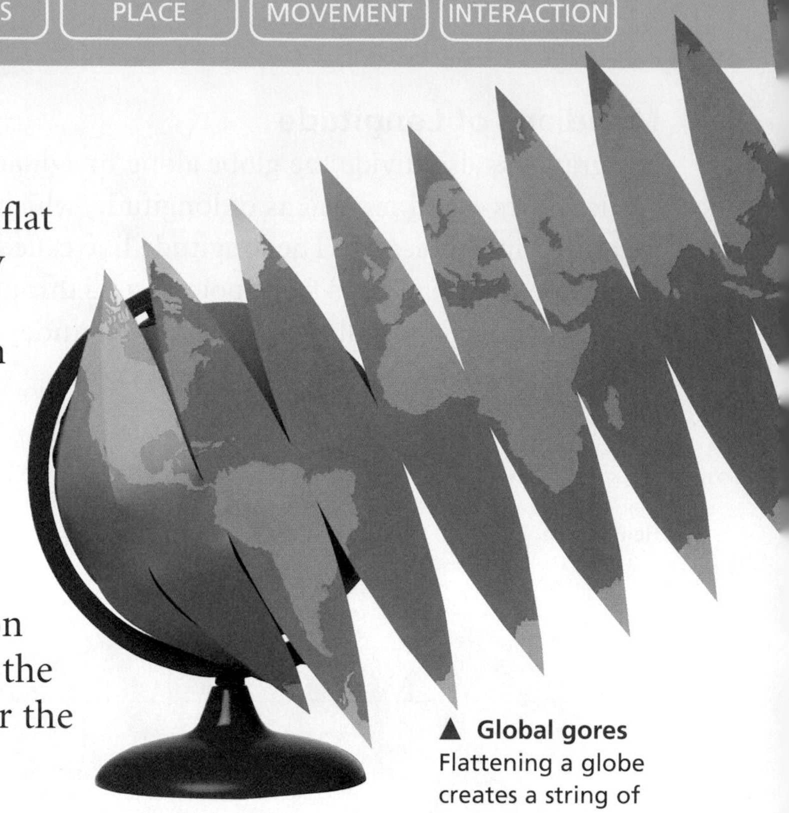

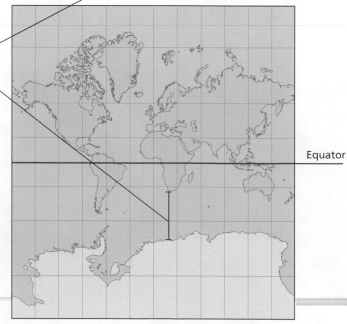

▲ **Global gores**
Flattening a globe creates a string of shapes called gores.

Same-Shape Maps

Map projections that accurately show the shapes of landmasses are called same-shape maps. However, these projections often greatly distort, or make less accurate, the size of landmasses as well as the distance between them. In the projection below, the northern and southern areas of the globe appear more stretched than the areas near the Equator.

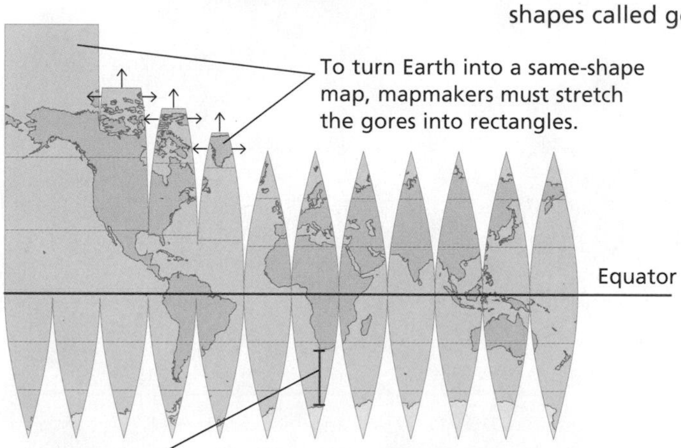

To turn Earth into a same-shape map, mapmakers must stretch the gores into rectangles.

Equator

Stretching the gores makes parts of Earth larger. This enlargement becomes greater toward the North and South Poles.

Equator

Mercator projection ▶
One of the most common same-shape maps is the Mercator projection, named for the mapmaker who invented it. The Mercator projection accurately shows shape and direction, but it distorts distance and size. Because the projection shows true directions, ships' navigators use it to chart a straight-line course between two ports.

Equal-Area Maps

Map projections that show the correct size of landmasses are called equal-area maps. In order to show the correct size of landmasses, these maps usually distort shapes. The distortion is usually greater at the edges of the map and less at the center.

PRACTICE YOUR GEOGRAPHY SKILLS

1 What feature is distorted on an equal-area map?

2 Would you use a Mercator projection to find the exact distance between two locations? Tell why or why not.

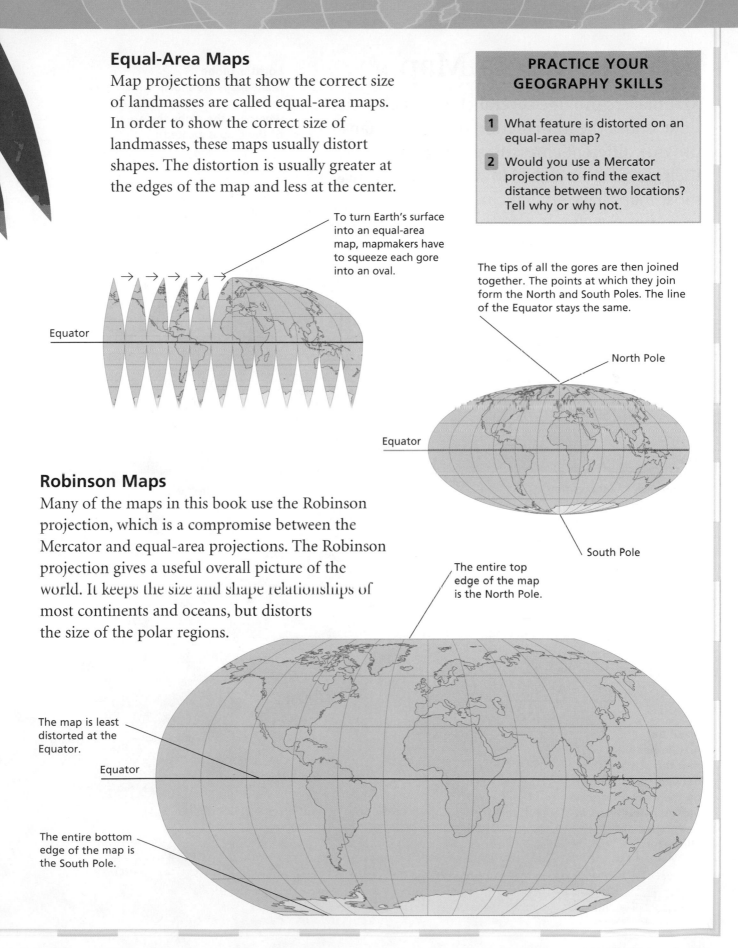

To turn Earth's surface into an equal-area map, mapmakers have to squeeze each gore into an oval.

Equator

The tips of all the gores are then joined together. The points at which they join form the North and South Poles. The line of the Equator stays the same.

North Pole

Equator

South Pole

Robinson Maps

Many of the maps in this book use the Robinson projection, which is a compromise between the Mercator and equal-area projections. The Robinson projection gives a useful overall picture of the world. It keeps the size and shape relationships of most continents and oceans, but distorts the size of the polar regions.

The entire top edge of the map is the North Pole.

The map is least distorted at the Equator.

Equator

The entire bottom edge of the map is the South Pole.

How to Use a Map

Mapmakers provide several clues to help you understand the information on a map. Maps provide different clues, depending on their purpose or scale. However, most maps have several clues in common.

Locator globe
Many maps are shown with locator globes. They show where on the globe the area of the map is located.

Title
All maps have a title. The title tells you the subject of the map.

Compass rose
Many maps show direction by displaying a compass rose with the directions north, east, south, and west. The letters N, E, S, and W are placed to indicate these directions.

Key
Often a map has a key, or legend. The key shows the symbols and colors used on the map, and what each one means.

Scale bar
A scale bar helps you find the actual distances between points shown on the map. Most scale bars show distances in both miles and kilometers.

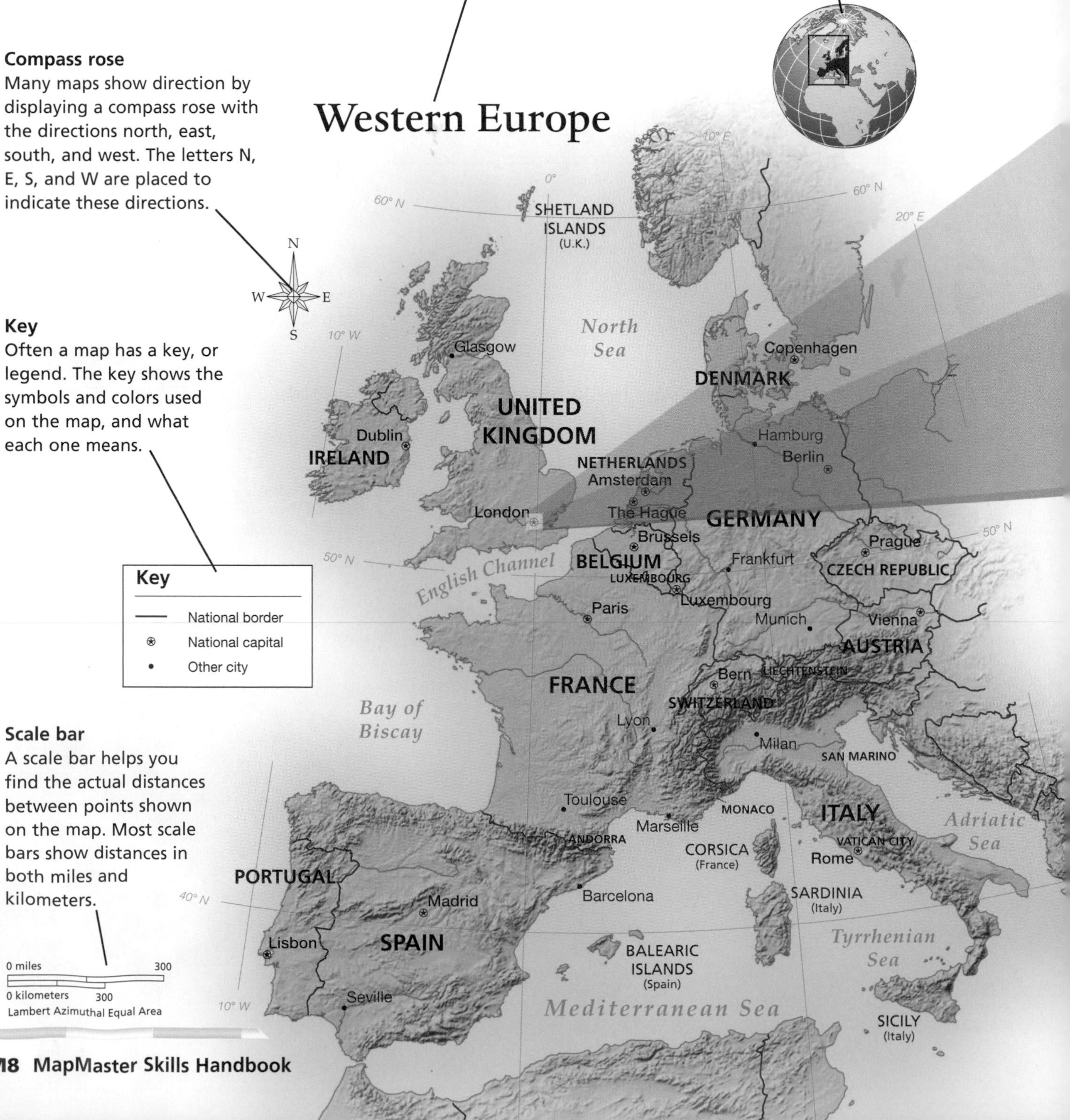

Western Europe

Key

——	National border
⊛	National capital
•	Other city

0 miles 300
0 kilometers 300
Lambert Azimuthal Equal Area

SHETLAND ISLANDS (U.K.)

North Sea

Glasgow

Copenhagen

DENMARK

UNITED KINGDOM

Hamburg
Berlin

Dublin

IRELAND

NETHERLANDS
Amsterdam

London

The Hague

GERMANY

Brussels

BELGIUM

Frankfurt

Prague

CZECH REPUBLIC

LUXEMBOURG

Luxembourg

Paris

Munich

Vienna

AUSTRIA

English Channel

Bay of Biscay

FRANCE

Bern LIECHTENSTEIN

SWITZERLAND

Lyon

Milan

SAN MARINO

Toulouse

MONACO

ITALY

Adriatic Sea

Marseille

ANDORRA

CORSICA (France)

VATICAN CITY

Rome

PORTUGAL

Madrid

Barcelona

SARDINIA (Italy)

Lisbon

SPAIN

BALEARIC ISLANDS (Spain)

Tyrrhenian Sea

Seville

Mediterranean Sea

SICILY (Italy)

60° N
0°
10° E
20° E
60° N
10° W
50° N
50° N
40° N
10° W

Maps of Different Scales

Maps are drawn to different scales, depending on their purpose. Here are three maps drawn to very different scales. Keep in mind that maps showing large areas have smaller scales. Maps showing small areas have larger scales.

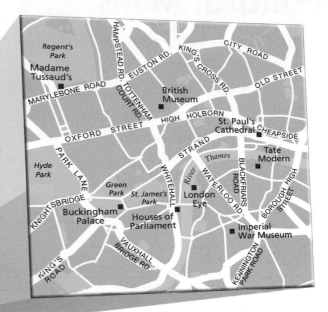

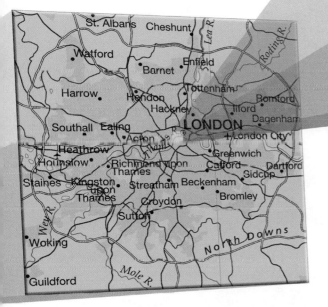

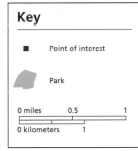

Key

■   Point of interest

▰   Park

0 miles   0.5   1
0 kilometers   1

▲ Central London

Find the gray square on the map of Greater London. This square represents the area shown on the map above. This map moves you closer into the center of London. Like the zoom on a computer or a camera, this map shows a smaller area but in greater detail. It has the largest scale (1 inch represents about 0.9 mile). You can use this map to explore downtown London.

▲ Greater London

Find the gray square on the main map of Western Europe (left). This square represents the area shown on the map above. It shows London's boundaries, the general shape of the city, and the features around the city. This map can help you find your way from the airport to the center of town.

Key

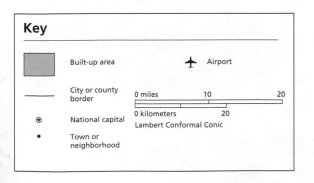

▨   Built-up area   ✈   Airport

——   City or county border

0 miles   10   20
0 kilometers   20
Lambert Conformal Conic

⊛   National capital

•   Town or neighborhood

PRACTICE YOUR GEOGRAPHY SKILLS

1 What part of a map explains the colors used on the map?

2 How does the scale bar change depending on the scale of the map?

3 Which map would be best for finding the location of the British Museum? Explain why.

Political Maps

Political maps show political borders: continents, countries, and divisions within countries, such as states or provinces. The colors on political maps do not have any special meaning, but they make the map easier to read. Political maps also include symbols and labels for capitals, cities, and towns.

PRACTICE YOUR GEOGRAPHY SKILLS

1 What symbols show a national border, a national capital, and a city?

2 What is Angola's capital city?

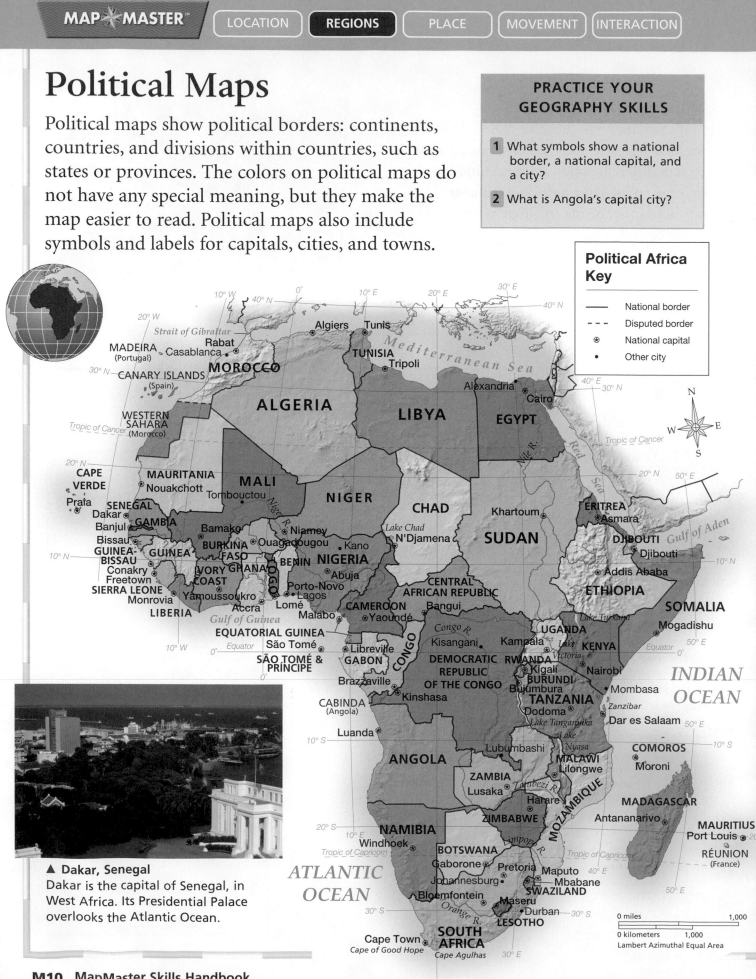

Political Africa Key

——	National border
- - -	Disputed border
⊛	National capital
•	Other city

▲ Dakar, Senegal

Dakar is the capital of Senegal, in West Africa. Its Presidential Palace overlooks the Atlantic Ocean.

0 miles 1,000
0 kilometers 1,000
Lambert Azimuthal Equal Area

Physical Maps

Physical maps represent what a region looks like by showing its major physical features, such as hills and plains. Physical maps also often show elevation and relief. Elevation, indicated by colors, is the height of the land above sea level. Relief, indicated by shading, shows how sharply the land rises or falls.

PRACTICE YOUR GEOGRAPHY SKILLS

1 Which areas of Africa have the highest elevation?

2 How can you use relief to plan a hiking trip?

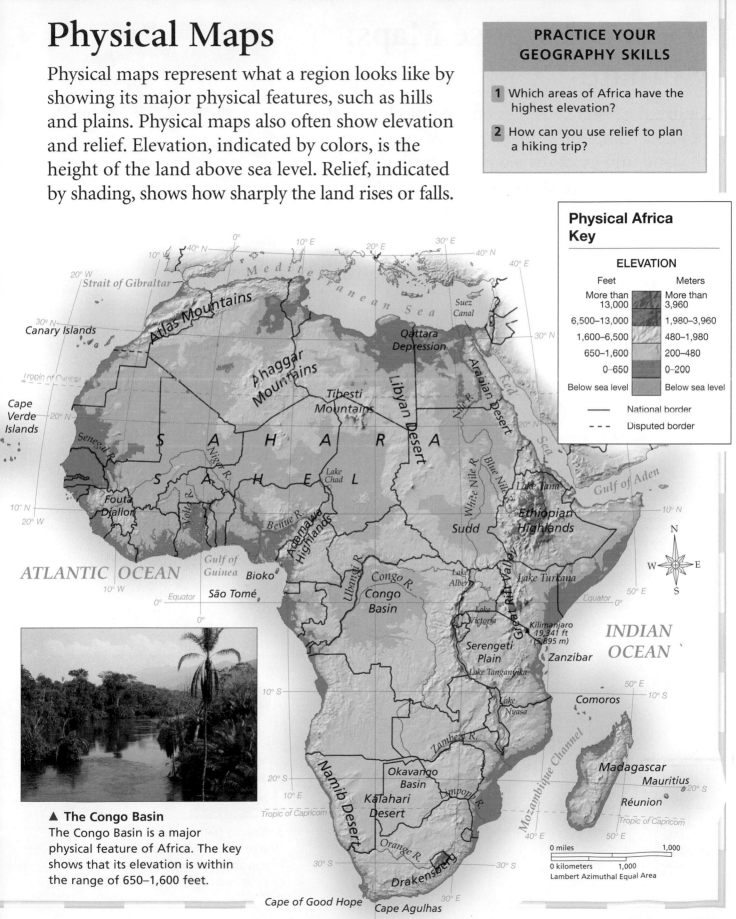

Physical Africa Key

ELEVATION

Feet	Meters
More than 13,000	More than 3,960
6,500–13,000	1,980–3,960
1,600–6,500	480–1,980
650–1,600	200–480
0–650	0–200
Below sea level	Below sea level

——— National border

- - - Disputed border

0 miles 1,000
0 kilometers 1,000
Lambert Azimuthal Equal Area

▲ **The Congo Basin**
The Congo Basin is a major physical feature of Africa. The key shows that its elevation is within the range of 650–1,600 feet.

Special-Purpose Maps: Climate

Unlike the boundary lines on a political map, the boundary lines on climate maps do not separate the land into exact divisions. For example, in this climate map of India, a tropical wet climate gradually changes to a tropical wet and dry climate.

PRACTICE YOUR GEOGRAPHY SKILLS

1 What part of a special-purpose map tells you what the colors on the map mean?

2 Where are arid regions located in India? Are there major cities in those regions?

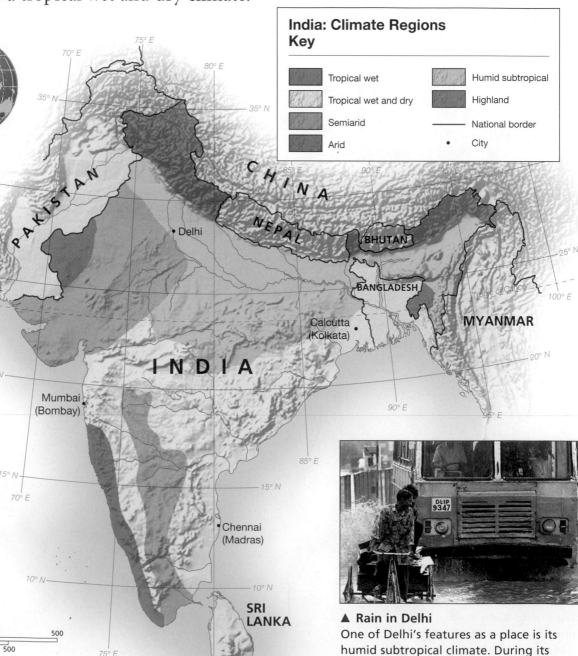

India: Climate Regions Key

- Tropical wet
- Tropical wet and dry
- Semiarid
- Arid
- Humid subtropical
- Highland
- —— National border
- • City

▲ **Rain in Delhi**
One of Delhi's features as a place is its humid subtropical climate. During its rainy season, Delhi receives heavy rainfall.

Special-Purpose Maps: Language

This map shows the official languages of India. An official language is the language used by the government. Even though a region has an official language, the people there may speak other languages as well. As in other special-purpose maps, the key explains how the different languages appear on the map.

PRACTICE YOUR GEOGRAPHY SKILLS

1 What color represents the Malayalam language on this map?

2 Where in India is Tamil the official language?

The Hindi language ▶
Hindi is the most widely spoken language in India. It is also the most popular language in Delhi.

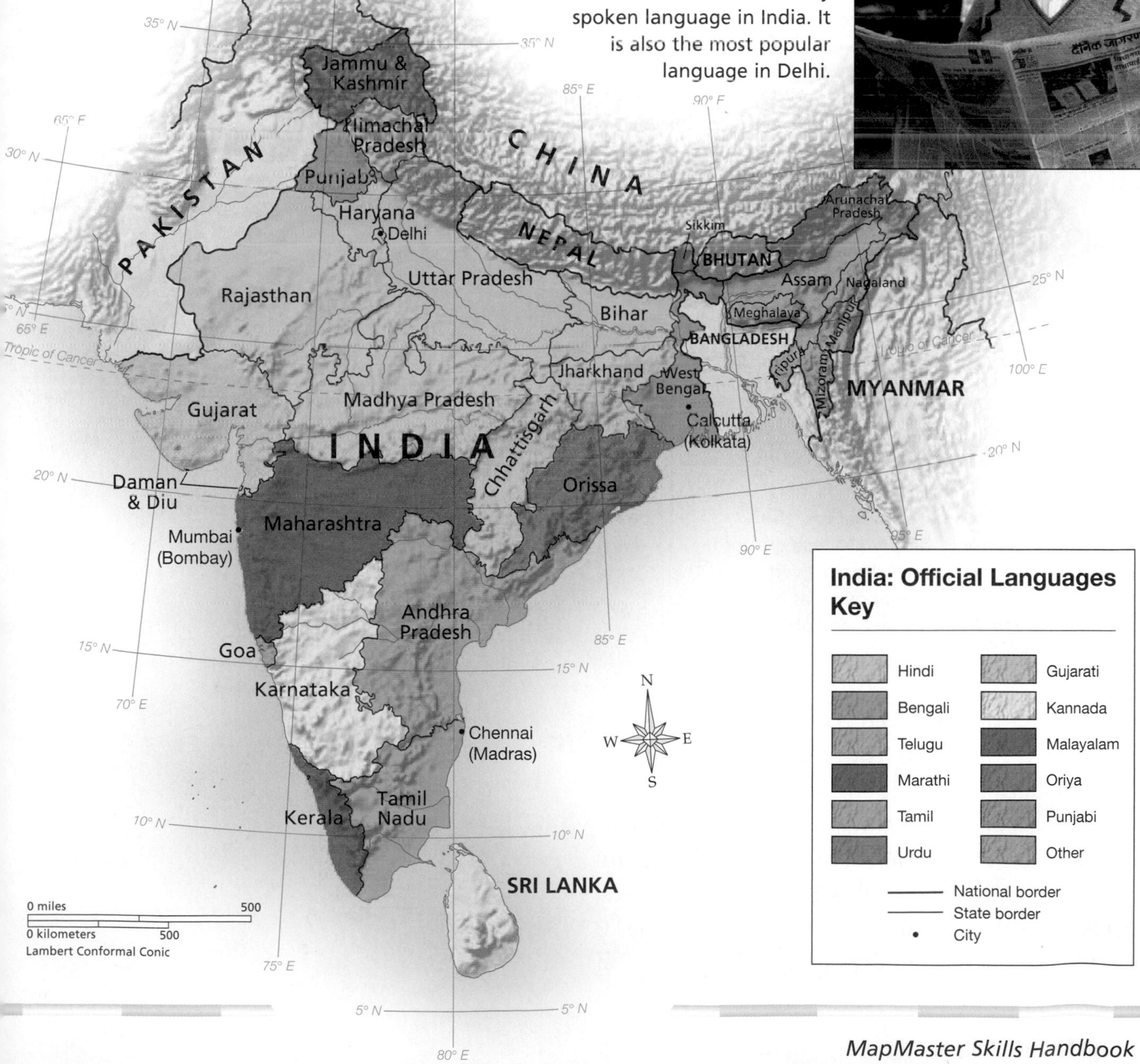

PAKISTAN

CHINA

NEPAL

BHUTAN

BANGLADESH

MYANMAR

INDIA

SRI LANKA

Jammu & Kashmir
Himachal Pradesh
Punjab
Haryana
Delhi
Rajasthan
Uttar Pradesh
Sikkim
Arunachal Pradesh
Assam
Nagaland
Meghalaya
Bihar
Jharkhand
West Bengal
Tripura
Mizoram
Manipur
Gujarat
Madhya Pradesh
Chhattisgarh
Calcutta (Kolkata)
Orissa
Daman & Diu
Maharashtra
Mumbai (Bombay)
Andhra Pradesh
Goa
Karnataka
Chennai (Madras)
Kerala
Tamil Nadu

Tropic of Cancer

35° N
30° N
25° N
20° N
15° N
10° N
5° N

65° E
70° E
75° E
80° E
85° E
90° E
95° E
100° E

N
W   E
S

0 miles   500
0 kilometers   500
Lambert Conformal Conic

India: Official Languages Key

Hindi	Gujarati
Bengali	Kannada
Telugu	Malayalam
Marathi	Oriya
Tamil	Punjabi
Urdu	Other

——— National border
——— State border
• City

Human Migration

Migration is an important part of the study of geography. Since the beginning of history, people have been on the move. As people move, they both shape and are shaped by their environments. Wherever people go, the culture they bring with them mixes with the cultures of the place in which they have settled.

Explorers arrive ▼
In 1492, Christopher Columbus set sail from Spain for the Americas with three ships. The ships shown here are replicas of those ships.

▲ Native American pyramid
When Europeans arrived in the Americas, the lands they found were not empty. Diverse groups of people with distinct cultures already lived there. The temple-topped pyramid shown above was built by Mayan Indians in Mexico, long before Columbus sailed.

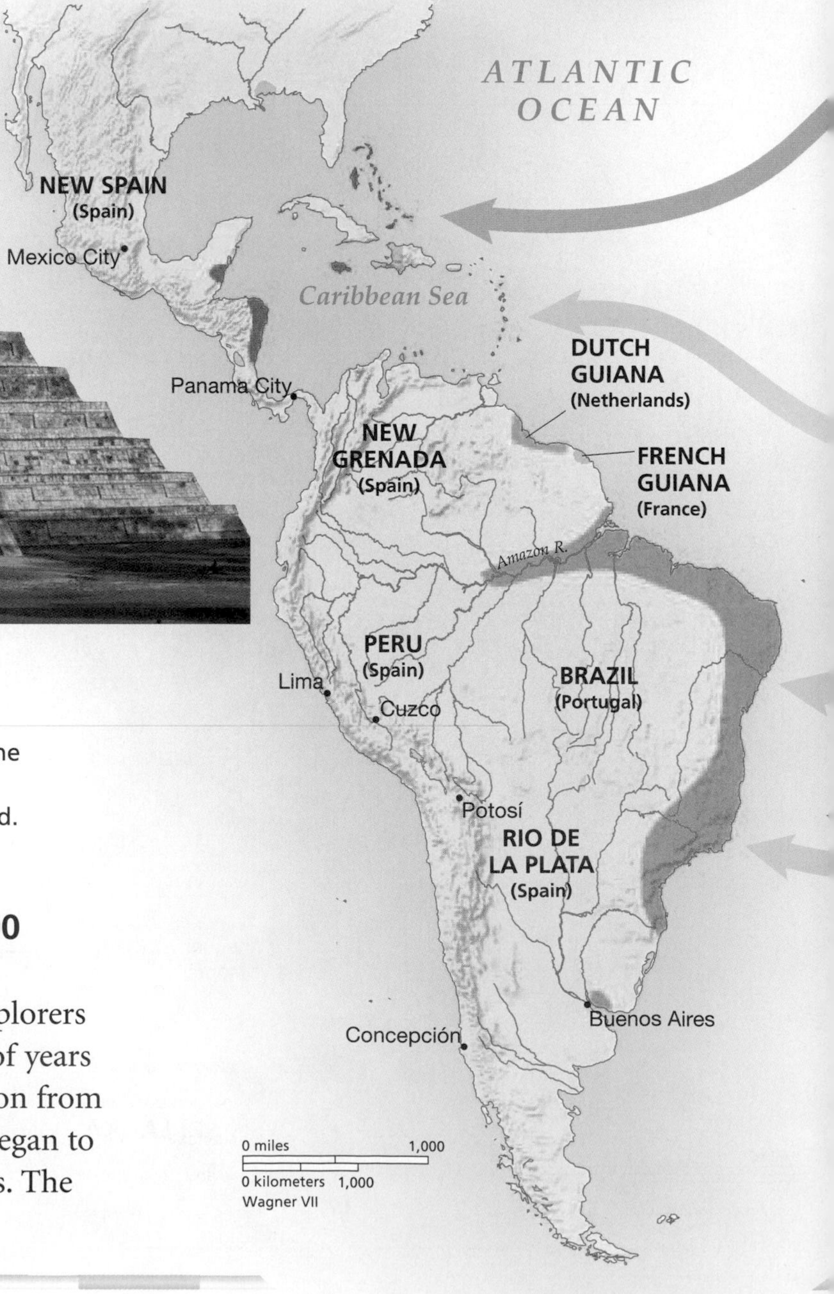

Migration to the Americas, 1500–1800

A huge wave of migration from the Eastern Hemisphere began in the 1500s. European explorers in the Americas paved the way for hundreds of years of European settlement there. Forced migration from Africa started soon afterward, as Europeans began to import African slaves to work in the Americas. The map to the right shows these migrations.

ATLANTIC OCEAN

NEW SPAIN
(Spain)
Mexico City

Caribbean Sea

Panama City

DUTCH GUIANA
(Netherlands)

NEW GRENADA
(Spain)

FRENCH GUIANA
(France)

Amazon R.

PERU
(Spain)
Lima
Cuzco

BRAZIL
(Portugal)

Potosí

RIO DE LA PLATA
(Spain)

Concepción

Buenos Aires

0 miles 1,000
0 kilometers 1,000
Wagner VII

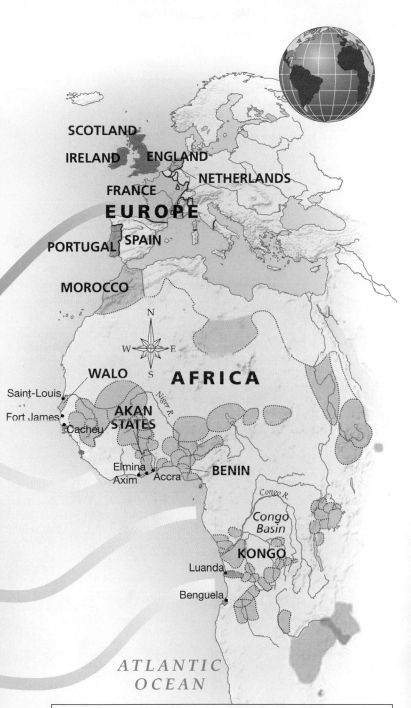

SCOTLAND

IRELAND   ENGLAND

                    NETHERLANDS

FRANCE

EUROPE

PORTUGAL SPAIN

MOROCCO

N
W   E
S

WALO   **AFRICA**

Saint-Louis

Fort James
                   Niger R.
Cacheu   AKAN
         STATES

Elmina
Axim   Accra   BENIN

                    Congo R.

                  Congo
                  Basin

         KONGO

Luanda

Benguela

*ATLANTIC
OCEAN*

PRACTICE YOUR GEOGRAPHY SKILLS

1 Where did the Portuguese settle in the Americas?

2 Would you describe African migration at this time as a result of both push factors and pull factors? Explain why or why not.

"Push" and "Pull" Factors

Geographers describe a people's choice to migrate in terms of "push" factors and "pull" factors. Push factors are things in people's lives that push them to leave, such as poverty and political unrest. Pull factors are things in another country that pull people to move there, including better living conditions and hopes of better jobs.

▲ **Elmina, Ghana**

Elmina, in Ghana, is one of the many ports from which slaves were transported from Africa. Because slaves and gold were traded here, stretches of the western African coast were known as the Slave Coast and the Gold Coast.

Migration to Latin America, 1500–1800 Key

◄ European migration	Spain and possessions
◄ African migration	Portugal and possessions
—— National or colonial border	Netherlands and possessions
·········· Traditional African border	France and possessions
African State	England and possessions

World Land Use

People around the world have many different economic structures, or ways of making a living. Land-use maps are one way to learn about these structures. The ways that people use the land in each region tell us about the main ways that people in that region make a living.

World Land Use Key

	Nomadic herding
	Hunting and gathering
	Forestry
	Livestock raising
	Commercial farming
	Subsistence farming
	Manufacturing and trade
	Little or no activity
——	National border
- - - -	Disputed border

▲ **Wheat farming in the United States**
Developed countries practice commercial farming rather than subsistence farming. Commercial farming is the production of food mainly for sale, either within the country or for export to other countries. Commercial farmers like these in Oregon often use heavy equipment to farm.

Levels of Development

Notice on the map key the term *subsistence farming*. This term means the production of food mainly for use by the farmer's own family. In less-developed countries, subsistence farming is often one of the main economic activities. In contrast, in developed countries there is little subsistence farming.

▲ **Growing barley in Ecuador**
These farmers in Ecuador use hand tools to harvest barley. They will use most of the crop they grow to feed themselves or their farm animals.

NORTH AMERICA

SOUTH AMERICA

0 miles 2,000
0 kilometers 2,000
Robinson

▲ Growing rice in Vietnam
Women in Vietnam plant rice in wet rice paddies, using the same planting methods their ancestors did.

PRACTICE YOUR GEOGRAPHY SKILLS

1 In what parts of the world is subsistence farming the main land use?

2 Locate where manufacturing and trade are the main land use. Are they found more often near areas of subsistence farming or areas of commercial farming? Why might this be so?

EUROPE

ASIA

AFRICA

N
W · E
S

AUSTRALIA

◀ Herding cattle in Kenya
Besides subsistence farming, nomadic herding is another economic activity in Africa. This man drives his cattle across the Kenyan grasslands.

How to Read Social Studies

🎯 Target Reading Skills

The Target Reading Skills introduced on this page will help you understand the words and ideas in this book and in other social studies reading you do. Each chapter focuses on one of these reading skills. Good readers develop a bank of reading strategies, or skills. Then they draw on the particular strategies that will help them understand the text they are reading.

🎯 Chapter 1 Target Reading Skill

Using the Reading Process Previewing can help you understand and remember what you read. In this chapter you will practice using these previewing skills: setting a purpose for reading, predicting what the text will be about, and asking questions before you read.

🎯 Chapter 2 Target Reading Skill

Clarifying Meaning If you do not understand something you are reading right away, you can use several skills to clarify the meaning of the word or idea. In this chapter you will practice these strategies for clarifying meaning: rereading, reading ahead, paraphrasing, and summarizing.

🎯 Chapter 3 Target Reading Skill

Using Cause and Effect Recognizing cause and effect will help you understand relationships among the situations and events you are reading about. In this chapter you will practice these skills: identifying cause and effect, recognizing multiple causes, and understanding effects.

🎯 Chapter 4 Target Reading Skill

Using Context Using the context of an unfamiliar word can help you understand its meaning. Context includes the words, phrases, and sentences surrounding a word. In this chapter you will practice using these context clues: definitions, contrast, and your own general knowledge.

🎯 Chapter 5 Target Reading Skill

Identifying the Main Idea Since you cannot remember every detail of what you read, it is important to identify the main ideas. The main idea of a section or paragraph is the most important point, the one you want to remember. In this chapter you will practice these skills: identifying both stated and implied main ideas, and identifying supporting details.

🎯 Chapter 6 Target Reading Skill

Comparing and Contrasting You can use comparison and contrast to sort out and analyze the information you are reading. Comparing means examining the similarities between things. Contrasting is looking at differences. In this chapter you will practice these skills: comparing and contrasting, identifying contrasts, and making comparisons.

LATIN AMERICA

The early peoples of Latin America created great civilizations from the riches of their land and their own ideas and skills. Their descendants have mixed with newcomers from around the world to create modern societies that blend the old and the new into vibrant and distinctive cultures.

Guiding Questions

The text, photographs, maps, and charts in this book will help you discover answers to these Guiding Questions.

 Geography What are the main physical features of Latin America?

2 **History** How has Latin America been shaped by its history?

3 **Culture** What factors have affected cultures in Latin America?

4 **Government** What types of government have existed in Latin America?

5 **Economics** How has geography influenced the ways in which Latin Americans make a living?

Project Preview

You can also discover answers to the Guiding Questions by working on projects. Several project possibilities are listed on page 198 of this book.

Investigate Latin America

Latin America is a vibrant region in the midst of change. The region's northern edge is marked by the boundary between the United States and Mexico. To the south, it extends to the tip of South America. Latin America covers about 14 percent of Earth's surface.

▲ San Cristóbal de las Casas, Mexico

LOCATION

1 Explore Latin America's Location

Recall from the MapMaster Skills Handbook that when it's winter north of the Equator it's summer south of the Equator, and vice versa. Trace the line of the Equator on the map above with your finger. Next, break into small groups. Tell each other in what season your birthdays fall. Work together to figure out in what season your birthdays would be if you all lived in Santiago, Chile. What would the seasons be if you lived in Brasília, Brazil? If you lived in Mexico City, Mexico?

REGIONS

2 Compare the Size of Latin America and the United States

How does Latin America's length compare to the length of the continental United States? Take a piece of string and curve it along the west coast of the United States from the border with Canada to the border with Mexico. Cut the string the same length as the coast. Now see how many string lengths fit along the west coast of Latin America. Start at northern Mexico. Finish at the southern tip of South America. How many times longer is Latin America's Pacific Coast than the coast of the United States?

Political Latin America

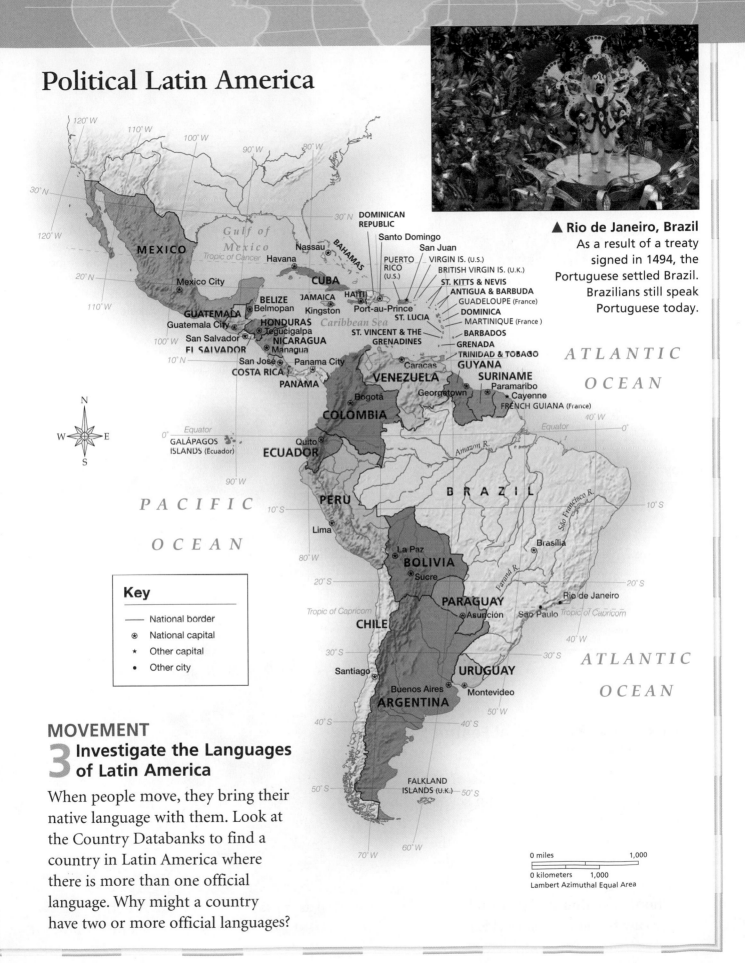

▲ **Rio de Janeiro, Brazil**
As a result of a treaty signed in 1494, the Portuguese settled Brazil. Brazilians still speak Portuguese today.

Key

— National border
⊛ National capital
★ Other capital
• Other city

0 miles _____ 1,000
0 kilometers ___ 1,000
Lambert Azimuthal Equal Area

MOVEMENT

3 Investigate the Languages of Latin America

When people move, they bring their native language with them. Look at the Country Databanks to find a country in Latin America where there is more than one official language. Why might a country have two or more official languages?

Physical Latin America

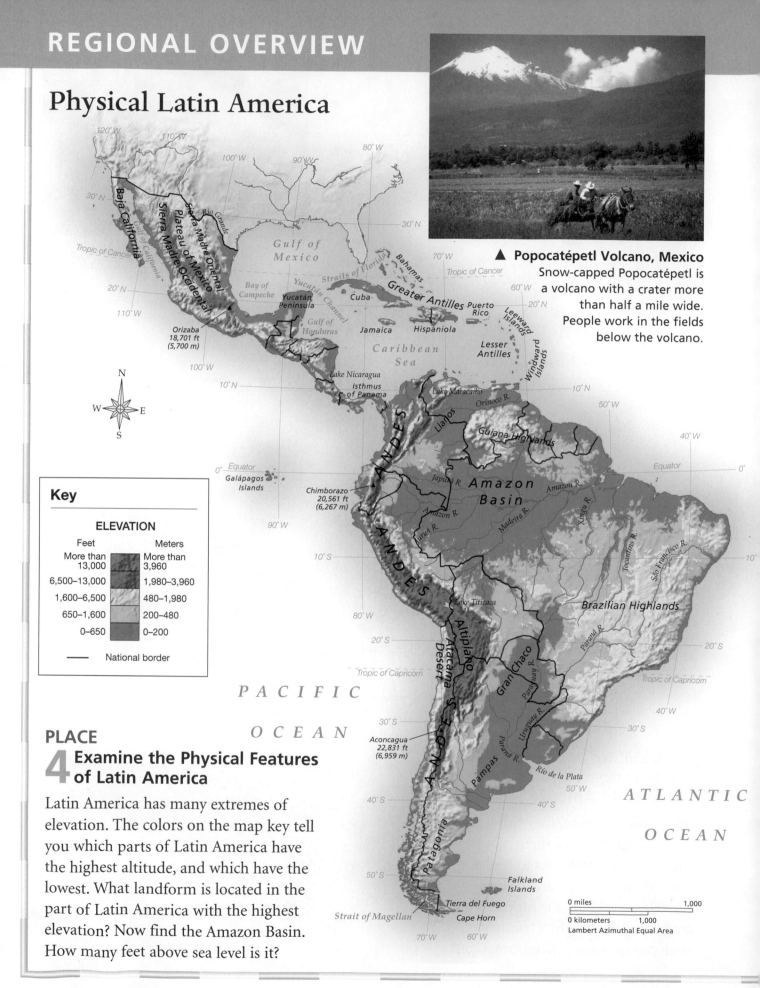

▲ Popocatépetl Volcano, Mexico
Snow-capped Popocatépetl is a volcano with a crater more than half a mile wide. People work in the fields below the volcano.

Key

ELEVATION

Feet		Meters
More than 13,000		More than 3,960
6,500–13,000		1,980–3,960
1,600–6,500		480–1,980
650–1,600		200–480
0–650		0–200
—— National border		

PLACE

4 Examine the Physical Features of Latin America

Latin America has many extremes of elevation. The colors on the map key tell you which parts of Latin America have the highest altitude, and which have the lowest. What landform is located in the part of Latin America with the highest elevation? Now find the Amazon Basin. How many feet above sea level is it?

Major Hydroelectric Plants

Electricity generated from water power is called hydroelectricity. One way to build a hydroelectric plant is to dam a river. The dam creates a large lake. When the dam gates open, water gushes from the lake to the river, turning huge paddles that create electricity. If you live in a region near a large river, your electricity may be generated in this way.

▲ **Itaipú Dam, Brazil/Paraguay**
Water surges through the gate at the Itaipú Dam. This dam supplies electricity to large areas of Brazil and Paraguay.

LOCATION

5 Investigate Latin America's Use of Hydroelectricity

The world's largest hydroelectric plant is located on the border of Brazil and Paraguay. Look at the circle graph below. How much of its power does Latin America get from hydroelectricity? From what energy source does Latin America get most of its power?

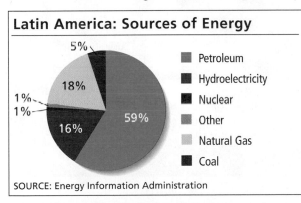

Latin America: Sources of Energy

5%
18%
1%
1%
16%
59%

- Petroleum
- Hydroelectricity
- Nuclear
- Other
- Natural Gas
- Coal

SOURCE: Energy Information Administration

Key

—— National border

■ Hydroelectric plant

PRACTICE YOUR GEOGRAPHY SKILLS

1 You are taking a trip through Latin America. You board your ship in Puerto Rico. You want to reach Panama. In which direction should you sail?

2 You are traveling through the Andes in Peru, looking for a large lake. What is it called?

3 You have traveled north again. You are looking for a hydroelectric plant in the far north of Brazil, near the coast. What is the plant called?

▲ **Lake Titicaca, Peru**

Focus on Countries in Latin America

Now that you've investigated the geography of Latin America, take a closer look at some of the countries that make up this region. The map shows all the countries of Latin America. The ten countries that you will study in depth in the second half of this book are shown in yellow on the map.

Go Online PHSchool.com Use Web Code **lfp-1010** for the **interactive maps** on these pages.

◄ Mexico

Mexico is the United States's southern neighbor. Its capital, Mexico City, is one of the largest cities on the planet. Many of the people who live and work in Mexico City have moved there from the countryside.

▲ Haiti

Haiti lies on the western third of the island of Hispaniola. It is the only nation in the Americas formed as a result of a successful revolt by enslaved Africans.

◄ Peru

Peru is a mountainous country that is home to many species of animals, including the llama. Llamas thrive in the mountains and their wool is used for clothing.

ATLANTIC
OCEAN

30° N

70° W

Mexico

BAHAMAS

Tropic of Cancer

60° W

CUBA

DOMINICAN
REPUBLIC

HAITI

20° N

BELIZE

JAMAICA

PUERTO
RICO
(U.S.)

ST. KITTS & NEVIS

ANTIGUA & BARBUDA

DOMINICA

HONDURAS

Caribbean Sea

ST. LUCIA

ST. VINCENT & THE GRENADINES

NICARAGUA

BARBADOS

GRENADA

50° W

COSTA RICA

TRINIDAD & TOBAGO

10° N

PANAMA

VENEZUELA

GUYANA

SURINAME

FRENCH GUIANA
(France)

40° W

COLOMBIA

Equator 0°

ECUADOR

B R A Z I L

PERU

10° S

10° S

80° W

BOLIVIA

20° S

20° S

Tropic of Capricorn

PARAGUAY

Tropic of Capricorn

PACIFIC
OCEAN

CHILE

40° W

30° S

30° S

URUGUAY

ARGENTINA

50° W

40° S

40° S

50° S

50° S

70° W

60° W

▲ Brazil

Brazil is the largest country in Latin America and is the home of São Paulo, the fastest-growing city in the world. Yet more than half of the country is made up of the Amazon rain forest, home to many diverse Native American groups who have lived there for thousands of years.

Key

— National border

☐ Countries with in-depth coverage

☐ Non-feature countries

0 miles   1,000

0 kilometers   1,000

Lambert Azimuthal Equal Area

Chile ▶

Chile is a long, narrow country with a dramatic, mountainous landscape. In some parts of Chile, people still live much as their ancestors did.

Chapter 1

Latin America: Physical Geography

Chapter Preview

This chapter will introduce you to the geography of Latin America and show how geography affects the people who live there.

Section 1
Land and Water

Section 2
Climate and Vegetation

Section 3
Resources and Land Use

Target Reading Skill

Reading Process In this chapter you will focus on the reading process by using previewing to help you understand and remember what you read.

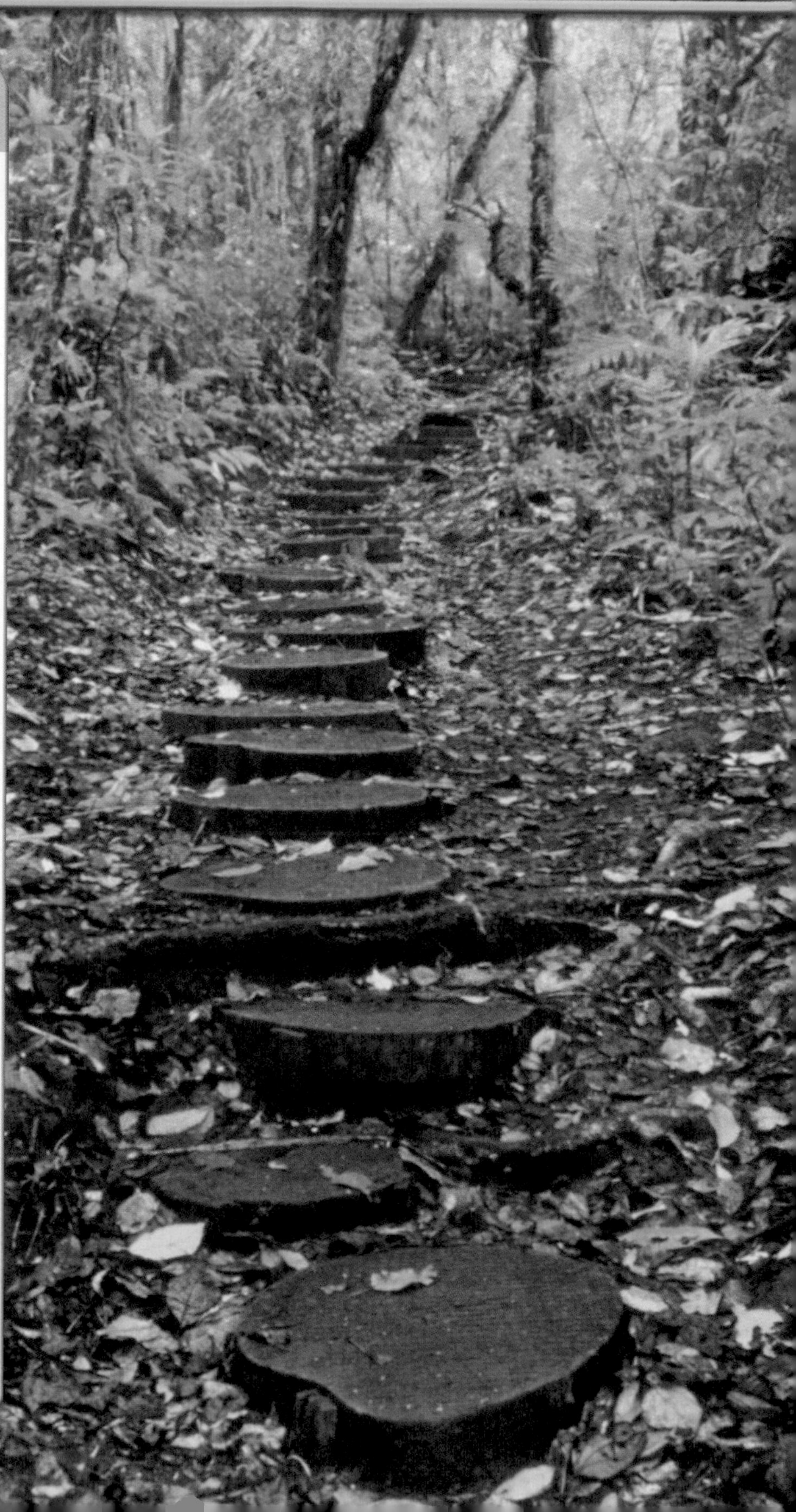

▶ Stepping stones through a rain forest in Costa Rica

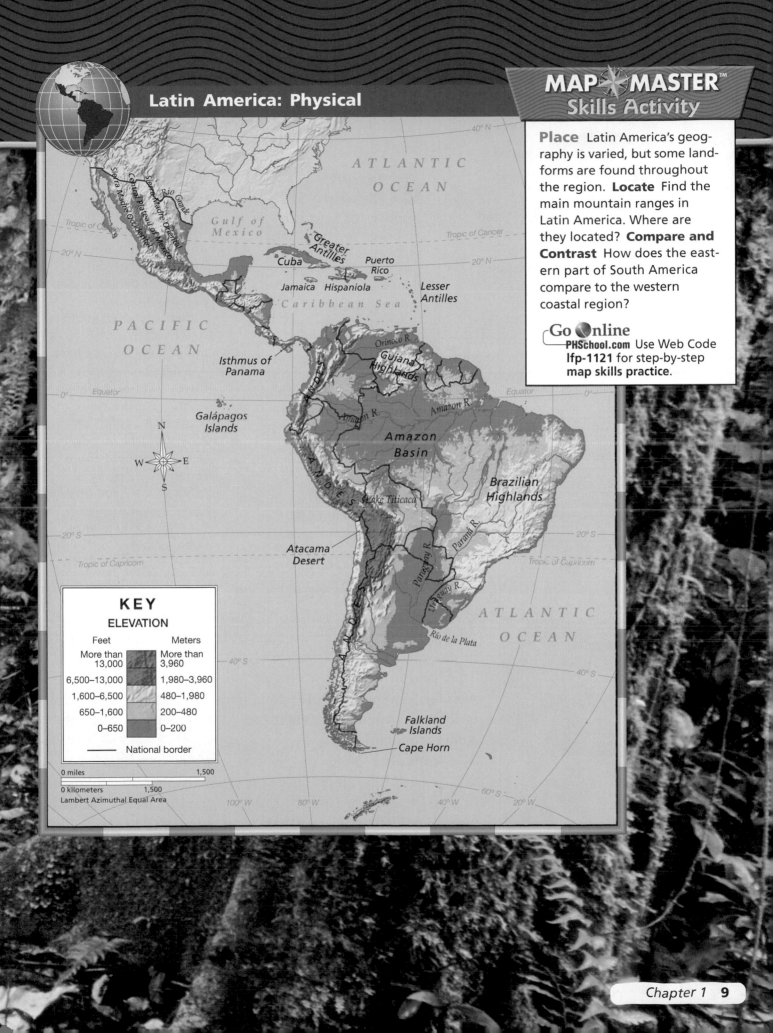

Latin America: Physical

Place Latin America's geography is varied, but some landforms are found throughout the region. **Locate** Find the main mountain ranges in Latin America. Where are they located? **Compare and Contrast** How does the eastern part of South America compare to the western coastal region?

Go Online
PHSchool.com Use Web Code **lfp-1121** for step-by-step **map skills practice**.

ATLANTIC OCEAN

PACIFIC OCEAN

Sierra Madre Occidental
Central Plateau of Mexico
Sierra Madre Oriental
Rio Grande
Tropic of Cancer
Gulf of Mexico
Greater Antilles
Cuba
Jamaica
Hispaniola
Puerto Rico
Lesser Antilles
Caribbean Sea
Isthmus of Panama
Orinoco R.
Guiana Highlands
ANDES
Galápagos Islands
Equator
Amazon R.
Amazon R.
Amazon Basin
Brazilian Highlands
Lake Titicaca
Atacama Desert
Paraguay R.
Paraná R.
Uruguay R.
Rio de la Plata
ATLANTIC OCEAN
Falkland Islands
Cape Horn

N W E S

Tropic of Capricorn

KEY

ELEVATION

Feet	Meters
More than 13,000	More than 3,960
6,500–13,000	1,980–3,960
1,600–6,500	480–1,980
650–1,600	200–480
0–650	0–200

—— National border

0 miles 1,500
0 kilometers 1,500
Lambert Azimuthal Equal Area

1 Land and Water

Prepare to Read

Objectives
In this section you will
1. Learn where Latin America is located.
2. Discover the important landforms of Latin America.
3. Find out how Latin America's waterways have affected the region.

Taking Notes
As you read this section, look for the main ideas about the geography of Latin America. Copy the table below and record your findings in it.

Geography of Latin America		
Region	Landforms	Waterways
Middle America		
Caribbean		
South America		

Target Reading Skill
Preview and Set a Purpose When you set a purpose for reading, you give yourself a focus. Before you read this section, look at the headings, photos, and maps to see what the section is about. Then set a purpose for reading, such as learning about Latin America's geography. Now read to meet your purpose.

Key Terms
- **Middle America** (MID ul uh MEHR ih kuh) *n.* Mexico and Central America

- **plateau** (pla TOH) *n.* a large raised area of mostly level land
- **isthmus** (IS mus) *n.* a strip of land with water on both sides that joins two larger bodies of land
- **pampas** (PAM puz) *n.* flat grasslands in South America
- **rain forest** (rayn FAWR ist) *n.* a dense evergreen forest that has abundant rainfall year-round
- **Amazon River** (AM uh zahn RIV ur) *n.* a long river in northern South America
- **tributary** (TRIB yoo tehr ee) *n.* a river or stream that flows into a larger river

La Paz, Bolivia

What would it be like to land at the highest major airport in the world? Many visitors to La Paz, Bolivia, do just that. They land at El Alto airport. *El Alto* (el AL toh) means "the high one" in Spanish. It is a good name for this airport, which is located more than 13,000 feet (3,962 meters) up in the Andes Mountains.

Shortly after leaving the plane, some visitors may get mountain sickness. The "thin" air of the Andes contains less oxygen than most people are used to. Oxygen starvation makes visitors' hearts beat faster and leaves them short of breath. Later on in the day, the visitors may get terrible headaches. It takes a few days for newcomers' bodies to get used to the mountain air. But the people who live in the Andes do not have these problems. Their bodies are used to the mountain environment.

Where Is Latin America?

When visitors land in La Paz, Bolivia, they have arrived in South America, one of the regions of Latin America. Find Bolivia on the map titled Political Latin America on page 3. As you can see, Latin America is located in the Western Hemisphere, south of the United States. Notice that Latin America includes all the nations from Mexico to the tip of South America. It also includes the islands that dot the Caribbean (ka ruh BEE un) Sea.

Geographic features divide Latin America into three smaller regions, as you can see in the map below. They are Mexico and Central America, which is also called **Middle America;** the Caribbean; and South America. South America is so large that geographers classify it as a continent.

Discovery
CHANNEL
SCHOOL
Video
Learn about the geography of Latin America.

✓ Reading Check **What three regions make up Latin America?**

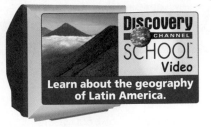

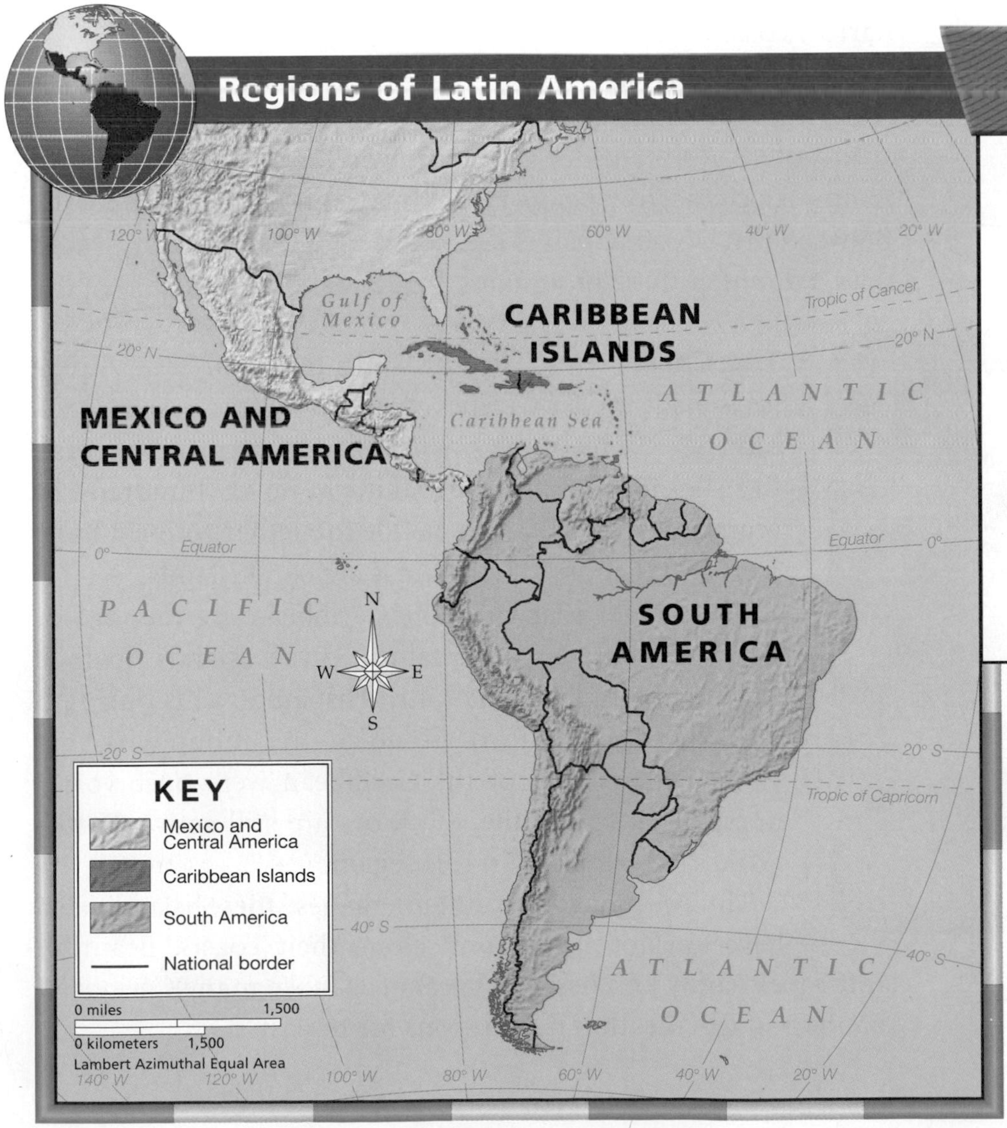

Regions of Latin America
Gulf of Mexico
CARIBBEAN ISLANDS
Tropic of Cancer
MEXICO AND CENTRAL AMERICA
Caribbean Sea
ATLANTIC OCEAN
Equator
PACIFIC OCEAN
SOUTH AMERICA
N
W
E
S
Tropic of Capricorn
KEY
Mexico and Central America
Caribbean Islands
South America
National border
0 miles 1,500
0 kilometers 1,500
Lambert Azimuthal Equal Area
ATLANTIC OCEAN
120° W
100° W
80° W
60° W
40° W
20° W
20° N
0°
20° S
40° S
140° W

MAP MASTER™ Skills Activity

Regions One of the three regions of Latin America is a continent, and one is made up of islands. **Identify** Find each region on the map. Which region is also called Middle America? **Infer** Why do you think that area is called Middle America and considered a separate region?

Go Online
PHSchool.com Use Web Code **lfp-1131** for step-by-step **map skills practice.**

Why "Latin" America?
Why are three distinct regions
called by one name, Latin
America? About 500 years
ago, Europeans sailed to the
Americas. Most of those who
settled in what is now called
Latin America came from
Spain and Portugal. These
European colonists brought
their own languages and
ways of life with them. Today,
most Latin Americans speak
Spanish, Portuguese, or
French. These languages have
their roots in the ancient
European language of Latin.
As a result, the entire region is
known as Latin America.

Landforms of Latin America

Picture mountains that pierce the clouds, and grassy plains that never seem to end. Imagine wet, dense forests and sun-baked deserts. This is Latin America, a region of variety and contrast.

Mexico and Central America Mexico and Central America stretch 2,500 miles (4,023 kilometers) from the United States border to South America. This distance is almost equal to the width of the United States from Los Angeles to New York City. Mountains dominate Middle America. These mountains are part of a long system of mountain ranges that extends from Canada through the United States all the way to the tip of South America.

Mexico's central plateau lies between two mountain ranges. A **plateau** (pla TOH) is a large raised area of mostly level land. Most of Mexico's people live there. However, the surrounding mountains make it difficult for people to travel to and from the central plateau. Along the east and west coasts of Mexico are narrow coastal plains.

Central America, located south of Mexico and north of South America, is an isthmus. An **isthmus** (IS mus) is a strip of land with water on both sides that joins two larger bodies of land. As in Mexico, narrow plains run along Central America's coasts. Between these coastal plains are steep, rugged mountains. More than a dozen of these mountains are active volcanoes.

The Caribbean The Caribbean region of Latin America is made up of two types of islands located in the Caribbean Sea. Some of the smaller islands are made of coral, the skeletons of tiny sea animals. Over hundreds of years, the skeletons have melded together to form large reefs and islands. The Bahamas are coral islands.

The larger islands of the Caribbean are the tops of huge underwater mountains. These islands include Cuba, Jamaica (juh MAY kuh), Hispaniola (his pun YOH luh), and Puerto Rico. Some of the mountains that formed the islands of the Caribbean were once volcanoes, and a few of the volcanoes are still active. Earthquakes are common in this region.

In addition to mountain ranges, these islands also have lowlands, or plains, along their coasts. Beautiful landscapes, sandy beaches, and coral reefs make many Caribbean islands popular vacation destinations for tourists.

A parrotfish swims by a coral reef in the Caribbean Sea.

South America The continent of South America has many types of landforms, but the Andes Mountains are probably the most impressive. The Andes run some 5,500 miles (8,900 kilometers) along the western coast of South America. In some places, the Andes rise to heights of more than 20,000 feet (6,100 meters). That's about as high as twenty 100-story buildings stacked one on top of another. Except for the Himalayan Mountains in Asia, the Andes are the highest mountains in the world.

The Andes are steep and difficult to cross. Even so, many people farm in this region. East of the Andes are rolling highlands. These highlands spread across parts of Brazil, Venezuela (ven uh ZWAY luh), Guyana (gy AN uh), and other South American countries. Farther south are the **pampas** (PAM puz), a large region of flat grasslands that stretches through Argentina (ahr jun TEE nuh) and Uruguay (YOOR uh gway). The pampas are similar to the Great Plains of the United States.

The eastern highlands and the Andes surround the Amazon River Basin. The Amazon River Basin contains the largest tropical rain forest in the world. A **rain forest** is a dense evergreen forest that has abundant rainfall throughout the year. This rain forest covers more than a third of the continent.

✓ **Reading Check** Describe the Andes mountain range.

Preview and Set a Purpose
If your purpose is to learn about the geography of Latin America, how does the paragraph at the left help you meet your goal?

Latin American Cowboys
These cowboys are herding cattle in the Patagonia region of Argentina.
Analyze Images *What details in the photo suggest that this scene is not taking place in the United States?*

Fishing the Rivers of Brazil
The families of these Brazilian fishers could not survive without their catch. **Infer** *Do you think these fishers sell their catch locally or send it to other countries? Use details from the photo to explain your answer.*

Latin America's Waterways

Latin America has some of the longest and largest bodies of water in the world. These waterways are important to the people of the region. Rivers serve as natural highways in places where it is hard to build roads. Fish from the rivers provide food. Rushing water from large rivers provides power to generate electricity.

Latin America's **Amazon** (AM uh zahn) **River** is the second-longest river in the world. Only the Nile in Africa is longer. The Amazon flows 4,000 miles (6,437 kilometers) from Peru across Brazil into the Atlantic Ocean. It carries more water than any other river in the world—about 20 percent of all the fresh river water on Earth! The Amazon gathers power from more than 1,000 tributaries that spill into it. **Tributaries** are the rivers and streams that flow into a larger river. With its tributaries, the Amazon drains an area of more than two million square miles.

The Paraná (pah rah NAH), Paraguay, and Uruguay rivers form the Río de la Plata system, which separates Argentina and Uruguay. In Venezuela, people travel on the Orinoco River and Lake Maracaibo (mar uh KY boh). Up in the Andes Mountains, Lake Titicaca is the highest lake in the world on which ships can travel. It lies 12,500 feet (3,810 kilometers) above sea level.

✓ **Reading Check** What rivers form the Río de la Plata system?

Section 1 Assessment

Key Terms
Review the key terms at the beginning of this section. Use each term in a sentence that explains its meaning.

Target Reading Skill
What was your purpose for reading this section? Did you accomplish it? If not, what might have been a better purpose?

Comprehension and Critical Thinking
1. (a) Name What are the three regions of Latin America?

(b) Synthesize Where are the regions located in relation to one another?
2. (a) Recall What are the main landforms of Latin America?
(b) Identify Cause and Effect How do mountain ranges affect life in Latin America?
3. (a) Identify Which is the largest river in Latin America?
(b) Analyze Information What are three important characteristics of that river?
(c) Generalize How do countries benefit from their waterways?

Writing Activity
If your family were planning to move to Latin America, which of its three regions would you prefer to live in? Write a paragraph explaining your choice.

Writing Tip Begin your paragraph with a topic sentence that states your main idea—your choice of region. Give at least two reasons for your choice. Support each reason with a specific detail.

Climate and Vegetation

Prepare to Read

Objectives

In this section you will
1. Find out what kinds of climate Latin America has.
2. Learn what factors influence climate in Latin America.
3. Understand how climate and vegetation influence the ways people live.

Taking Notes

As you read this section, look for the ways different factors affect climate and vegetation. Copy the table below and record your findings in it.

Factor	Effect on Climate	Effect on Vegetation

Target Reading Skill

Preview and Predict
Making predictions about your text helps you set a purpose for reading and remember what you read. Before you begin, look at the headings, photos, and anything else that stands out. Then predict what the text might be about. For example, you might predict that this section will tell about Latin America's climate and plants. As you read, if what you learn doesn't support your prediction, revise your prediction.

Key Terms

- **El Niño** (el NEEN yoh) *n.* a warming of the ocean water along the western coast of South America
- **elevation** (el uh VAY shun) *n.* the height of land above sea level
- **economy** (ih KAHN uh mee) *n.* the ways that goods and services are produced and made available to people

Every few years, something strange happens off the western coast of South America. Fish that usually thrive in the cold waters of the Pacific Ocean are driven away. At the same time, other changes occur on land. Areas that usually have dry weather get heavy rains, and low-lying regions are flooded. In other parts of Latin America, drought plagues the land and the people.

What brings this disaster to Latin America? It is **El Niño** (el NEEN yoh), a warming of the ocean water along the western coast of South America. It occurs every few years and influences global weather patterns. El Niño is Spanish for "the little boy." Peruvian fishermen gave it this name, which refers to the baby Jesus, because the warm water currents usually reach Peru around Christmas time. El Niño is one of many factors that affect climate in Latin America.

The warm water current of El Niño appears red in this view from space.

Latin America: Climate Regions

Location The Equator runs through parts of Latin America, but it is far from other parts of the region. **Locate** Find the Equator on the map. Which climates are most common in Latin America, and how far is each climate region from the Equator? **Draw Conclusions** How do climates change as you move away from the Equator?

Go Online
PHSchool.com Use Web Code lfp-1142 for step-by-step map skills practice.

UNITED STATES

ATLANTIC OCEAN

Gulf of Mexico

Monterrey
MEXICO
Guadalajara
Mexico City

BAHAMAS
Havana
CUBA
JAMAICA HAITI
DOMINICAN REPUBLIC
San Juan
PUERTO RICO (U.S.)

Tropic of Cancer

BELIZE
HONDURAS
GUATEMALA
EL SALVADOR
NICARAGUA
COSTA RICA
PANAMA

Caribbean Sea

Caracas
VENEZUELA
GUYANA
SURINAME
FRENCH GUIANA (France)
Bogotá
COLOMBIA
ECUADOR

PACIFIC OCEAN

GALÁPAGOS ISLANDS (Ecuador)

Equator

PERU
Lima

BRAZIL

Brasília

BOLIVIA

Tropic of Capricorn

PARAGUAY

Rio de Janeiro
São Paulo

CHILE
Santiago
Buenos Aires
URUGUAY
ARGENTINA

ATLANTIC OCEAN

FALKLAND ISLANDS (U.K.)

SOUTH GEORGIA (U.K.)

KEY

- Tropical wet
- Tropical wet and dry
- Semiarid
- Arid
- Mediterranean
- Humid subtropical
- Marine west coast
- Tundra
- Highland
- — National border
- • City

0 miles 1,000
0 kilometers 1,000
Lambert Azimuthal Equal Area

N
W E
S

The Climates of Latin America

What is the climate like where you live? Is it hot? Cold? Rainy? Dry? If you lived in Latin America, the climate might be any of these. Climate in Latin America can vary greatly even within the same country.

Hot, Cold, Wild, and Mild In parts of the Andes, below-zero temperatures can set your teeth chattering. Travel to the Amazon Basin, and you may be sweating in 90°F (32°C) heat. And don't forget your umbrella! This part of Latin America receives more than 80 inches (203 centimeters) of rain each year. If you prefer dry weather, visit the Atacama (ah tah KAH mah) Desert in Chile or the Sonoran Desert in Mexico. These areas are two of the driest places on Earth.

The weather in the Caribbean is usually sunny and warm. From June to November, however, the region is often hit with fierce hurricanes. In 2005, Hurricane Wilma shattered the sunny Caribbean weather with a wild blast. Winds howled at more than 185 miles per hour (300 kilometers per hour). Waves nearly 20 feet (6 meters) high smashed into the coast. The storm tore roofs off houses, shattered windows, and yanked huge trees from the ground. Wilma turned out to be the most intense hurricane ever recorded in the region.

Hurricanes are a part of life for people living in the Caribbean. But people in other parts of Latin America have to deal with other climates. For example, people who live in the mountains need to protect themselves against the cold. That's because the higher up the mountains you go, the cooler it gets.

Climate Regions of Latin America Look at the map titled Latin America: Climate Regions. You will notice that many parts of Latin America have a tropical wet climate. A tropical wet climate means hot, humid, and rainy weather all year round.

Other parts of Latin America have a tropical wet and dry climate. These areas are equally hot, but the rainy season does not last all year long. Parts of Mexico and Brazil and most of the Caribbean have a tropical wet and dry climate.

Much of Argentina, Uruguay, and Paraguay has a humid sub-tropical climate. Here, the summers are hot and wet while the winters are cool and damp. Farther south, the climate turns arid, or dry. This colder, drier area is called Patagonia (pat uh GOH nee uh).

✓ **Reading Check** Describe a tropical wet and dry climate.

Links to
Science

What is a Hurricane?
A hurricane is a strong tropical storm with winds of 73 miles per hour (117 kilometers per hour) or more. Hurricanes get their energy from warm, humid air at the ocean's surface. As the warm air rises and forms clouds, more air is pulled into the developing storm. The winds spiral inward. As the storm grows, it creates very high winds and heavy rains. At the center of the hurricane is the "eye," an area of calm. After the eye passes over an area, the hurricane resumes. It can still cause serious damage, as Hurricane Mitch did in 1998 in countries such as Honduras and Nicaragua (photo below).

What Factors Affect Climate?

Have you ever hiked in the mountains? If so, you've probably noticed that as you climbed higher the temperature dropped.

One key factor affecting the climate of mountainous Latin America is **elevation**, the height of land above sea level. Look at the diagram titled Vertical Climate Zones. It shows how elevation affects climate. As you can see, the higher the elevation, the colder the temperature. Near the Equator, it may be a warm 80°F (27°C) at sea level. But above 10,000 feet (3,048 meters), the temperature may remain below freezing—too cold for people to live.

Location also affects Latin America's climate. Regions close to the Equator are generally warmer than those farther away. Look at the map titled Latin America: Climate Regions on page 16. Find the Equator. Which parts of Latin America are closest to the Equator? These regions are likely to have the warmest weather.

Wind patterns affect climate too. Winds move cold air from the North and South poles toward the Equator. They also move warm air from the Equator toward the poles. In the Caribbean, sea breezes help to keep temperatures moderate. Winds also affect rainfall in the Caribbean. More rain falls on the sides of islands facing the wind than on the sides facing away.

✓ **Reading Check** How does nearness to the Equator affect climate?

■ Diagram Skills

Even near the Equator, temperature varies with elevation. Notice the tree line. Above the tree line, it is too cold and windy for trees to grow. **Identify** What is the elevation of the tree line? Above what elevation is there snow year-round? **Draw Conclusions** Why is land between the tree line and the snow line used for grazing?

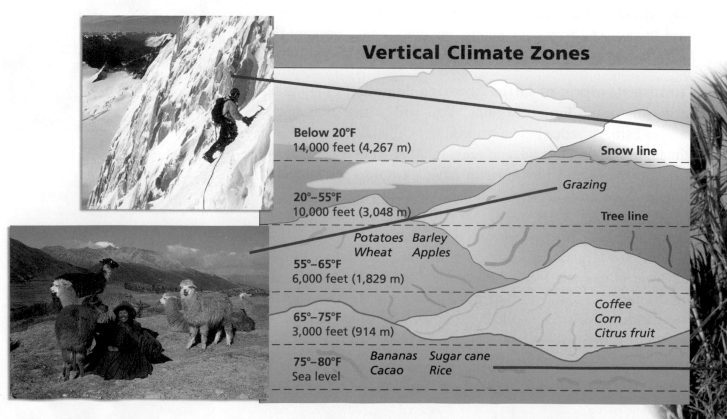

Vertical Climate Zones

Below 20°F
14,000 feet (4,267 m) — Snow line

20°–55°F
10,000 feet (3,048 m) — Grazing — Tree line

55°–65°F
6,000 feet (1,829 m) — Potatoes Barley Wheat Apples

65°–75°F
3,000 feet (914 m) — Coffee Corn Citrus fruit

75°–80°F
Sea level — Bananas Sugar cane Cacao Rice

Climate, Plants, and People

Imagine a forest so dense and lush that almost no sunlight reaches the ground. Broad green leaves, tangled vines, and thousands of species of trees and plants surround you. The air is hot and heavy with moisture. Welcome to the Amazon rain forest.

Now, suppose you have traveled to the coast of northern Chile. You're in the Atacama Desert. Winds carry no moisture to this barren land, and there are few signs of life. The Andes shield this parched region from rain. Parts of the desert have not felt a single raindrop in hundreds of years.

Vegetation Regions Latin America's varied climate and physical features make such extremes possible. Look at the map titled Latin America: Vegetation Regions on the next page. Notice which countries in Latin America have areas of tropical rain forest. Now, find these countries on the climate map. How do the tropical climate and heavy rainfall in these countries influence the vegetation that grows there?

Of course, not all of Latin America is either rain forest or desert. Many regions of Latin America with less extreme climates have different kinds of vegetation. For example, the pampas of Argentina and Uruguay are grassy plains where cattle are raised. Herding is also a way of life on grasslands high in the Andes Mountains, where Native Americans have raised llamas for centuries. Llamas are used mostly as pack animals. Their relatives, alpacas and vicuñas, provide fine wool.

Preview and Predict
Based on what you've read so far, is your prediction on target? If not, revise or change your prediction now.

Life in the Climate Zones
A mountain climber ascends above the snow line in Argentina (facing page, top), and llamas graze above the tree line (facing page, bottom). In the photo on this page, a woman harvests sugar cane in Barbados. **Generalize** *At what elevations would you expect to find most farms? Explain why.*

Latin America: Vegetation Regions

Location Different kinds of vegetation grow in different regions of Latin America. **Identify** Find the two largest vegetation regions on the map. Name the kind of vegetation found in these regions. **Compare** Compare this map with the climate map on page 16. What connection do you see between vegetation regions and climate regions?

Go Online
PHSchool.com Use Web Code lfp-1152 for step-by-step map skills practice.

UNITED STATES

ATLANTIC OCEAN

Gulf of Mexico

Monterrey
MEXICO
Guadalajara
Havana
Mexico City
BELIZE
GUATEMALA   HONDURAS
EL SALVADOR   NICARAGUA
COSTA RICA
PANAMA

BAHAMAS
CUBA
JAMAICA   HAITI
DOMINICAN REPUBLIC
San Juan   PUERTO RICO (U.S.)
Caribbean Sea

Tropic of Cancer

Caracas
VENEZUELA
Bogotá
COLOMBIA
ECUADOR

GUYANA
SURINAME
FRENCH GUIANA (France)

PACIFIC OCEAN

GALÁPAGOS ISLANDS (Ecuador)

Equator

PERU
Lima

BRAZIL
Brasília

BOLIVIA

PARAGUAY

Rio de Janeiro
São Paulo

Tropic of Capricorn

CHILE
Santiago

Buenos Aires   URUGUAY
ARGENTINA

ATLANTIC OCEAN

FALKLAND ISLANDS (U.K.)

SOUTH GEORGIA (U.K.)

KEY

- Tropical rain forest
- Deciduous forest
- Mixed forest
- Coniferous forest
- Mediterranean vegetation
- Tropical savanna
- Temperate grassland
- Desert scrub
- Desert (little or no vegetation)
- Highland (vegetation varying with elevation)
- — National border
- • City

0 miles   1,000
0 kilometers   1,000
Lambert Azimuthal Equal Area

Crops and Climate Temperature and rainfall affect not only what plants grow naturally in a region, but also what crops people can grow there. Sugar cane, coffee, and bananas require warm weather and abundant rainfall. These crops are important to the economies of many countries around the Caribbean Sea. The **economy** is the ways that goods and services are produced and made available to people. Look again at the climate map on page 16. Why do you think the area around the Caribbean is well suited to growing these crops?

Elevation and Vegetation Elevation also affects vegetation. For example, palm trees and fruit trees that grow well in the coastal plains of Mexico and Central America would not survive high in the Andes. To grow at higher elevations, plants must be able to withstand cooler temperatures, strong winds, and irregular rainfall.

Look again at the diagram on page 18 titled Vertical Climate Zones. Notice the tree line and the snow line. It is too cold and windy for trees to grow above the tree line, but plants that grow low to the ground, such as grasses, are found in this area. Birds, bats, mice, foxes, and llamas also live here. Above the snow line, snow does not melt, and there is almost no wildlife.

Harvesting bananas in Honduras

✔ **Reading Check** **Describe how elevation affects the vegetation of a region.**

Section 2 Assessment

Key Terms
Review the key terms at the beginning of this section. Use each term in a sentence that explains its meaning.

Target Reading Skill
What did you predict about this section? How did your prediction guide your reading?

Comprehension and Critical Thinking
1. (a) Recall Describe Latin America's climate regions.

(b) Synthesize How does climate affect the ways that Latin Americans live?

2. (a) Identify Name three factors that affect climate.

(b) Apply Information Why might two areas near the Equator have very different climates?

3. (a) Name What two factors affect the kinds of vegetation that grow in a region?

(b) Infer Why do some farmers in Argentina raise apples while farmers in other parts of the country raise sheep?

Writing Activity
Would you pack differently for trips to the Atacama Desert and the Andes Mountains? Write a paragraph describing what you would take to each place and why.

Go Online
PHSchool.com

For: An activity on the rain forest
Visit: PHSchool.com
Web Code: lfd-1102

Analyzing and Interpreting Climate Maps

> **Travel agent:** Thanks for calling South America Travel Service. May I help you?
>
> **Customer:** I'd like to visit South America, but I can't decide where to go. Could you send me brochures of places you recommend?
>
> **Travel agent:** Certainly. And you might want to visit our Web site, which features a climate map of South America. You'll see that the region has many climates, offering activities from water skiing to snow skiing.

A special purpose map shows information about a particular topic. The climate map on the next page is a type of special purpose map. The travel agent knows that for most people, climate is an important factor in deciding where to vacation.

Learn the Skill

Use these steps to analyze and interpret a climate map.

1. **Read the map title and look at the map to get a general idea of what it shows.** Notice the area for which climate is being shown.

2. **Read the key to understand how the map uses symbols, colors, and patterns.** A climate map usually uses colors to represent different climates.

3. **Use the key to interpret the map.** Look for the different colors on the map. Notice where different climates are located, and what landforms and waterways are also in those locations.

4. **Draw conclusions about what the map shows.** Facts you discover when you analyze a climate map can help you draw conclusions about a place: what kinds of plants and animals live there or how the people make a living.

Practice the Skill

If you were the caller on page 22, where would you want to go on your vacation? List your favorite vacation activities, and then use the map on this page to identify several places you would like to visit.

1 Jot down the purpose of the map. What does it show?

2 Look at the key to see the different climates in South America. Identify the climates in which you could probably do the vacation activities on your list.

3 On the map, find the places that have the climates you have identified.

4 Use the climate map to draw conclusions about each place you found. Might the place have ocean views? Rock walls to climb? Forests with fascinating wildlife? Write your conclusions for each place, and choose a vacation destination.

South America: Climate Regions

KEY

- Tropical wet
- Tropical wet and dry
- Semiarid
- Arid
- Mediterranean
- Humid subtropical
- Marine west coast
- Tundra
- Highland
- ——— National border
- • City

0 miles 1,500
0 kilometers 1,500
Lambert Azimuthal Equal Area

Apply the Skill

Now take the role of the travel agent. You get an e-mail from an author. "I am writing a book that takes place in a desert region of South America that is also near the ocean. Where should I go to do my research?"

Turn to your map. (**a**) In what climate are you likely to find a desert? (**b**) What places in South America have that type of climate? (**c**) Among those places, which is closest to the ocean? Write a reply to the author. Suggest a location and explain why it will suit her needs.

Resources and Land Use

Prepare to Read

Objectives

In this section you will
1. Find out what Latin America's most important natural resources are.
2. Learn why depending on a one-resource economy has been a problem for Latin American nations.

Taking Notes

As you read this section, look for the major resources of each region of Latin America. Copy the chart below and record your findings in it.

```
                 Major Resources
   ┌──────────────┬──────────────┬──────────────┐
   │    Middle    │   Caribbean  │    South     │
   │   America    │              │   America    │
   ├──────────────┼──────────────┼──────────────┤
   │  •           │  •           │  •           │
   │  •           │  •           │  •           │
   └──────────────┴──────────────┴──────────────┘
```

Target Reading Skill

Preview and Ask Questions Before you read this section, preview the headings and illustrations to see what the section is about. Then write two questions that will help you understand or remember something important in the section. For example, you might ask, "What are the resources of Middle America?" Then read to answer your questions.

Key Terms

- **natural resources** (NACH ur ul REE sawrs uz) *n.* things found in nature that people can use to meet their needs
- **hydroelectricity** (hy droh ee lek TRIS ih tee) *n.* electric power produced by rushing water
- **one-resource economy** (wun REE sawrs ih KAHN uh mee) *n.* a country's economy based largely on one resource or crop
- **diversify** (duh VUR suh fy) *v.* to add variety

Quechua Indian women sort ore at a Bolivian tin mine.

Bolivia has long depended on its mineral resources for wealth. At first, silver helped to bring money into Bolivia's treasury. Soon, however, tin became even more important. For many years, Bolivia enjoyed the wealth that tin brought to the economy. Then, in the 1920s and 1930s, a worldwide economic crisis hit. Industries stopped buying tin, as well as other natural resources. Bolivia suffered as its main resource failed to bring in money. This economic crisis hit all of Latin America hard. It brought home a problem that many Latin American nations have: They rely too much on one resource.

Latin America's Resources

What do the following things have in common: fish, petroleum, water, silver, and forests? They are all natural resources of Latin America. **Natural resources** are things found in nature that people can use to meet their needs. Latin America's resources are as varied as its physical features and climate.

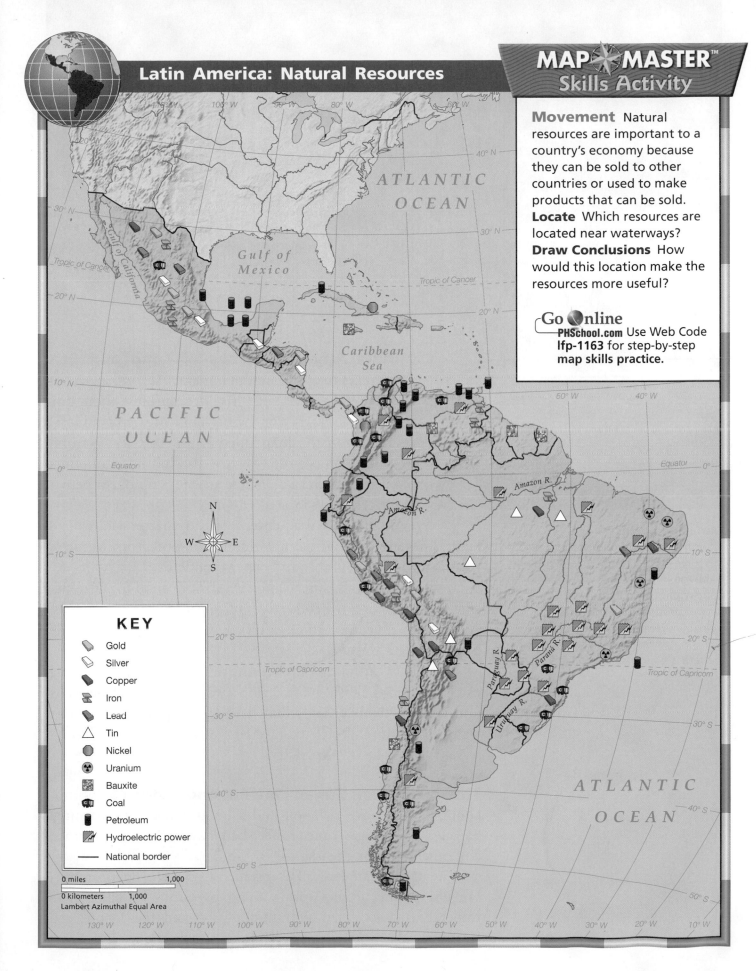

Latin America: Natural Resources

Movement Natural resources are important to a country's economy because they can be sold to other countries or used to make products that can be sold.
Locate Which resources are located near waterways?
Draw Conclusions How would this location make the resources more useful?

Go Online
PHSchool.com Use Web Code lfp-1163 for step-by-step map skills practice.

ATLANTIC OCEAN

Gulf of Mexico

Caribbean Sea

PACIFIC OCEAN

Tropic of Cancer

Equator

Amazon R.

Amazon R.

Paraguay R.

Paraná R.

Uruguay R.

Tropic of Capricorn

ATLANTIC OCEAN

KEY

- Gold
- Silver
- Copper
- Iron
- Lead
- Tin
- Nickel
- Uranium
- Bauxite
- Coal
- Petroleum
- Hydroelectric power
- National border

0 miles 1,000
0 kilometers 1,000
Lambert Azimuthal Equal Area

N
W E
S

Middle America: Riches of Land and Sea

Mexico is a treasure chest of minerals. It has deposits of silver, gold, copper, coal, iron ore, and just about any other mineral you can name. Find Mexico's mineral resources on the map titled Latin America: Natural Resources on page 25. Mexico also has huge amounts of oil and natural gas. Where are Mexico's oil, or petroleum, resources located?

In addition, trees cover nearly a quarter of Mexico's land. Trees are another natural resource. Wood from Mexico's trees is turned into lumber and paper products.

Central America's climate and rich soil are good for farming. The people there grow coffee, cotton, sugar cane, and bananas. They also plant cacao (kuh KAY oh) trees. Cacao seeds are made into chocolate and cocoa.

Not all of Central America's resources are on land. The people catch fish and shellfish in the region's waters. Central Americans also have built huge dams that harness the power of rushing water to produce electricity. Electric power created by rushing water is called **hydroelectricity.**

The Caribbean: Sugar, Coffee, and More Caribbean countries also have rich soil and a good climate for farming. Farmers grow sugar cane, coffee, bananas, cacao, citrus fruits, and other crops on the islands.

The Caribbean has other resources as well. For example, Jamaica is one of the world's main producers of bauxite—a mineral used to make aluminum. Cuba and the Dominican Republic have nickel deposits. Trinidad is rich in oil.

Varied Resources
Countries depend on a variety of resources, from commercially grown cabbage in the Dominican Republic (upper photo) to hydroelectric power produced by this dam in Brazil (lower photo). **Generalize** *Explain how each resource could benefit a country's economy.*

Commercial Fishing
Workers unload their catch at a dock in Argentina. The fish shown below are tuna.
Compare and Contrast
How is this example of fishing different from that shown on page 14?

South America: A Wealth of Resources Like Mexico, South America is rich in minerals. It has gold, copper, tin, bauxite, and iron ore. Look again at the map titled Latin America: Natural Resources on page 25. Where are these resources located? South America also has oil. Much of South America's oil is found in Venezuela.

South America's plants and fish are natural resources, too. Forests cover about half the continent. Trees from these forests provide everything from wood for building to coconuts for eating. Mahogany and rosewood are used to make fine furniture. Some woods are used by local people for fuel. The rain forests of South America contain a wide variety of trees and other vegetation. Some of these plants are used to make medicines. Scientists are studying other plants to see if they, too, might have medical uses.

The people of South America harvest many kinds of fish. Tuna, anchovies, and other species of fish are plentiful in the waters off the Pacific coast. Shellfish, such as shrimp, are also important to the region's economy. Freshwater fish, those found in rivers, are an important food source in South America.

Like other parts of Latin America, South America has rich soil. Farmers grow many different crops there. For example, coffee is a key crop in Brazil and Colombia. Wheat is important in Argentina. Many South American economies rely on the production of sugar cane, cotton, and rice.

✓ **Reading Check** **What kinds of products are made from South America's forests?**

World Coffee Prices, 1965–2005

Prices adjusted for inflation, using U.S. dollars.
SOURCE: World Bank, International Coffee Association

Graph Skills

World coffee prices affect not only the economies of many Latin American countries but also ordinary people, such as this Guatemalan coffee-picker. **Describe** What is the pattern of coffee prices over the 40 years shown in the graph above? **Analyze Information** What years were good years for coffee growers? What year might have been the worst? Explain your answer.

Resources and the Economy

Not every country shares equally in the wealth of Latin America's resources. Some Latin American countries have many resources, while others have few. Some countries do not have the money they need to develop all of their resources. Even when countries do develop their resources, not everyone in that country always enjoys the benefits. And sometimes countries rely too much on one resource or crop.

Problems of a One-Resource Economy Sometimes having a great deal of a valuable resource can lead to economic problems. That's because some countries then develop what is called a **one-resource economy,** an economy that depends largely on one resource or crop. Why is this a problem? Here is an example: When world copper prices are high, the copper mining industry is very successful. But suppose copper prices drop sharply. Then copper exports are not worth as much. When this happens, the mining industry loses money. Mining workers may lose their jobs. People and businesses—even a whole country—can go into debt. Chile is the leading producer of copper in the world. When prices plunge, Chile's whole economy suffers.

The World Economy Oil is one of Latin America's most valuable resources. But world oil prices go up and down, sometimes very suddenly. Mexico and Venezuela are major oil producers. In the mid-1980s, oil companies produced more oil than the world needed. As a result, prices dropped. Mexico earned much less income than it had expected.

Many people in Latin America make their living by farming. Some Latin American countries depend on only one or two crops, such as coffee, bananas, or sugar. Certain factors outside the country—such as increased production of coffee by other countries—may cause the price of the crop to drop. When the price of a crop goes down, exports of that crop bring less money into the country.

Weather Effects Weather brings challenges, too. Hurricanes, droughts, and plant diseases may damage crops. Weather can also hurt the fishing industry. Usually, the cold water of the Pacific supports a large number of small water plants on which fish feed. But when El Niño strikes, the warm water kills the plants and the fish die or move to other areas. The fishing industry of Peru has suffered great economic losses due to El Niño effects.

In each case described above, dependence on a particular resource—copper, oil, one particular crop, or fishing—has hurt the economy of the country that depended on it. That is because, if something unexpected happens to the major resource of a country with a one-resource economy, that country is left with few other sources of income.

Preview and Ask Questions
Ask a question that will help you learn something important from the paragraph at the left. Now read the paragraph and answer your question.

At the Mercy of the Weather
In 2001, a severe drought in Guatemala caused many crops to dry up. This man is sowing beans on top of his failed corn crop. **Predict** *What might be the result if this farmer depended only on corn?*

An automobile factory in Quito, Ecuador

Latin America Begins to Diversify

Because Latin American nations have learned the risks of depending on one resource or crop, they began to diversify their economies in the 1960s and 1970s. To **diversify** is to add variety. Many Latin American nations are building factories. Factories make products that can be sold to bring more money into the economy. Factories also provide jobs.

Rather than depending so much on oil, Venezuela has been promoting investment in its agriculture, steel, and tourism industries. The island nation Trinidad and Tobago also has large deposits of natural resources such as oil and natural gas. However, tourism and international business are also important parts of the economy.

El Salvador used to depend too heavily on its coffee crop. Now, cotton, sugar, corn, and other crops play an important role in the nation's economy. Brazil, too, has been building up its industries so that it does not have to depend so much on agriculture. In addition to farm products, Brazil now exports machinery, steel, and chemicals. The governments of Latin America continue to look for ways to protect their nations from the hazards of a one-resource economy.

✓ **Reading Check** How is Brazil diversifying its economy?

Section 3 Assessment

Key Terms
Review the key terms at the beginning of this section. Use each term in a sentence that explains its meaning.

Target Reading Skill
What questions helped you learn something important from this section? What are the answers to your questions?

Comprehension and Critical Thinking
1. (a) Identify Name the important natural resources of each region of Latin America.

(b) Compare How are the resources of South America similar to those of Middle America?
(c) Draw Conclusions How can rich soil and a mild climate benefit the economy of a region?
2. (a) Recall What resources have Venezuela and El Salvador depended on in the past?
(b) Synthesize Was depending on these resources good for the economies of these countries?
(c) Identify Cause and Effect Suppose a disease destroyed El Salvador's coffee crop. How would this loss affect coffee-plantation workers and the economy of El Salvador? Explain your answer.

Writing Activity
Suppose you are the president of a Latin American country. Your nation depends on sugar cane for nearly all of its income. Outline the arguments you would use in a speech to persuade your people of the need to diversify. Then write an introduction to your speech.

Writing Tip A persuasive speech is like a persuasive essay. Be sure you have three reasons to support your main idea. Use persuasive language to introduce those ideas in your opening paragraph.

Review and Assessment

◆ Chapter Summary

Section 1: Land and Water
- Latin America is located south of the United States and is made up of three regions.
- Mountain ranges and rain forests dominate Latin America, but there are also islands, plains, plateaus, and deserts.
- Waterways such as the Amazon River provide transportation, food, and electric power to the people of Latin America.

Section 2: Climate and Vegetation
- Latin America has a wide range of climate regions.
- Climate is shaped by elevation, nearness to the Equator, and wind patterns.
- Latin America's diverse climate regions affect vegetation patterns and how people live.

Section 3: Resources and Land Use
- Latin America's resources include minerals, good farmland, forests, and fish.
- Depending on only a few resources, such as one crop or mineral, can lead to economic problems.
- Latin American countries are now diversifying their economies.

Argentina

Honduras

Brazil

◆ Key Terms

Each of the statements below contains a key term from the chapter. Decide whether each statement is true or false. If it is true, write *true*. If it is false, rewrite the sentence to make it true.

1. A plateau is a narrow strip of land that has water on both sides and joins two larger bodies of land.

2. A tributary is smaller than the river into which it flows.

3. Pampas are flat grasslands.

4. Rain forests thrive in hot, dry climates.

5. Elevation is the distance from the Equator.

6. The goods a country produces are its natural resources.

7. Hydroelectricity is electric power produced from rushing water.

8. To diversify an economy is to produce more of one resource.

◆ Comprehension and Critical Thinking

9. (a) Recall In what part of Mexico do most Mexicans live?
(b) Describe What is this part of Mexico like?
(c) Identify Causes What makes travel to and from this area difficult?

10. (a) Identify What is the major mountain range in South America?
(b) Identify Effects Describe two effects this mountain range has on the climate, the vegetation, or the people.
(c) Evaluate Do you think that the mountains help or hurt South America? Explain.

11. (a) Define What is El Niño?
(b) Identify Effects What are some of El Niño's effects on land and sea?
(c) Synthesize How can El Niño affect the economy of Latin America?

12. (a) Recall How does elevation affect climate?
(b) Contrast How are the different vegetation regions in Latin America shaped by their climates?
(c) Infer How do climate and vegetation affect how people live and work?

13. (a) Identify What are the major resources of Middle America?
(b) Categorize Which of these resources helps produce power?
(c) Analyze Explain what happens when too much of one resource is produced worldwide.

14. (a) Define What is a one-resource economy?
(b) Summarize Describe how one Latin American country is diversifying its economy.
(c) Generalize Why is it important for countries to diversify their economies?

◆ Skills Practice

Analyzing and Interpreting Climate Maps
In the Skills for Life activity in this chapter, you analyzed and interpreted a climate map. The skill you learned can be applied to other special-purpose maps.

Review the steps you followed to learn the skill. Then turn to the map titled Latin America: Vegetation Regions on page 20. Take the role of the travel agent again. This time respond to

two people: one who wants to visit a rain forest and another who wants to visit grassy plains to observe Latin American cowboys.

◆ Writing Activity: Science

Suppose you are the television meteorologist for a small Caribbean island. As part of your weather report, you are doing an overview of the weather for the past three months. Explain to your broadcast audience why one side of your island has been rainy and the other side has been sunny. You can create a mental picture or a map of the geography of your island (including mountains and rivers) to aid in your explanation.

MAP MASTER™
Skills Activity

Latin America

Place Location For each place listed below, write the letter from the map that shows its location.

1. South America
2. Caribbean Sea
3. Amazon River
4. Equator
5. Mexico
6. Central America
7. Andes Mountains

Go Online
PHSchool.com Use Web Code **lfp-1123** for an **interactive map**.

Standardized Test Prep

Test-Taking Tips

Some questions on standardized tests ask you to make mental maps. Read the passage below. Then follow the tips to answer the question.

TIP Try to picture the locations of the Southern Hemisphere and the Amazon River in your mind. Think of maps you have seen.

Pick the letter that best answers the question.

Zach's geography teacher asked his class to write clues for a game called What Country Is It? Zach wrote the following set of clues:
This country is mostly in the Southern Hemisphere. The Amazon River runs through it. It is larger than Argentina.

  A ~~Mexico.~~
  B Brazil.
  C ~~Canada.~~
  D Peru.

TIP First rule out answer choices that don't make sense. Pick the BEST answer from the remaining choices.

Think It Through Canada and Mexico are both in the Northern Hemisphere, so you can rule out answers A and C. The Amazon River runs across northern South America, including both Peru and Brazil. But Peru is smaller than Argentina. That leaves Brazil, answer B.

Practice Questions

Choose the letter of the best answer.

1. What two bodies of land does the isthmus of Central America connect?
   A the Caribbean and South America
   B Mexico and the United States
   C Mexico and the Caribbean
   D South America and North America

2. Which of the following factors does NOT affect a region's climate?
   A hurricanes
   B elevation
   C location
   D wind patterns

3. Throughout much of Latin America, people use rushing water to create
   A wells.
   B swimming pools.
   C water parks.
   D hydroelectricity.

4. The largest tropical rain forest in the world is located in
   A Mexico's central plateau.
   B the Amazon River Basin.
   C the isthmus of Central America.
   D the coral reefs of the Caribbean.

Read the following passage and answer the question that follows.

Yoshi is writing clues for a game called Name That Region. He wrote the following set of clues:
This region in Latin America is located in the Northern Hemisphere. It is made up of islands. Farming is especially good in this region.

5. What region do Yoshi's clues describe?
   A South America
   B the Caribbean
   C Mexico
   D North America

Go Online PHSchool.com
Use Web Code lfa-1101 for a **Chapter 1 self-test.**

The Surveyor
By Alma Flor Ada

Prepare to Read

Background Information
Do people in your family tell you stories about their past? Are some of those stories repeated many times? What stories do you remember the best? What do you learn from these stories?

The stories that family members tell each other become a part of a family's history. They are important because they teach us about our cultural heritage. They connect us to events, to places, and to people. They show us the world from a particular, personal point of view.

Alma Flor Ada (AL muh flawr AY duh) grew up in Cuba. The following selection shows what Ada learned from one of the stories her father used to tell her.

Objectives
In this selection you will

1. Discover how a story from the past can shape the present.

2. Learn how geography can have an important effect on people's lives.

surveyor (sur VAY ur) n. a person who measures land and geographic features

Small farmers in Cuba live in villages like this one.

My father, named Modesto after my grandfather, was a surveyor. Some of the happiest times of my childhood were spent on horseback, on trips where he would allow me to accompany him as he plotted the boundaries of small farms in the Cuban countryside. Sometimes we slept out under the stars, stringing our hammocks between the trees, and drank fresh water from springs. We always stopped for a warm greeting at the simple huts of the neighboring peasants, and my eyes would drink in the lush green forest crowned by the swaying leaves of the palm trees.

Since many surveying jobs called for dividing up land that a family had inherited from a deceased parent or relative, my father's greatest concern was that justice be achieved. It was not enough just to divide the land into equal portions. He also had to ensure that all parties would have access to roads, to water sources, to the most fertile soil. While I was able to join him in some trips, other surveying work involved large areas of land. On these jobs, my father was part of a team, and I would stay home, eagerly awaiting to hear the stories from his trip on his return.

Surveyors use instruments like this one to help them take measurements.

Latin American families tend not to limit their family boundaries to those who are born or have married into it. Any good friend who spends time with the family and shares in its daily experiences is welcomed as a member. The following story from one of my father's surveying trips is not about a member of my blood family, but instead concerns a member of our extended family.

Félix Caballero, a man my father always liked to <u>recruit</u> whenever he needed a team, was rather different from the other surveyors. He was somewhat older, unmarried, and he kept his thoughts to himself. He came to visit our house daily. Once there, he would sit silently in one of the living room's four rocking chairs, listening to the lively conversations all around him. An occasional nod or a single word were his only contributions to those conversations. My mother and her sisters sometimes made fun of him behind his back. Even though they never said so, I had the impression that they questioned why my father held him in such high regard.

recruit (rih KROOT) *v.* to enlist or hire to join a group

Then one day my father shared this story.

"We had been working on foot in mountainous country for most of the day. Night was approaching. We still had a long way to go to return to where we had left the horses, so we decided to cut across to the other side of the mountain, and soon found ourselves facing a deep <u>gorge</u>. The gorge was <u>spanned</u> by a railroad bridge, long and narrow, built for the sugarcane trains. There were no side rails or walkways, only a set of tracks resting on thick, heavy crossties suspended high in the air.

gorge (gawrj) *n.* a narrow canyon with steep walls
span (span) *v.* to extend across a space

"We were all upset about having to climb down the steep gorge and up the other side, but the simpler solution, walking across the bridge, seemed too dangerous. What if a cane train should appear? There would be nowhere to go. So we all began the long descent . . . all except for Félix. He decided to risk

✓ **Reading Check**

What kind of work does Ada's father do?

dissuade (dis SWAYD) *v.* to persuade not to do something

ominous (AHM uh nus) *adj.* threatening

resilient (rih ZIL yunt) *adj.* able to withstand shock and bounce back from changes

walking across the railroad bridge. We all tried to <u>dissuade</u> him, but to no avail. Using an old method, he put one ear to the tracks to listen for vibrations. Since he heard none, he decided that no train was approaching. So he began to cross the long bridge, stepping from crosstie to crosstie between the rails, balancing his long red-and-white surveyor's poles on his shoulder.

"He was about halfway across the bridge when we heard the <u>ominous</u> sound of a steam engine. All eyes rose to Félix. Unquestionably he had heard it, too, because he had stopped in the middle of the bridge and was looking back.

"As the train drew closer, and thinking there was no other solution, we all shouted, 'Jump! Jump!', not even sure our voices would carry to where he stood, so high above us. Félix did look down at the rocky riverbed, which, as it was the dry season, held little water. We tried to encourage him with gestures and more shouts, but he had stopped looking down. We could not imagine what he was doing next, squatting down on the tracks, with the engine of the train already visible. And then, we understood. . . .

"Knowing that he could not manage to hold onto the thick wooden crossties, Félix laid his thin but <u>resilient</u> surveyor's poles across the ties, parallel to the rails. Then he let his body slip down between two of the ties, as he held onto the poles. And there he hung, below the bridge, suspended over the gorge but safely out of the train's path.

A train on a narrow railroad bridge travels high above the trees.

"The cane train was, as they frequently are, a very long train. To us, it seemed interminable. . . . One of the younger men said he counted two hundred and twenty cars. With the approaching darkness, and the smoke and shadows of the train, it was often difficult to see our friend. We had heard no human sounds, no screams, but could we have heard anything at all, with the racket of the train crossing overhead?

"When the last car began to curve around the mountain, we could just make out Félix's lonely figure still hanging beneath the bridge. We all watched in relief and amazement as he pulled himself up and at last finished walking, slowly and calmly, along the tracks to the other side of the gorge."

After I heard that story, I saw Félix Caballero in a whole new light. He still remained as quiet as ever, prompting a smile from my mother and her sisters as he sat silently in his rocking chair. But in my mind's eye, I saw him crossing that <u>treacherous</u> bridge, stopping to think calmly of what to do to save his life, emerging all covered with soot and smoke but triumphantly alive—a lonely man, hanging under a railroad bridge at dusk, suspended from his surveyor's poles over a rocky gorge.

If there was so much courage, such an ability to calmly confront danger in the quiet, aging man who sat rocking in our living room, what other wonders might lie hidden in every human soul?

About the Selection

"The Surveyor" appears in a collection of real-life stories set in Cuba, *Where the Flame Trees Bloom,* by Alma Flor Ada.

treacherous (TRECH ur us) *adj.* dangerous

✓ Reading Check

What makes Félix think he will be safe?

About the Author

Alma Flor Ada (b. 1938) was born in Camagüey (kah mah GWAY), Cuba. Her relatives were great storytellers. Their stories—part truth, part fiction—and her own childhood experiences are woven into her writing. Dr. Ada now lives in California where she is a professor at the University of San Francisco and an author and translator.

Review and Assessment

Thinking About the Selection

1. (a) **Respond** What is your reaction to what Félix did?
(b) **Infer** What qualities did Ada's father see in Félix that shaped his opinion of the man?
2. (a) **Recall** How did Ada's mother and her sister treat Félix?
(b) **Analyze** Why did the women have such a response to Félix?
3. (a) **Recall** What parts of the story tell us about Ada and her father?

(b) **Evaluate Information** What has Ada learned and from whom did she learn it? What did you learn?

Writing Activity

Write a Short Story Choose a story you have heard from a friend or a family member, or a story that you have told about an event that was important or meaningful to you. Write the story. Include an introduction and a conclusion that explain why the story is important to you.

Chapter Preview

This chapter presents the history of Latin America and shows how that history affects the region to this day.

Section 1
Early Civilizations of Middle America

Section 2
The Incas: People of the Sun

Section 3
European Conquest

Section 4
Independence

Section 5
From Past to Present

Target Reading Skill

Clarifying Meaning In this chapter you will focus on skills you can use to clarify meaning as you read.

▶ Decorated wall of a Mayan building at Uxmal, Mexico

Latin America: Early Civilizations

Gulf of Mexico

Tropic of Cancer

120° W

20° N

Tenochtitlan

Yucatán Peninsula

Tikal

CENTRAL AMERICA

Caribbean Sea

ATLANTIC OCEAN

60° W

40° W

20° N

0° Equator

PACIFIC OCEAN

ANDES

Amazon R.

Cuzco

SOUTH AMERICA

0°

N
W   E
S

20° S

Tropic of Capricorn

20° S

ATLANTIC OCEAN

40° S

40° S

KEY

Aztec Empire, 1325–1521

Mayan civilization, about 250–900

Incan Empire, early 1400s–1533

Other native peoples

0 miles   2,000
0 kilometers   2,000
Lambert Azimuthal Equal Area

100° W   80° W   60° W   40° W   20° W   0°
60° S

Regions This map shows three civilizations that flourished in Latin America before Europeans arrived in the region. **Identify** Name the civilizations shown on the map. Which is the oldest? **Draw Conclusions** Which one is likely to have been influenced by another civilization shown on the map? Explain why.

Go Online
PHSchool.com Use Web Code lfp-1221 for step-by-step map skills practice.

Early Civilizations of Middle America

Prepare to Read

Objectives

In this section you will
1. Find out what Mayan civilization was like.
2. Learn how the Aztecs built their empire and understand what kind of society they created.

Taking Notes

As you read this section, look for similarities and differences in the Mayan and Aztec civilizations. Copy the diagram below and record your findings in it.

Ancient Civilizations

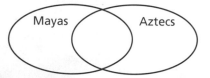

 Target Reading Skill

Reread Rereading can help you understand words and ideas in the text. If you do not understand a sentence or a paragraph, read it again to look for connections among the words and sentences. For example, rereading the first paragraph below can make it clear that the game being described took place long ago. Now you can better understand the surprising comparison of pok-ta-tok to basketball.

Key Terms

- **hieroglyphics** (hy ur oh GLIF iks) *n.* a system of writing using signs and symbols
- **maize** (mayz) *n.* corn
- **Tenochtitlán** (teh nawch tee TLAHN) *n.* capital city of the Aztec empire, located where Mexico City now stands

Fans cheered as the players brought the ball down the court. Suddenly, the ball flew into the air and sailed through the hoop. Fans and players shouted and screamed. Although this may sound like a championship basketball game, it is actually a moment in a game played more than 1,000 years ago. The game was called pok-ta-tok.

Pok-ta-tok was a game played by the ancient Mayas. Using only their leather-padded hips and elbows, players tried to hit a four-pound (1.9 kilogram), six-inch (15.2 centimeter) rubber ball through a stone hoop mounted 30 feet (9.1 meters) above the ground.

The Mayas

How do we know about this ancient game? Crumbling ruins of pok-ta-tok courts and ancient clay statues of players have been found at sites in Central America and southern Mexico. In these areas, Mayan civilization thrived from about A.D. 250 to A.D. 900. By studying ruins, scientists have learned much about Mayan civilization.

Mayan Civilization The Mayas built great cities, such as Copán (koh PAHN) in the present-day country of Honduras, and Tikal (tee KAHL) in present-day Guatemala. Mayan cities were economic, political, and religious centers. Large pyramid-shaped temples often stood in the middle of Mayan cities. Rival Mayan cities also engaged in frequent warfare with one another.

Mayan priests studied the stars and planets. They developed two calendars. They used one to schedule religious celebrations and the other, as we do today, to follow the seasons. The Mayas also developed a system of writing using signs and symbols called **hieroglyphics** (hy ur oh GLIF iks). Hieroglyphics found in books and in carvings have helped scientists understand Mayan culture.

Farmers worked in fields surrounding the cities. Their most important crop was **maize, or corn,** the main food of the Mayas. They also grew beans, squash, peppers, avocados, and papayas.

The Great Mystery of the Mayas About A.D. 900, the Mayan cities began to decline. No one knows why. Crop failures, war, disease, drought, or famine may have killed many Mayas. Or perhaps people rebelled against the control of the priests and nobles. The Mayas stayed in the region, however. Millions of Mayas still live in Mexico, Belize, and Guatemala.

✓ **Reading Check** What is the "great mystery of the Mayas"?

Links to Math

The Concept of Zero

The Mayas created a number system that included zero. Zero is important in math because it is a symbol that shows that there is none of something. For example, to write the number 308, you need a symbol to show that there are no tens. The idea of zero, which also developed in Asia, is considered to be one of the greatest inventions in mathematics. In the Mayan book above, the zero looks like a shell (circled above). Other numbers are made up of bars and dots.

Mayan Ruins
The Mayan city of Chichén Itzá had a pok-ta-tok court as well as this huge temple. **Infer** *What does this great temple suggest about Mayan culture and technology?*

The Aztec Empire

In the 1400s, another great civilization arose in Middle America. It was created by the Aztecs, who had arrived in the Valley of Mexico in the 1100s.

The Aztecs settled on an island in Lake Texcoco in 1325. They changed the swampy lake into a magnificent city. **Tenochtitlán** (teh nawch tee TLAHN), the Aztec capital, stood on the site of present-day Mexico City. When Europeans explored the area in the 1500s, they found the Aztecs ruling a rich empire from the city of Tenochtitlán.

Building an Empire In the 1400s, Aztec warriors began conquering the other people in the region. They forced the conquered people to pay tribute, or taxes. Tribute could be paid in food, cotton, gold, or slaves. The Aztecs grew rich from the tribute.

The Aztec emperor ruled over all Aztec lands. Nobles helped the emperor to govern. Soldiers fought in wars to expand the empire. They also protected the empire's trade routes. Priests were not only religious leaders, but were also important in society. People of the upper classes wore feathered garments and carried feathered fans as symbols of their status.

Farming Most of the people in the Aztec empire were farmers. The Aztecs used irrigation, or artificial systems for watering crops. As you can see in Eyewitness Technology: Aztec Farming on the next page, they also created new farmland by constructing artificial floating gardens called chinampas. Aztec farmers grew corn, squash, and beans on these chinampas.

Culture and Religion Tenochtitlán was a magnificent capital city. It had huge temples, busy markets, wide streets and canals, and floating gardens. It even had a zoo. The markets were filled with food, gold and silver jewelry, feathers, and fine crafts. The emperor and nobles lived in splendid palaces and had many slaves to serve them.

In the temples, priests performed rituals, including human sacrifice, or the offering of human lives, to please their gods. Aztec priests also used an advanced calendar based on the Maya calendar. Aztec astronomers also predicted eclipses and the movements of planets. They kept records using hieroglyphics similar to those used by the Mayas.

Aztec calendar
The face of the Aztec sun god is shown in the center of this stone calendar. The symbols surrounding the face represent the twenty days in each Aztec month.
Draw Conclusions *Why would the Aztec sun god be associated with the calander?*

Reread
Read the paragraph at the right again to find out two things Aztec astronomers did.

Aztec Farming

The Aztec city of Tenochtitlán, in central Mexico, grew quickly. The Aztecs soon used up all the farmland that was available on the island. To grow more crops, they learned how to create new farmland. At the outskirts of town, Aztec farmers dug canals through the marshy land to make small plots called *chinampas*, or "floating beds." People could paddle canoes through the many canals running among the chinampas.

The Floating City: Tenochtitlán
This painting shows what Tenochtitlán looked like. Built on a small island in the middle of a lake, it grew to a city of 200,000 people.

2 Mud and vegetation are piled onto mats that rest on the water's surface.

1 Wooden posts are set up to hold the sides of each plot in place.

3 Willow trees are planted to keep the mud in place. Over time, their roots will anchor the chinampas to the bottom of the lake.

4 Woven reeds are placed along the sides of the mud and vegetation to hold them in.

5 More layers of mud and fertile manure are added until the land is ready to plant.

6 Maize grows tall on a fully developed chinampa.

Modern-Day Living
Today, most of the lakes used by the Aztecs have been drained and covered by city growth. However, some chinampas are still used as farmland. The photo at the left shows Mexicans farming chinampas today.

ANALYZING IMAGES
How did the planting of willow trees make the Aztecs' chinampas more stable?

Past Meets Present
This girl is sketching an Aztec statue at the site of the Great Temple of the Aztecs in Mexico City. **Generalize** *Why do you think people still flock to see and study Aztec ruins?*

Aztec Medicine Aztec doctors were able to make more than 1,000 medicines from plants. They used the medicines to lower fevers, cure stomachaches, and heal wounds. Aztec doctors also set broken bones and practiced dentistry.

Trade Because of the power of the Aztec army, traders could travel long distances in safety. Crops from distant parts of the empire were brought to the capital and to other cities. Crafts, weapons, and tools were also carried throughout the empire and beyond. Luxury goods such as jaguar skins, cacao beans, and fine jewelry were also traded. These goods were carried by people called porters, because the Aztecs did not have pack animals to carry loads. Trade was usually done by barter, or the exchange of goods without the use of money.

The End of the Aztec Empire The Aztecs did not abandon their fine cities as the Mayas had done. Instead, they were conquered by newcomers from a faraway land. You will read about how the Aztec empire fell later in this chapter.

✓ **Reading Check** **How was trade carried out in the Aztec empire?**

Section 1 Assessment

Key Terms
Review the key terms at the beginning of this section. Use each term in a sentence that explains its meaning.

Target Reading Skill
What word or idea were you able to clarify by rereading? Explain how rereading helped.

Comprehension and Critical Thinking
1. (a) **Identify** Describe the main features of Mayan civilization.

(b) **Conclude** What do the facts that Mayas created accurate calendars and great cities tell about their civilization?
(c) **Infer** What can you infer about the mathematical skills of the Mayas?
2. (a) **Describe** How was Aztec society organized?
(b) **Sequence** Tell how the Aztecs created their large and powerful empire.
(c) **Infer** How do you think the conquered peoples felt about being ruled by the Aztecs? Explain your answer.

Writing Activity
If you could interview an ancient Maya or Aztec about his or her life, what would you ask? Write some questions that would help you understand one of these civilizations. Organize your questions into at least three different topics.

Writing Tip First decide which civilization to focus on. Then use the blue headings in the section to help you decide on topics. Reread the text under the headings to get ideas for your questions.

The Incas: People of the Sun

Prepare to Read

Objectives

In this section you will

1. Find out how the Incas created their empire.
2. Understand what Incan civilization was like.
3. Learn how the descendants of the Incas live today.

Taking Notes

As you read this section, look for details of Incan civilization. Copy the web below and fill in the ovals with information about the Incas.

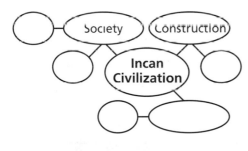

Target Reading Skill

Read Ahead Reading ahead can help you understand something you are not sure of in the text. If you do not understand a certain word or passage, keep reading. The word or idea may be clarified further on. For example, at first you may not understand why a second runner begins running beside the first one in the first paragraph below. Read the second paragraph to find the term *relay runners*. That will help you understand the idea in paragraph one.

Key Terms

- **Cuzco** (KOOS koh) *n.* capital of the Incan empire
- **Topa Inca** (TOH puh ING kuh) *n.* emperor of the Incas, who expanded their empire
- **census** (SEN sus) *n.* an official count of all the people in an area
- **quipu** (KEE poo) *n.* knotted strings on which the Incas recorded information
- **aqueduct** (AK wuh dukt) *n.* a pipe or channel that carries water from a distant source

The runner sped along the mountain road. He lifted a horn made from a shell to his lips and blew. A second runner appeared and began running beside him. Without stopping, the first runner gave the second runner the message he carried. The second runner was gone like the wind. He would not stop until he reached the next runner.

The Incas used relay runners to spread news from one place in their empire to another. Incan messengers carried news at a rate of 250 miles (402 kilometers) a day. Without these runners, controlling the vast empire would have been very difficult.

An Incan runner blowing a conch shell and carrying a quipu

Read Ahead
The paragraph at the right says that the Incan empire was "large and powerful." Read ahead to find out how big it was. Where did you find the answer?

Timeline Skills

Three great civilizations are shown on the timeline. Vertical lines indicate specific events. Horizontal brackets show periods of time. **Identify** Which civilization lasted the longest? Which empire lasted the shortest time? **Analyze Information** Why does the timeline show two dates for the Aztecs before the beginning of their empire?

The Rise of the Incas

The large and powerful empire of the Incas had small beginnings. In about 1200, the Incas settled in **Cuzco** (KOOS koh), a village in the Andes that became the Incan capital city. It is now a city in the country of Peru. Most Incas were farmers. They grew maize and other crops. Through wars and conquest, the Incas won control of the entire Cuzco Valley, one of many valleys that dot the Andes Mountains.

In 1438, Pachacuti (pahch ah KOO tee) became ruler of the Incas. The name Pachacuti means "he who shakes the earth." Pachacuti conquered the people of the Andes and the Pacific coast, from Lake Titicaca north to the city of Quito in present-day Ecuador. Pachacuti demanded loyalty from the people he conquered. If they were disloyal, he forced them off their land. He replaced them with people loyal to the Incas.

Later, Pachacuti's son, **Topa Inca,** became emperor of the Incas. He expanded the empire. In time, it stretched some 2,500 miles (4,023 kilometers) from what is now Ecuador south along the Pacific coast through Peru, Bolivia, Chile, and Argentina. The 12 million people ruled by the Incas lived mostly in small villages.

✓ **Reading Check** How did Pachacuti make sure conquered peoples were loyal to the Incas?

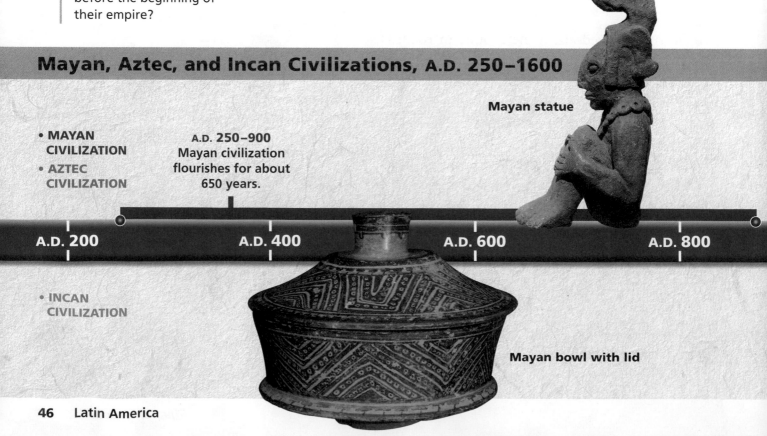

Mayan, Aztec, and Incan Civilizations, A.D. 250–1600

Mayan statue

- **MAYAN CIVILIZATION**
- **AZTEC CIVILIZATION**

A.D. 250–900
Mayan civilization flourishes for about 650 years.

A.D. 200　　　A.D. 400　　　A.D. 600　　　A.D. 800

- **INCAN CIVILIZATION**

Mayan bowl with lid

Incan Civilization

The Incas were excellent farmers, builders, and managers. The Incan capital, Cuzco, was the center of government, trade, learning, and religion. In the 1500s, one of the first Spaniards to visit Cuzco described it as "large enough and handsome enough to compare to any Spanish city."

The emperor, along with the nobles who helped him run the empire, lived in the city near the central plaza. Nobles wore special headbands and earrings that showed their high rank. Most of the farmers and workers outside Cuzco lived in mud-brick huts.

Government and Records The government of the Incan empire was carefully organized. The emperor chose nobles to govern each province. Each noble conducted a census so that people could be taxed. A **census** is an official count of all the people in an area. Local officials collected some of each village's crops as a tax. The villagers also had to work on government building projects. However, the government took care of the poor, the sick, and the elderly.

The Incas did not have a written language. Incan government officials and traders used **quipus** (KEE pooz), knotted strings on which they recorded information. Each quipu had a main cord with several colored strings attached to it. Each color represented a different item, and knots of different sizes at certain distances stood for numbers.

Keeping Count
Incan quipus like this one recorded information about births, deaths, trade, and taxes. **Generalize** *What would be some advantages and disadvantages of this system of record keeping?*

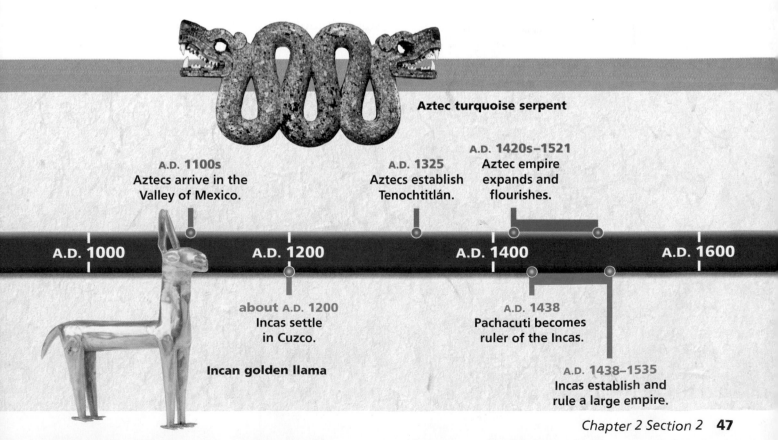

Aztec turquoise serpent

A.D. **1100s**
Aztecs arrive in the Valley of Mexico.

A.D. **1325**
Aztecs establish Tenochtitlán.

A.D. **1420s–1521**
Aztec empire expands and flourishes.

A.D. **1000**   A.D. **1200**   A.D. **1400**   A.D. **1600**

about A.D. **1200**
Incas settle in Cuzco.

A.D. **1438**
Pachacuti becomes ruler of the Incas.

Incan golden llama

A.D. **1438–1535**
Incas establish and rule a large empire.

Roads, Bridges, and Aqueducts The Incas built more than 14,000 miles (22,530 kilometers) of roads. The roads went over some of the most mountainous land in the world. The road system helped the Incas to govern their vast empire. Not only did runners use the roads to deliver messages, but Incan armies and trade caravans also used the roads for speedy travel.

In addition to roads, the Incas needed bridges to span the deep gorges of the Andes Mountains. Gorges are narrow passes or valleys between steep cliffs. In the Andes, swift-moving rivers often flow through gorges. The Incas developed rope bridges to carry people safely over these dangerous spaces. The bridges were made of braided vines and reeds. Similar bridges are still in use today in the Andes.

The Incas also built canals and aqueducts to carry water to dry areas. An **aqueduct** is a pipe or channel that carries water from a distant source. One stone aqueduct carried water from a mountain lake almost 500 miles (805 kilometers) to its destination. The system of canals and aqueducts allowed the Incas to irrigate land that was otherwise too dry to grow crops.

Incan Buildings The Incas were masters of building with stone. They constructed cities, palaces, temples, and fortresses without the use of modern tools. Using only hammers and chisels, Incan stoneworkers cut large stones so precisely that they fit together without mortar or cement. The stones fit together so tightly that even today a piece of paper cannot be slipped between them. Many Incan structures can still be seen in Peru. The most famous Incan ruin is Machu Picchu (MAH choo PEEK choo), a city that includes buildings, stairs carved into the side of the mountain, and roads cut into bare rock.

Religion Like the Mayas and the Aztecs, the Incas worshipped many gods and practiced human sacrifice. The sun god, Inti, was one of their most important gods. The Incas believed that Inti was their parent, and they referred to themselves as "children of the sun." Another important Incan god was Viracocha (vee ruh KOH chuh), the creator of all the people of the Andes.

✔ **Reading Check** Describe Incan stone buildings.

Links to
Science

Earthquake-Proof Buildings
The land under the Incan empire was often shaken by earthquakes. Incan buildings swayed but did not collapse. That is because their walls tilt in at about an 80° angle rather than standing straight up at 90°. The doors and windows are shaped like trapezoids, wider at the base than at the top. This gives them stability when the ground shakes. The Spanish conquerors of the Incas built in the European style—and when earthquakes hit Cuzco, the Spanish buildings collapsed while the Incan stonework remained.

The Quechua: Descendants of the Incas

The Spanish conquered the Incan empire in the 1500s. However, descendants of the Incas still live in present-day Peru, Ecuador, Bolivia, Chile, and Colombia. They speak Quechua (KECH wuh), the Incan language.

Today, many of the Quechua live high in the Andes. Although they are isolated from many aspects of modern life, they have been influenced by it. For example, their religion combines elements of Roman Catholic and traditional practices.

Most Quechua who live in the mountains grow only enough food to feed their families. They continue to use farming methods similar to those of the ancient Incas. They also continue the weaving traditions of the Incas. They spin wool and weave fabric much as their ancestors did. They use this brightly colored cloth with complex patterns for their own clothing and also sell it to outsiders. Their clothing styles, such as the distinctive poncho, also reflect their Incan heritage.

Terrace Farming
The Incas built terraces into the sides of steep slopes to increase their farmland and to keep soil from washing down the mountains. **Infer** *Why do you think terrace farming is still used in the Andes Mountains today?*

✓ **Reading Check** How do the Quechua preserve Incan culture?

Section 2 Assessment

Key Terms
Review the key terms at the beginning of this section. Use each term in a sentence that explains its meaning.

Target Reading Skill
What word or idea were you able to clarify by reading ahead? Where did you find this clarification?

Comprehension and Critical Thinking
1. (a) Recall Where and when did the Incas create their empire?

(b) Sequence List the major events in the creation of the Incan empire in order.

2. (a) Identify What were the major achievements of Incan civilization?

(b) Draw Conclusions Why were a good network of roads and record keeping important to the Incan empire?

3. (a) Describe How do the descendants of the Incas live now?

(b) Infer Why do you think the Quechua still do many things the way their ancestors did?

Writing Activity
Which of the Incan achievements do you think was most important in creating their large and rich empire? Explain your choice in a paragraph. Give at least two reasons for your choice.

For: An activity on the Incas
Visit: PHSchool.com
Web Code: lfd-1202

Prepare to Read

Objectives

In this section you will

1. Learn why Europeans sailed to the Americas.
2. Find out how the conquistadors conquered the Aztecs and the Incas.
3. Understand how the Spanish empire was organized and how colonization affected the Americas.

Taking Notes

As you read this section, look for the major events in the European conquest of Latin America. Copy the timeline below, and record the events in the proper places on it.

Columbus arrives
in the Americas.

```
|----+----+----+----+----|
1490 1492
```

🎯 Target Reading Skill

Paraphrase When you paraphrase, you restate what you have read in your own words. This process can help you understand and remember what you read.

Key Terms

- **Moctezuma** (mahk tih ZOO muh) *n.* ruler of the Aztec empire at the time the Spanish arrived there
- **Christopher Columbus** (KRIS tuh fur kuh LUM bus) *n.* Italian explorer sponsored by Spain who landed in the West Indies in 1492

- **conquistador** (kahn KEES tuh dawr) *n.* one of the conquerors who claimed and ruled land in the Americas for the Spanish government in the 1500s
- **Hernán Cortés** (hur NAHN kohr TEZ) *n.* conquistador who conquered the Aztec empire
- **Francisco Pizarro** (frahn SEES koh pea SAHR oh) *n.* conquistador who conquered the Incas
- **mestizo** (meh STEE zoh) *n.* in Latin America, a person of mixed Spanish and Native American ancestry
- **hacienda** (hah see EN dah) *n.* a large farm or plantation

Cortés meets Moctezuma, in a 1976 mural by Roberto Cueva del Rio.

One day in 1519, the Aztec ruler **Moctezuma** (mahk tih ZOO muh) received startling news. Something strange had appeared offshore. He sent spies to find out about it. The spies reported back to Moctezuma:

> **❝We must tell you that we saw a house in the water, out of which came white men, with white hands and faces, and very long, bushy beards, and clothes of every color: white, yellow, red, green, blue, and purple, and on their heads they wore round hats.❞**
>
> —*An Aztec spy*

The white men with round hats were a Spanish military force. They had sailed to the coast of Mexico in search of treasure. They would bring great changes to the land of the Aztecs.

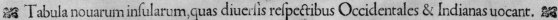

Columbus thought he had reached these islands in 1492.

Many explorers set sail from Spain.

This flag shows that Spain claimed this land.

This flag shows Portugal's claim to this land.

Europeans Arrive in the Americas

In the 1400s, the European nations of Spain and Portugal were searching for new trade routes to Asia. They knew that in Asia they would find goods such as spices and silks. These goods could be traded for huge profits in Europe.

Columbus Reaches America Christopher Columbus, an Italian explorer, thought he could reach Asia by sailing west across the Atlantic Ocean. Columbus knew the world was round, as did most educated Europeans. But Columbus believed the distance around the world was shorter than it is. First Columbus asked Portugal to sponsor his voyage. Portugal refused. Then he asked Spain. Queen Isabella of Spain finally agreed.

Columbus set sail in early August, 1492. Some 10 weeks later, on October 12, he spotted land. Columbus thought he had reached the East Indies in Asia, so he called the people he met Indians.

Mapping the Americas
This 1540 map is based on information supplied by Columbus and other explorers. Also shown is an astrolabe, a navigational instrument from the 1500s. **Infer** *Find the islands Columbus was looking for, and the Caribbean islands he found instead. Why do you think he thought they were the same?*

Dividing a Continent Spain and Portugal each sent explorers to the Americas and tried to stop the other country from claiming land there. In 1494, the two nations signed an important treaty. (A treaty is an agreement in writing made between two or more countries.) The Treaty of Tordesillas (tawr day SEE yahs) set an imaginary line from the North Pole to the South Pole at about 50°W longitude, called the Line of Demarcation. It gave Spain the right to settle and trade west of the line. Portugal could do the same east of the line. The only part of South America that is east of the line is roughly the eastern half of present-day Brazil. Because of the Treaty of Tordesillas, the language and background of Brazil are Portuguese.

✓ **Reading Check** Why did Spain and Portugal become rivals?

The Success of the Conquistadors

Spanish explorers heard stories of wealthy kingdoms in the Americas. They hoped to find gold and other treasures there. Spanish rulers did not pay for the expeditions of the explorers. Instead, they gave the **conquistadors** (kahn KEES tuh dawrs), or conquerors, the right to hunt for treasure and to settle in the Americas. In exchange, conquistadors agreed to give Spain one fifth of any treasures they found.

Sculpture of the Aztec god Quetzalcoatl

Cortés Conquers the Aztecs Aztec rulers demanded heavy tribute from the peoples they had conquered. When the conquistador **Hernán Cortés** arrived in Mexico in 1519, he found many of these groups willing to help him against the Aztecs.

Cortés headed for Tenochtitlán with 500 soldiers and 16 horses. Aztec spies saw them coming. They had never seen horses before. Moctezuma's spies described the Spanish as "supernatural creatures riding on hornless deer, armed in iron, fearless as gods."

Moctezuma thought Cortés might be the god Quetzalcoatl (ket sahl koh AHT el). Quetzalcoatl had promised to return and rule the Aztecs. With a heavy heart, Moctezuma welcomed Cortés and his soldiers. Cortés tried to convince Moctezuma to surrender to Spain and then seized him as a hostage. After a brief period of peace, Spanish soldiers killed some Aztecs. Then the Aztecs rebelled against the Spanish. By the end of the fighting, Moctezuma was dead, and Cortés and his army barely escaped.

With the help of the Aztecs' enemies, Cortés defeated the Aztecs in 1521. By then, about 240,000 Aztecs had been killed and so had 30,000 of Cortés's allies. Tenochtitlán and the Aztec empire lay in ruins, but the region had been claimed for Spain.

Pizarro Conquers the Incas Francisco Pizarro (frahn SEES koh pea SAHR oh) was also a Spanish conquistador. He heard stories about the rich Incan empire. In 1531, Pizarro sailed to the Pacific coast of South America with a force of 180 Spanish soldiers. The Spanish captured and killed the Incan emperor and many other Incan leaders. By 1535, Pizarro had conquered most of the Incan empire, including the capital, Cuzco.

In only 15 years, the conquistadors had defeated the two most powerful empires in the Americas. How did they do it? The Spanish had guns and cannons and horses, all of which the Native Americans had never seen. Native American weapons were far less powerful. The Europeans also carried diseases such as smallpox, measles, and chicken pox. The Native Americans had never been exposed to these diseases, and entire villages got sick and died. Also, because of local rivalries, some Native Americans were eager to help the Spanish conquistadors.

✓ **Reading Check** What are two reasons the conquistadors were able to conquer the Aztecs and the Incas?

Advantages of the Conquistadors
This illustration shows conquistadors using guns ❶ to fight Aztec soldiers armed with spears ❷ . For protection, the Spanish have metal helmets, ❸ while the Aztecs use feather and animal skin shields ❹ .
Contrast *What other items in the picture might have contributed to the Spanish victory?*

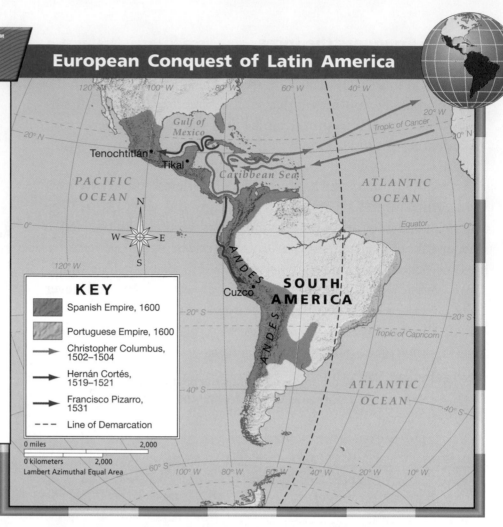

Movement The map shows Columbus's last voyage from Spain and the voyages of the conquistadors who conquered the Aztecs and the Incas. **Locate** Cortés and Pizarro were already in Latin America when they began their conquests. Find their starting points. **Identify Causes** Why were much of the Portuguese and Spanish empires located along the coasts? Why might the Spanish Empire have extended inland in certain areas?

Go Online
PHSchool.com Use Web Code lfp-1213 for an interactive map.

KEY

- Spanish Empire, 1600
- Portuguese Empire, 1600
- → Christopher Columbus, 1502–1504
- → Hernán Cortés, 1519–1521
- → Francisco Pizarro, 1531
- – – – Line of Demarcation

0 miles 2,000
0 kilometers 2,000
Lambert Azimuthal Equal Area

Colonization

By the 1600s, Spain claimed land throughout much of the Americas. Spain's lands stretched from southern South America all the way north into the present-day United States, and included some islands in the Caribbean Sea. Later, the French and English also claimed some Caribbean islands. Portugal claimed Brazil.

European Settlers Arrive Settlers from Spain, Portugal, and other European nations began arriving in what came to be called Latin America. Some of them were missionaries, sent by the Catholic Church to spread Christianity to the peoples of the Americas. Others came to look for gold and other mineral riches. Still others wanted to settle and farm the land. If the Native American people resisted, the newcomers used their superior force to suppress them. The Europeans created the kinds of colonies that would benefit them and the countries from which they had come.

Paraphrase
Read the paragraph at the right carefully and then paraphrase it, or restate it in your own words. In your paraphrase, you might number the reasons people came to the Americas.

Spain Organizes Its Empire Spain controlled the largest portion of the Americas south of what is now the United States. The king of Spain wanted to keep strict control over his empire, so the territory was divided into provinces. The king appointed viceroys, or representatives who ruled the provinces in the king's name. Other settlers who had been born in Spain helped the viceroys rule. Meanwhile, a council in Spain supervised the colonial officials to make sure they did not become too powerful.

The two most important provinces in Spain's American empire were New Spain and Peru. The capital of New Spain was Mexico City. Lima became the capital of Peru.

Spanish social classes determined where people lived in Lima. The most powerful citizens lived in the center of the city. They either came from Spain or had Spanish parents. **Mestizos, people of mixed Spanish and Native American ancestry,** lived on the outskirts of Lima. Many mestizos were poor, but some were middle class or even quite wealthy. Native Americans were the least powerful class. Most Native Americans continued to live in the countryside. The Spanish forced them to work on haciendas. A **hacienda** (hah see EN dah) was a plantation owned by Spaniards or the Catholic Church.

Learn how Pizarro conquered the Incan empire.

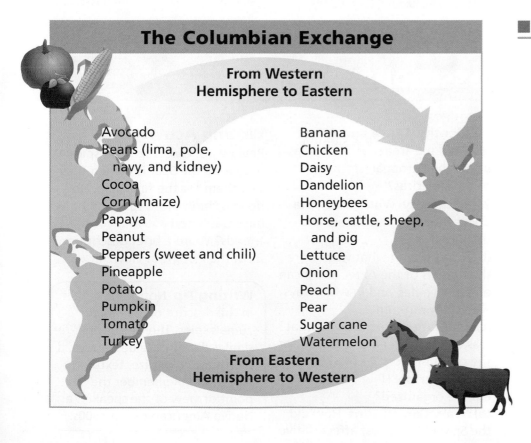

The Columbian Exchange

From Western Hemisphere to Eastern

Avocado
Beans (lima, pole, navy, and kidney)
Cocoa
Corn (maize)
Papaya
Peanut
Peppers (sweet and chili)
Pineapple
Potato
Pumpkin
Tomato
Turkey

Banana
Chicken
Daisy
Dandelion
Honeybees
Horse, cattle, sheep, and pig
Lettuce
Onion
Peach
Pear
Sugar cane
Watermelon

From Eastern Hemisphere to Western

Diagram Skills

Goods, as well as people, crossed the Atlantic Ocean in the years after Columbus's voyages. **Identify** Which animals were part of the exchange? **Infer** Which animal had the potential for making the greatest change in its new home? Explain your answer.

Devastating Diseases
This 1500s illustration shows a medicine man treating an Aztec for smallpox. Native Americans had never been exposed to European diseases. **Explain** *How did these diseases contribute to the success of Spanish rule?*

The Effect of European Rule Spain gave its settlers encomiendas (en koh mee EN dahs), which were rights to demand taxes or labor from Native Americans. At first, the Native Americans were forced to work only on the haciendas. But when silver was discovered in Mexico and Peru, the Spanish forced them to work in the mines as well. Many Native Americans died from overwork, malnutrition, and European diseases. Others rebelled unsuccessfully against the Spanish.

In the first 50 years of Spanish rule, the Native American population of New Spain declined from an estimated 25 million to 3 million. The Spanish now needed more workers for their haciendas and mines. They began importing enslaved Africans in large numbers. In Europe, the demand for products from the Americas continued to grow. Even more workers were needed. Millions more slaves were brought from Africa.

Brazil The situation was somewhat different in Brazil, which was a colony of Portugal. Most settlers remained near the coast. They took land from the Native Americans for sugar plantations and cattle ranches. Brazil also came to depend on the forced labor of Native Americans and enslaved Africans.

✓ **Reading Check** Why did the Native American population decline?

Section 3 Assessment

Key Terms
Review the key terms at the beginning of this section. Use each term in a sentence that explains its meaning.

Target Reading Skill
Paraphrase the second paragraph on this page. Present ideas in the order they appear in the paragraph.

Comprehension and Critical Thinking
1. (a) **Recall** Explain why Europeans came to the Americas in the 1500s.

(b) **Identify Cause and Effect** How did the Treaty of Tordesillas affect the European settlement of the Americas?
2. (a) **Identify** Which conquistadors conquered the Aztecs and the Incas?
(b) **Compare** In what ways were the defeats of the Aztec and Incan empires similar, and in what ways were they different?
(c) **Evaluate Information** What was the most important reason for the conquistadors' success? Explain.
3. (a) **Describe** How was Spain's empire organized?
(b) **Draw Conclusions** How did the Spanish conquest affect Native Americans and Africans?

Writing Activity
Review how Moctezuma's spies described the Spanish when they saw them for the first time. How do you think those spies might have described you and your friends? Write a brief description from their point of view.

Writing Tip Notice the details in the description by Moctezuma's spies. Then focus on similar details. Use descriptive words for color, size, texture, and sound. Remember the point of view of the speaker: a Native American of the 1500s.

Independence

Prepare to Read

Objectives

In this section you will

1. Learn what events inspired revolutions in Latin America.
2. Find out how Mexico gained its independence.
3. Discover how Bolívar and San Martín helped bring independence to South America.

Taking Notes

As you read the section, look for the ways revolutionary leaders helped bring independence to Latin America. Copy the table below and use it to record the name and accomplishments of each person.

Leader	Country	Accomplishment

Target Reading Skill

Summarize When you summarize, you restate the main points you have read in the correct order. Because you leave out less important details, a summary is shorter than the original text. Summarizing is a good technique to help you comprehend and study. As you read, pause to summarize occasionally.

Key Terms

• **Toussaint L'Ouverture** (too SAN loo vehr TOOR) n. leader of Haiti's fight for independence

• **revolution** (rev uh LOO shun) n. overthrow of a government, with another taking its place
• **criollo** (kree OH yoh) n. a person with Spanish parents who was born in Latin America
• **Simón Bolívar** (see MOHN boh LEE vahr) n. a South American revolutionary leader
• **José de San Martín** (hoh SAY deh sahn mahr TEEN) n. a South American revolutionary leader
• **caudillo** (kaw DEE yoh) n. a military officer who rules a country very strictly

On August 24, 1791, the night sky over Saint-Domingue (san duh MAYNG) glowed red and gold. The French Caribbean colony was on fire. The slaves were sick of being mistreated by their white masters. They finally had rebelled. Now they were burning every piece of white-owned property they could find. This Night of Fire was the beginning of the first great fight for freedom in Latin America. **Toussaint L'Ouverture** (too SAN loo vehr TOOR), a former slave, led the people of Saint-Domingue in this fight for independence for more than 10 years. Eventually they won, and they founded the independent country of Haiti (HAY tee) in 1804.

The Seeds of Revolution

The flame of liberty lit in Haiti soon spread across Latin America. By 1825, most of the region was independent. Latin Americans would no longer be ruled by Europe.

Toussaint L'Ouverture

People across Latin America were also inspired by two other revolutions. A **revolution** is the overthrow of a government, with another taking its place. During the 1770s and early 1780s, the British colonies in North America freed themselves from Britain's rule. In 1789, the people of France staged a violent uprising against their royal rulers.

Criollos (kree OH yohz) paid particular attention to these events. A **criollo** had Spanish parents, but had been born in Latin America. Criollos often were the best-educated and wealthiest people in the Spanish colonies, but they had little political power. Only people born in Spain could hold government office. Many criollos attended school in Europe. There, they learned about the ideas that inspired revolution in France and the United States.

The criollos especially liked the idea that people had the right to govern themselves. However, they were frightened by the slave revolt in Haiti. The criollos wanted independence from Spain but power for themselves.

✓ **Reading Check** **Which revolutions inspired ideas of independence in Latin America?**

Independence in Mexico

Mexico began its struggle for self-government in 1810. That's when Miguel Hidalgo (mee GEL hee DAHL goh), a criollo priest, began planning the Mexican revolution. He appealed to local mestizos and Native Americans.

Cry of Dolores
This section of a mural by Juan O'Gorman shows Hidalgo and his followers. **Analyze Images** *Look carefully at the people behind Hidalgo. What does the painter suggest about the Mexican Revolution by showing these people?*

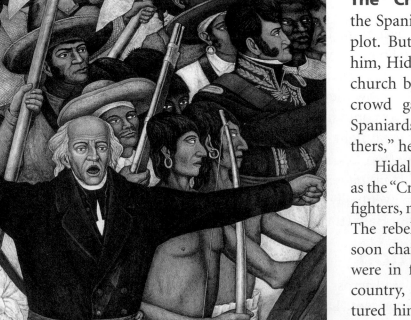

The "Cry of Dolores" In September 1810, the Spanish government discovered Hidalgo's plot. But before the authorities could arrest him, Hidalgo took action. He wildly rang the church bells in the town of Dolores. A huge crowd gathered. "Recover from the hated Spaniards the land stolen from your forefathers," he shouted.

Hidalgo's call for revolution became known as the "Cry of Dolores." It attracted some 80,000 fighters, mostly mestizos and Native Americans. The rebels won some victories, but their luck soon changed. By the beginning of 1811, they were in full retreat. Hidalgo tried to flee the country, but government soldiers soon captured him. He was convicted of treason and then executed by firing squad in July 1811.

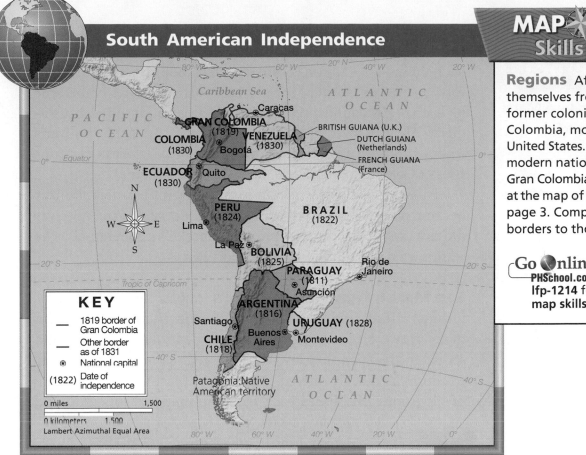

South American Independence

MAP MASTER™
Skills Activity

Regions After freeing themselves from Spain, several former colonies formed Gran Colombia, modeled after the United States. **Identify** Which modern nations were part of Gran Colombia? **Compare** Look at the map of South America on page 3. Compare Peru's modern borders to those of 1831.

Go Online
PHSchool.com Use Web Code lfp-1214 for step-by-step map skills practice.

KEY

— 1819 border of Gran Colombia
— Other border as of 1831
⊛ National capital
(1822) Date of independence

0 miles 1,500
0 kilometers 1,500
Lambert Azimuthal Equal Area

Mexico Becomes Independent The Spanish could execute the revolution's leaders, but they could not kill its spirit. Small rebel groups kept fighting. Then a high-ranking officer in the Spanish army, Agustín de Iturbide (aw guh STEEN deh ee toor BEE day), joined the rebels. Many wealthy people who had viewed Hidalgo as a dangerous hothead trusted Iturbide to protect their interests. He was a criollo and an army officer. They decided to support the rebellion. In 1821, Iturbide declared Mexico independent.

✓ **Reading Check** What groups made up most of Hidalgo's army?

South American Independence

Simón Bolívar (see MOHN boh LEE vahr), one of South America's most important revolutionary leaders, was born in Venezuela in 1783. His family was one of the richest and most important families in Latin America. When Bolívar was at school in Spain, he met Prince Ferdinand, the heir to the Spanish throne. He played a game similar to present-day badminton with the prince. Custom required that Bolívar show respect for the prince by losing. Instead, Bolívar played hard and tried to win. He even knocked the prince's hat off with his racquet! The angry prince demanded an apology. Bolívar refused. He claimed it was an accident.

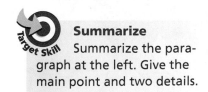

Summarize
Summarize the paragraph at the left. Give the main point and two details.

To Be a Leader: José Martí

José Martí grew up in Cuba when it was still a Spanish colony. At the age of 16, he started a newspaper dedicated to Cuban independence. After he supported an 1868 uprising, Martí was sent to prison. He spent many years in exile, working for Cuban freedom by writing and publishing, and by helping to form a revolutionary party. In 1895, Martí led an invasion of Cuba to free the island from Spanish rule. He was killed on the battlefield a month later—seven years before Cuba achieved independence. This statue of Martí is in New York City's Central Park.

Bolívar, The Liberator Many years later, Bolívar and Ferdinand faced off again. This time, Bolívar knocked Spanish America right out from under Ferdinand's feet. Bolívar joined the fight for Venezuelan independence in 1807. Six years later he became its leader. His confidence, courage, and daring inspired his soldiers. They enjoyed victory after victory. By 1822, Bolívar's troops had freed a large area from Spanish rule (the future countries of Colombia, Venezuela, Ecuador, and Panama).

This newly liberated region formed Gran Colombia. Bolívar became its president. Even though his country was free, Bolívar did not give up the cause of independence. "The Liberator," as he was now known, turned south toward Peru.

San Martín Fights for Freedom Another important revolutionary leader was **José de San Martín** (hoh SAY deh sahn mahr TEEN). He was an Argentine who had lived in Spain and served in the Spanish army. When Argentina began its fight for freedom, he quickly offered to help. San Martín took good care of his troops. He shared each hardship they had to suffer, and they loved him for it. Many said they would follow San Martín anywhere—even over the snow-capped Andes Mountains.

In 1817, his soldiers had to do just that. San Martín led them through high passes in the Andes into Chile. This bold action took the Spanish completely by surprise. In a matter of months, Spain was defeated. San Martín declared Chile's independence. Then he, too, turned his attention to Peru.

Again, San Martín planned a surprise. This time, he attacked from the sea. The Spanish were not prepared, and their defenses quickly collapsed. In July 1821, San Martín pushed inland and seized Lima, the capital of Peru.

An Important Meeting A year later, San Martín met with Bolívar to discuss the fight for independence. Historians do not know what happened in that meeting. But afterward, San Martín suddenly gave up his command. He left Bolívar to continue the fight alone. Eventually, Bolívar drove the remaining Spanish forces out of South America altogether. By 1825, only Cuba and Puerto Rico were still ruled by Spain.

Brazil Takes a Different Route Portugal's colony, Brazil, became independent without fighting a war. In the early 1800s, during a war in Europe, French armies invaded Spain and Portugal. Portugal's royal family fled to Brazil for safety. The king returned to Portugal in 1821. However, he left his son, Dom Pedro, to rule the colony. Dom Pedro took more power than the king expected. He declared Brazil independent in 1822. Three years later, Portugal quietly admitted that Brazil was independent.

Independence Brings Challenges Simón Bolívar dreamed of uniting South America as one country, a "United States of South America." Gran Colombia was the first step. But Bolívar found that his dream was impossible. Latin America was a huge area, divided by the Andes and dense rain forests. Also, the leaders of the countries in Gran Colombia wanted little to do with Bolívar. In poor health, he retired from politics.

Even though he did not remain in office, Bolívar set the standard for Latin American leaders. Most were **caudillos** (kaw DEE yohz), military officers who ruled very strictly. Bolívar cared about the people he governed. However, many caudillos did not. These later caudillos only wanted to stay in power and get rich. You will read about how these caudillos affected the nations they governed in the next section.

This July 2000 parade in Bogotá celebrates 181 years of Colombian independence.

✓ **Reading Check** What are two reasons that South America was not united into one country?

Section 4 Assessment

Key Terms
Review the key terms at the beginning of this section. Use each term in a sentence that explains its meaning.

Target Reading Skill
Write a summary of the last two paragraphs on this page. Include a main point and several details from each paragraph.

Comprehension and Critical Thinking
1. (a) Identify What events inspired independence movements in Latin America?

(b) Identify Cause and Effect Why were many criollos in favor of independence?

2. (a) Describe How did Hidalgo begin the Mexican Revolution?

(b) Analyze Information Explain why Iturbide was successful and Hidalgo was not.

3. (a) Recall What were the achievements of Bolívar, San Martín, and Dom Pedro?

(b) Infer What do you think Bolívar had in mind when he wanted to create the "United States of South America"?

Writing Activity
Suppose you are a soldier in Bolívar's or San Martín's army. Describe what you are doing, why you are doing it, and how you feel about your commander.

Writing Tip Remember to write your description in the first person, using the pronouns *I* or *we*. Use vivid words, such as *terrified, exhausted,* or *thrilled,* to describe your feelings.

Making a Timeline

If you want to show where cities and towns are located along a certain route, you can draw a road map. But how do you show when events occurred? In that case, you can draw a timeline.

You might say that a timeline is a map of time. It has a beginning date and an ending date. It shows when events occurred during that time period, and in what order. Look at pages 46 and 47 for an example of a historical timeline. Use a timeline whenever you need to organize a series of dates.

Golden bird made by the Incas

Learn the Skill

Use these steps to make a timeline.

1. **Create a title for your timeline.** Decide what your timeline will show. It might be "History of the Incas" or "The Life of Simón Bolívar."

2. **Put events in order.** On sticky notes or index cards, write down four or five important events. They will be the entries for your timeline. Put one entry on each sticky or card. Write the date and a short description of the event. Now arrange the entries in chronological order—that is, from the earliest to the latest date.

3. **Select a time span.** Choose a starting date that is earlier than your first entry. Choose an ending date that is later than your last entry.

4. **Build your timeline.** On a sheet of paper, draw a straight line across the page. Make a large dot on the line at each end, and label those dots with the starting and ending dates of your timeline.

5. **Mark the divisions of time periods.** Divide your timeline into equal time periods. Label each one.

6. **Put your entries on the timeline.** Put a dot at the appropriate place on the timeline for each entry. From each dot, draw a straight line upward or downward. Write the text of the entry next to the straight line.

Portrait of Simón Bolívar

Practice the Skill

Now make a timeline of your own life, the life of someone you know, or the life of someone famous. Create the timeline by following the steps below.

1 Your timeline can cover an entire life or some portion of it. Choose a title that reflects the topic and the time span.

2 Decide which important events you want to include. Write the events with their dates on sticky notes or index cards, and arrange them chronologically, that is, from the earliest to the latest date.

3 Choose starting and ending dates that include all your entries.

4 Draw your timeline and mark the starting and ending dates.

5 Add the time periods to your drawing. For instance, if you used 1995 as your starting date, your next date might be 1998 or 2000. Make sure the dates are equally spaced along the line.

6 Add your entries to the appropriate places on your timeline.

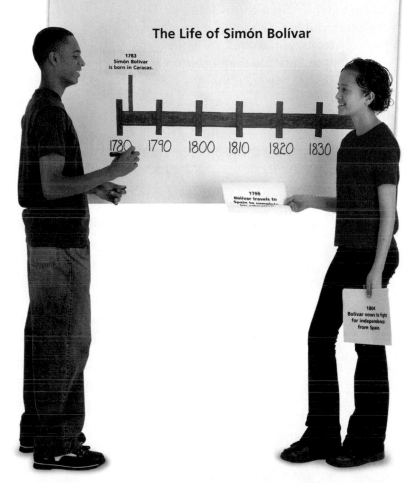

Apply the Skill

Identify what you think are the most important events in Section 4, Independence. Then create a timeline of the major events in the section, using no more than five entries.

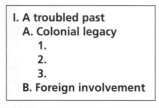

From Past to Present

Prepare to Read

Objectives

In this section you will

1. Learn how Latin American caudillos and foreign involvement contributed to the region's troubled past.
2. Find out how Latin American nations are struggling to improve their economies and the welfare of their people.

Taking Notes

As you read the section, look for the main ideas and details. Copy the format below, and use it to outline the section.

```
I. A troubled past
   A. Colonial legacy
      1.
      2.
      3.
   B. Foreign involvement
```

Target Reading Skill

Reread or Read Ahead Both rereading and reading ahead can help you understand words and ideas in the text. If you do not understand a word or passage, use one or both of these techniques. In some cases, you may wish to read ahead first to see if the word or idea is clarified later on. If not, try going back and rereading the original passage.

Key Terms

- **dictator** (DIK tay tur) *n.* a ruler with complete power
- **export** (eks PAWRT) *v.* to send products from one country to be sold in another
- **import** (im PAWRT) *v.* to bring products into one country from another
- **foreign debt** (FAWR in det) *n.* money owed by one country to other countries
- **regime** (ruh ZHEEM) *n.* a particular administration or government

Slaves building a street in Rio de Janeiro, from an 1824 lithograph

Before independence, when Latin America was ruled by European nations, many of the ordinary people of the region were very poor. In the Spanish colonies, people born in Spain held government office. Criollos were often wealthy and owned large haciendas, or plantations. However, most mestizos and Native Americans owned little land. African Americans were slaves.

A Troubled Past

Latin America has changed a great deal since the nations of the region became independent. On the other hand, many problems with their roots in the colonial past still remain today.

Colonial Legacy After Spain's Latin American colonies became independent, the criollos gained political power. However, most mestizos and Native Americans remained poor. Many continued to work on the haciendas as they had before. Even after slavery was ended, former slaves had little opportunity for a better life.

Many of the new Latin American countries were ruled by caudillos. These "strongmen" ignored the democratic constitutions that had been established by their new nations. They became **dictators**, or rulers with complete power. There were revolts, and some dictators were overthrown. Often they were replaced by other caudillos. Life changed little for the ordinary people.

Before independence, Latin American colonies exported farm products, minerals, and other resources to Spain and Portugal. To **export** is to send products from one country to be sold in another. The colonies bought manufactured products from the European countries that ruled them. After independence, the new nations of Latin America were free to trade with other countries. The United States became an important trading partner for Latin America. But Latin American countries still relied on exporting farm products and minerals. And they still imported manufactured goods. To **import** is to bring products into one country from another.

Working on the Railroad
This railroad linking El Salvador to Guatemala was built in the 1920s by an American company, using local laborers. **Identify Causes** *Why do you think an American company was interested in building a railroad there?*

Reread or Read Ahead
Reread or read ahead
to see why the United States
became involved in Latin America. Which technique helped
you clarify what you reread?

Foreign Involvement Foreign companies began to buy large farms, mines, and other land in Latin America. They built seaports and railroads that made it easier to export their products. These companies were interested in taking resources out of Latin America. The United States and other foreign nations supported Latin American governments that helped these companies.

In 1903, the United States wanted to build a canal across the Isthmus of Panama, in the nation of Colombia. A canal would benefit American trade and the American navy. When Colombia refused permission to build a canal, U.S. President Theodore Roosevelt backed a revolt by the people of Panama against Colombia. Once Panama was independent, it allowed the United States to build the Panama Canal.

As owner of the Panama Canal, the United States had even more interest in Latin America. In 1904, President Roosevelt claimed that the United States had a right to keep law and order there. He also said the United States could force Latin American nations to pay their **foreign debt,** or money they owed to other countries. For the next 20 years, the United States used Roosevelt's policy to intervene in Latin America.

✓ **Reading Check** **What role did President Roosevelt think the United States should have in Latin America?**

Graph Skills

Many Latin American nations have gone into debt to foreign countries and to world organizations. **Identify** Which country in the graph has the highest foreign debt? Which has the lowest? **Identify Cause and Effect** Brazil, Mexico, and Argentina are among the most industrialized Latin American countries. Why might building industries lead to debt?

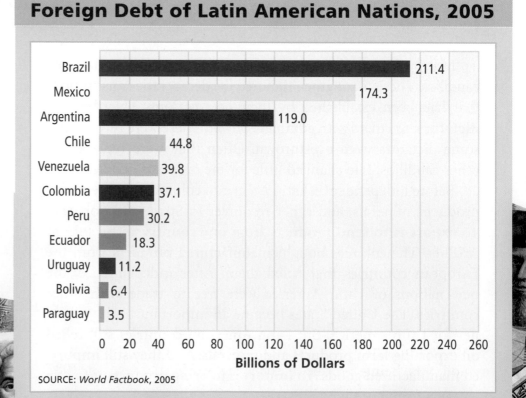

Foreign Debt of Latin American Nations, 2005

Country	Billions of Dollars
Brazil	211.4
Mexico	174.3
Argentina	119.0
Chile	44.8
Venezuela	39.8
Colombia	37.1
Peru	30.2
Ecuador	18.3
Uruguay	11.2
Bolivia	6.4
Paraguay	3.5

SOURCE: *World Factbook,* 2005

The Struggle Continues

In the mid-1900s, there were still big gaps between the few who were rich and the many who were poor. Most of Latin America's land was owned by a small percentage of the people. Many businesses were owned by foreign companies.

The Beginnings of Reform At the same time, some groups wanted to improve conditions for the poor. Reformers of the 1930s and 1940s wanted to divide the land more equally and to diversify the economies of their countries. Some Latin American countries did begin to make reforms.

As demands for reform continued in the 1960s and 1970s, military regimes seized power in many Latin American countries. A regime is a particular administration or government. These military regimes ruled harshly. They censored the press, outlawed political parties, and imprisoned—or even killed—those who opposed them.

By the 1980s, however, some of these harsh regimes were replaced by elected governments. But problems still remained. Some elected leaders abused their power. President Alberto Fujimori of Peru, for example, dissolved Peru's legislature and later dismissed the high court justices when they disagreed with him. And many Latin American nations still had huge economic problems. One of these problems was foreign debt.

Foreign Debt Latin American countries had borrowed money to improve their economies. In the 1980s, oil prices went up at the same time that prices of many Latin American products fell. Latin American countries had to spend more money, but they were making less and less. To make up the difference, they borrowed money from wealthy countries such as the United States. Then they had to borrow more money to pay off their debts.

Although Mexico was a major oil producer, it too suffered an economic crisis. In the 1970s, Mexico began to rely more and more on oil exports to fuel its economy. But in the 1980s, more oil was being produced than the world needed. In 1982, Mexico found that it could not repay its debt.

Protests in Buenos Aires
In Argentina, foreign debt contributed to an economic crisis. In this 2003 protest, unemployed Argentines lift shovels as they march to demand jobs. **Apply Information** *Use the text to help explain how foreign debt might lead to unemployment.*

Plaza in Montevideo, Uruguay
Although Latin American countries are still working to improve their economies, they do have large, thriving modern cities.

Two international organizations stepped in. The World Bank and the International Monetary Fund lent Mexico money—but there were strict conditions. Mexico found that it had to cut back on programs that helped the poor. Other Latin American countries also borrowed under these strict conditions. They had to allow more foreign ownership of businesses and farms. In Argentina, debt, unemployment, and other economic problems caused riots in the streets. In 2000, the president of Argentina was forced to resign.

Looking Toward the Future Recently, Latin American countries have tried to improve their economies by joining trade organizations. In 1994, another trade treaty came into effect—the North American Free Trade Agreement (NAFTA). It made trade easier among Mexico, the United States, and Canada.

Efforts to improve the economies and the welfare of people in Latin America continue. You will read more about these efforts in the Focus on Countries chapters later in this book.

✓ **Reading Check** What happened when Mexico could not pay its debt?

Section 5 Assessment

Key Terms
Review the key terms at the beginning of this section. Use each term in a sentence that explains its meaning.

Target Reading Skill
What words or ideas in this section were you able to clarify by rereading or reading ahead?

Comprehension and Critical Thinking
1. (a) **Describe** How did caudillos rule their countries?

(b) **Explain** Describe foreign involvement in Latin America.
(c) **Compare and Contrast** How did Latin America's economy change after independence? How did it remain the same?
2. (a) **Recall** How did Mexico end up with a large foreign debt?
(b) **Draw Conclusions** The powerful groups that own the most land also run the governments of some Latin American countries. Why do you think these groups resist reform?

Writing Activity
What do you think is the most important challenge facing Latin America today? Write a paragraph explaining your choice.

For: An activity on Venezuela
Visit: PHSchool.com
Web Code: lfd-1205

Review and Assessment

◆ Chapter Summary

Section 1: Early Civilizations of Middle America

- The Mayas built great cities, created an advanced number system and calendars, and then mysteriously abandoned their cities.
- The Aztecs of central Mexico ruled a rich empire from their capital at Tenochtitlán, which was a center of trade and learning.

Mexico

Section 2: The Incas

- The Incas built a huge empire based in what is now Peru.
- The Incas built excellent roads and aqueducts, and used quipus rather than a written language to manage their empire.
- The descendants of the Incas still live in the Andes Mountains.

Section 3: European Conquest

- Europeans came to the Americas for riches and for land.
- The conquistadors conquered the Aztecs and Incas in 15 years.
- Spain ruled a large empire in the Americas, bringing disease and enslavement to the Native Americans and importing enslaved Africans.

Section 4: Independence

- Revolutions in North America, France, and Haiti helped inspire Latin Americans to seek independence.
- Mexico's revolution began with Hidalgo's "Cry of Dolores" and was completed by Iturbide.
- Bolívar and San Martín were the liberators of South America.

Section 5: From Past to Present

- Many problems in Latin America are the result of the region's colonial past, foreign involvement, and undemocratic governments.
- Reform movements are working to help the poor, elected governments have replaced military ones, and nations are struggling with their foreign debt.

◆ Key Terms

Define each of the terms below.

1. hieroglyphics
2. maize
3. census
4. regime
5. conquistador
6. mestizo
7. hacienda
8. revolution
9. criollo
10. caudillo
11. import
12. foreign debt

◆ Comprehension and Critical Thinking

13. (a) Recall Describe Mayan civilization.
(b) Compare How were the Aztec and Incan civilizations similar and different?
(c) Generalize What lessons in empire-building can be learned from the Aztecs and the Incas?

14. (a) Name Which Europeans were the first to explore Central and South America?
(b) Identify Causes Why did the Spanish want to explore the Americas?
(c) Conclude Why did many Native Americans help Hernán Cortés defeat the Aztecs?

15. (a) Recall How did Spain organize its empire?
(b) Explain What were encomiendas and what effect did they have on Native Americans?
(c) Identify Causes Why did the Spanish start to import enslaved Africans to the Americas? Why did this practice increase over time?

16. (a) Identify Who led the Mexican Revolution?
(b) Compare Compare the ways Mexico, Haiti, and Peru gained their independence.
(c) Draw Conclusions How did independence affect criollos? Native Americans?

17. (a) Recall Describe how caudillos ruled their countries.
(b) Identify Causes Why did foreign nations build seaports and railroads in Latin America?
(c) Explain What is one way a nation can develop foreign debt?

◆ Writing Activity: Math

Look again at the photo of the quipu on page 47. Suppose you have five strings of different colors to record the number of people in your class: girls, boys, and the teacher. How would you show this information? Use string or make a drawing with colored pencils. Now write directions for using the mathematical system you just invented. Have another student read and follow your directions. Evaluate how well your partner used your mathematical system.

◆ Skills Practice

Making a Timeline In the Skills for Life activity in this chapter, you learned to create a timeline. Review the steps you followed to learn the skill.

Use an encyclopedia or other reliable source to research one of the people you read about in this chapter. Then make a timeline of the important events in that person's life.

MAP◆MASTER™
Skills Activity

Latin America

Place Location For each place listed below, write the letter from the map that shows its location.
1. Peru
2. Venezuela
3. Cuzco
4. Mexico City
5. Brazil
6. Panama
7. Mexico

Go Online
PHSchool.com Use Web Code lfp-1215 for an interactive map.

Standardized Test Prep

Test-Taking Tips

Some questions on standardized tests ask you to analyze a point of view. Read the paragraph below. Then follow the tips to answer the sample question.

Pick the letter that best answers the question.

In 1519, the Spanish conquistador Hernán Cortés marched toward the great Aztec capital, Tenochtitlán, with 500 soldiers. Somebody watching the troops whispered: *This is a happy day! These white gods could mean the end to Moctezuma and his bloodthirsty followers. Let us help them on their way.*

Which onlooker might have made those comments?

A a spy of Moctezuma

B a soldier of Francisco Pizarro

C a Native American neighbor of the Aztecs

D a wife of Moctezuma

Think It Through Moctezuma's own spies would not want an end to him or call themselves bloodthirsty. The same would be true for his wife. Francisco Pizarro was a conqueror who didn't arrive in South America until years after Cortés. A neighbor of the Aztecs might have been happy to see Cortés, because Moctezuma was a powerful enemy who conquered many of his neighbors. So the best answer is C.

TIP Make sure you understand the question. Restate it in your own words: *The person who said those words was probably _____.*

TIP Use what you know about history along with common sense to choose the BEST answer.

Practice Questions

Choose the letter of the best answer.

1. Unlike the Incas and Aztecs, the Mayas did NOT have
   A an emperor.
   B a calendar.
   C cities.
   D a form of writing.

2. Brazil's language and culture—Portuguese—were established by
   A the voyage of Columbus.
   B Pizarro's conquest.
   C the Treaty of Tordesillas.
   D the encomienda system.

3. What is one way that Latin American countries have been trying to improve their economies?
   A by cooperating with one another
   B by increasing their foreign debt
   C by giving more land to large companies
   D by depending on one resource

Read the following passage and answer the question that follows.

The following is taken from a speech made by someone living in Latin America in the early 1800s: "I love my country, but I deserve to govern myself. I learned plenty about governing when I attended school in Europe!"

4. Who most likely made this speech?
   A the king of Spain
   B a criollo
   C a poor mestizo
   D a Native American

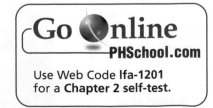

Use Web Code lfa-1201 for a **Chapter 2 self-test.**

Chapter 3

Cultures of Latin America

Chapter Preview

This chapter will introduce you to the cultures of the three regions of Latin America.

Section 1
The Cultures of Mexico and Central America

Section 2
The Cultures of the Caribbean

Section 3
The Cultures of South America

Target Reading Skill

Cause and Effect In this chapter you will focus on recognizing cause and effect in the text you are reading. Recognizing cause and effect will help you understand relationships among situations or events.

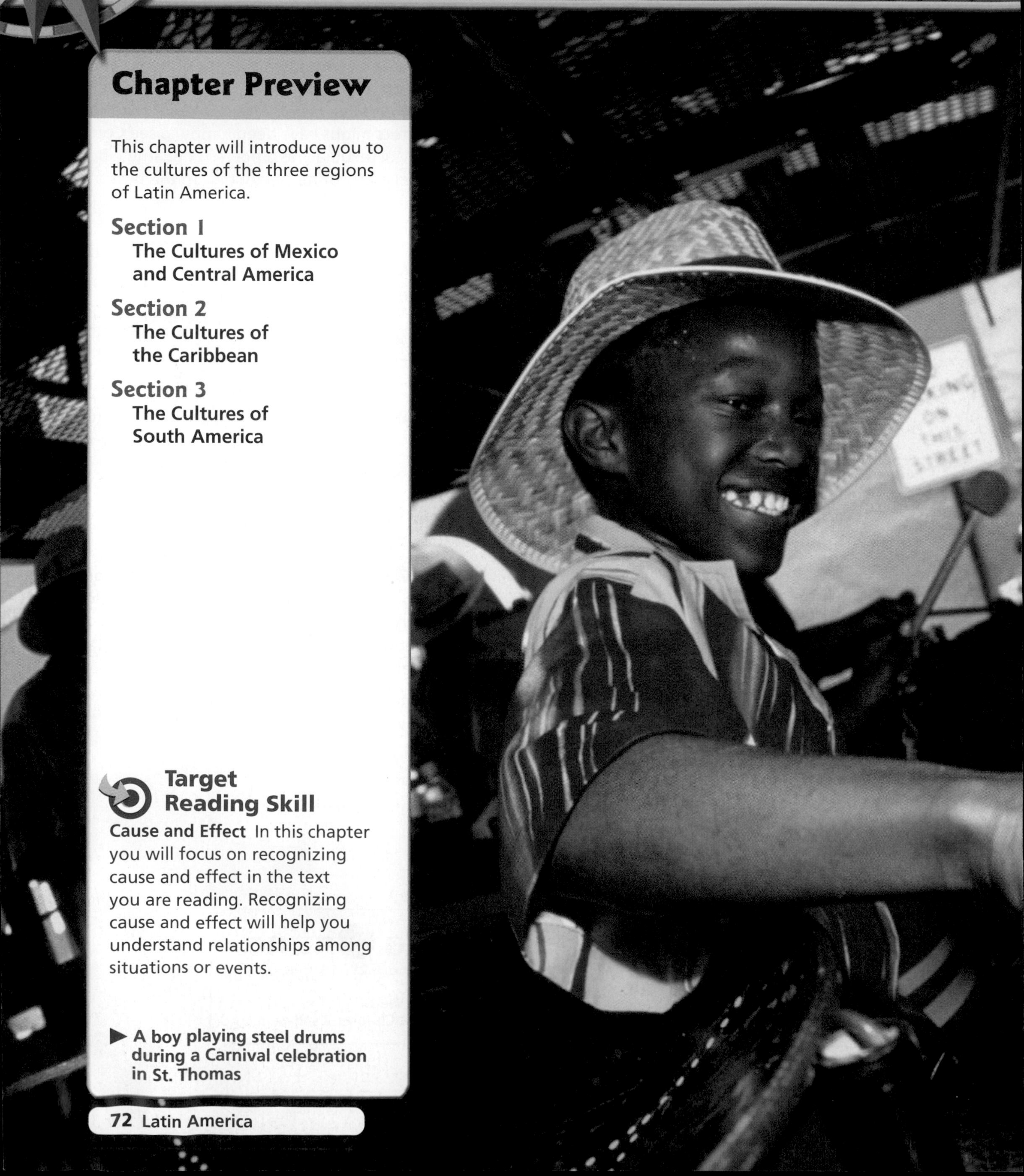

▶ **A boy playing steel drums during a Carnival celebration in St. Thomas**

Latin America: Languages

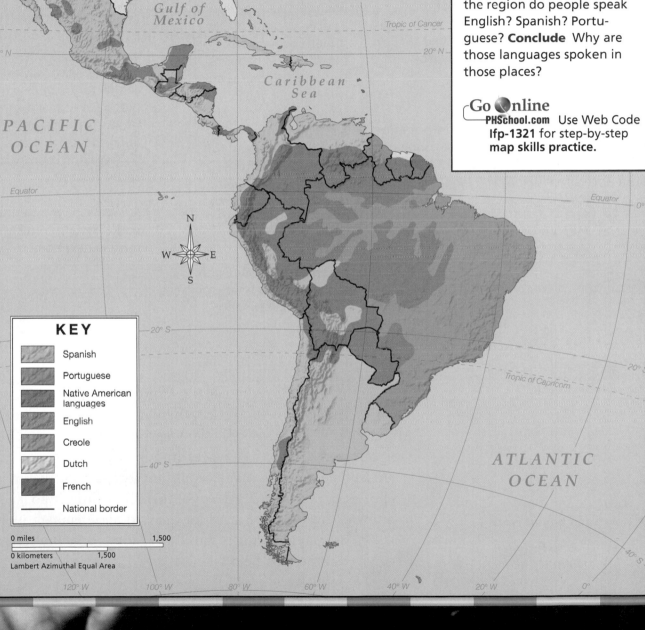

ATLANTIC OCEAN

Gulf of Mexico

Tropic of Cancer

20° N

20° N

Caribbean Sea

PACIFIC OCEAN

Equator

Equator

0°

N
W   E
S

20° S

Tropic of Capricorn

20° S

ATLANTIC OCEAN

40° S

40° S

100° W   80° W   60° W   40° N

120° W   100° W   80° W   60° W   40° W   20° W   0°

KEY

- Spanish
- Portuguese
- Native American languages
- English
- Creole
- Dutch
- French
- —— National border

0 miles   1,500
0 kilometers   1,500
Lambert Azimuthal Equal Area

Regions Notice that many languages are spoken in Latin America and that language regions do not follow political boundaries. **Locate** Where in the region do people speak English? Spanish? Portuguese? **Conclude** Why are those languages spoken in those places?

Go Online
PHSchool.com Use Web Code
lfp-1321 for step-by-step map skills practice.

Cultures of Mexico and Central America

Prepare to Read

Objectives

In this section you will
1. Discover the cultural heritage of the people of Middle America.
2. Find out why many people in this region have been moving away from the countryside.

Reading to Learn

As you read this section, look for information on the cultures of Middle America. Copy the web diagram below and record information about ancestry, religion, and language.

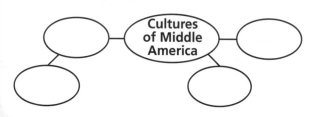

Target Reading Skill

Identify Causes and Effects A cause makes something happen. An effect is what happens. Determining causes and effects helps you understand relationships among situations and events. As you read this section, think of the cultures of Middle America as effects. What are the causes of these effects?

Key Terms

- **campesino** (kahm peh SEE noh) *n.* a poor Latin American farmer or farm worker
- **indigenous people** (in DIJ uh nus PEA pul) *n.* descendants of the people who first lived in a region
- **maquiladora** (mah kee luh DOHR ah) *n.* a Mexican factory that assembles parts to make products for export
- **emigrate** (EM ih grayt) *v.* to leave one country to settle in another
- **immigrant** (IM uh grunt) *n.* a person who comes into a foreign country to make a new home

Seven nations form the narrow, crooked isthmus of Central America. Together with Mexico, these nations make up Middle America. The nations of Middle America share a cultural heritage, but there are also differences among them.

In Middle America, many people are **campesinos** (kahm peh SEE nohz), or poor farmers. Most of them have little or no land of their own. Therefore, it is hard for them to make enough money to support their families. Today, organizations of campesinos help farmers get loans to buy seeds and farm machinery.

Cultural Heritage

There is much diversity, or variety, among the people of Middle America. Many people are mestizo. That means they have both Spanish and indigenous ancestors. **Indigenous people** are descendants of the people who first lived in a region. In Latin America, indigenous people are also called Native Americans or Indians.

A Honduran boy at work

One Region, Many Faces In Honduras, most of the people are mestizo. About one third of Guatemala's people are mestizo. Another 60 percent are indigenous. Many Costa Ricans are direct descendants of Spaniards. And more than 40 percent of the people of Belize are of African or mixed African and European descent.

The countries of Central America have many languages, too. Guatemala is home to more than 20 languages. Spanish is the language of government and business, but the indigenous people in Guatemala speak their own languages. So do indigenous people in Panama, El Salvador, and Nicaragua. Spanish is the main language in six of the seven countries. People in Belize speak English.

Mexico also blends Native American and Spanish influences. Spanish is the first language for most Mexicans, but some Mexicans speak Native American languages as well. About 30 percent of the people of Mexico are indigenous, and about 60 percent of the population are mestizos.

Art of Middle America Art made by Native Americans before the arrival of Europeans is called Pre-Columbian art. Archaeologists have found beautiful wall paintings and painted vases, sculptures, and metalwork in Mexico and Central America. Gold jewelry was a specialty of the Mixtec people, while the Olmecs created huge stone heads and lovely figures made of jade.

This 1930 self-portrait is by the Mexican artist Frida Kahlo.

Mexican History
This detail of *Sugar Cane* (1931) by Diego Rivera shows some people hard at work. Because the Aztecs and Mayas had painted murals, these more recent artworks revived a Native American art form. **Infer** *Which people are not hard at work? What do you learn about Mexican history from these details?*

A Blend of Cultures
Indigenous people attend a church service in the Mexican state of Chiapas. **Infer** *What evidence is there in the photo that these people have blended Christianity with their traditional culture?*

The art of Mexico reflects both its Spanish and its Native American cultures. In the 1920s, the government invited Mexican artists to create murals on public buildings. Murals are large pictures painted directly on walls. The murals by such artists as Diego Rivera (dee AY goh rih VEHR uh) and José Clemente Orozco (ho SAY kleh MEN teh oh ROHS koh) show the history of Mexico, including the contributions of the indigenous people to the nation.

The Church Religion is important to the people of Mexico and Central America. The Spanish settlers who came to the region were Roman Catholic. In the 1500s and 1600s, Spanish missionaries converted many Native Americans to Christianity. The Catholic Church has been important to this region ever since. Most of the people are Catholic. Native Americans have blended many elements of their religions with Christianity.

Fighting Injustice In Middle America, priests and bishops have spoken out against injustice. Following the Church's lead, citizens have taken steps to end poverty and injustice. Ordinary people have started health clinics, farms, and organizations.

Elvia Alvarado (el VEE uh al vuh RAH doh) works for one of these organizations, and her work is not easy. "The communities we work in are hard to get to," she says. "Sometimes I don't eat all day, and in the summertime the streams dry up and there's often no water to drink." Sometimes Alvarado does not get paid. "But I couldn't be happy if my belly was full while my neighbors didn't have a plate of beans and tortillas to put on the table," she says.

✓ **Reading Check** **Name two ways people have worked to fight poverty and injustice.**

Leaving the Countryside

The population of Mexico and Central America is growing rapidly. This rapid population growth has made it hard for young people in rural areas to find jobs. Many have left their homes to look for work in the cities. Today, most people in Middle America live in cities.

In Mexico, some people move to towns and cities along the border with the United States. There, they can work in factories owned by American companies. These companies place their factories in Mexico because wages and other costs are lower there. Border factories that assemble imported parts to make products for export are called **maquiladoras** (mah key luh DOHR ahs).

Other urban areas in the region also offer jobs and other opportunities. Many rural people have moved to large cities such as Mexico City in Mexico, Panama City and Colón in Panama, and San José, the capital of Costa Rica. As a result, these cities have grown rapidly and often have trouble providing housing and services for new arrivals.

Identify Causes and Effects
What factor makes it difficult for young people in rural areas to find jobs? List that as a cause. What is the result of this unemployment? List that as an effect.

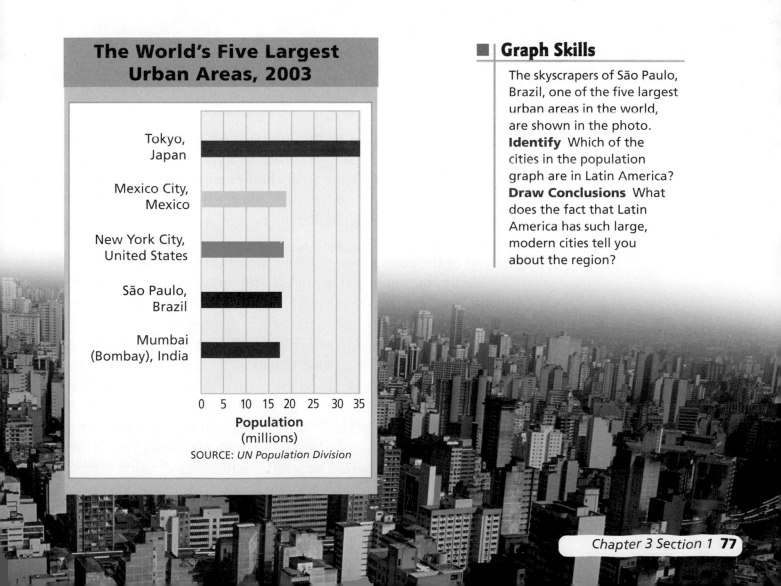

The World's Five Largest Urban Areas, 2003

Tokyo, Japan

Mexico City, Mexico

New York City, United States

São Paulo, Brazil

Mumbai (Bombay), India

Population (millions)
0 5 10 15 20 25 30 35

SOURCE: *UN Population Division*

■ Graph Skills

The skyscrapers of São Paulo, Brazil, one of the five largest urban areas in the world, are shown in the photo. **Identify** Which of the cities in the population graph are in Latin America? **Draw Conclusions** What does the fact that Latin America has such large, modern cities tell you about the region?

A Market in Guatemala
Guatemalans shop at a traditional market in Totonicapán, one of the country's largest cities.
Analyze Images *What details in this photo reflect Guatemalan culture?*

Life in the City In many cities in the region, there are sharp contrasts between the lives of the wealthy and the lives of the poor. Wealthy people live in big houses on wide streets. They go to good schools and can afford to pay for medical care. Many of them have a lifestyle similar to that of wealthy people in the United States.

For the poor, however, life in the city can be hard. There is a shortage of housing. It is not easy to find work. Sometimes, the only way to make a living is selling fruit or soda on street corners. It is hard to feed a family on the income that can be earned this way.

Nevertheless, many people are willing to live with the hardships they find in the cities. Cecilia Cruz can explain why. She moved with her husband and their two sons to Mexico City from the southern state of Oaxaca (wah HAH kah). They live in a two-room house made of cinder blocks. It is on the outermost boundary of the city. "We came here for the schools," says Cruz. "There are more choices here. The level of education is much higher." Most newcomers to the city would agree.

Moving to the United States Most people in Mexico and Central America move somewhere else within their own country if they cannot find work. However, there are also thousands of people who emigrate. To **emigrate** is to leave one country and settle in another. Most leave to find jobs. Many of them emigrate to the United States.

Fermin Carrillo (fehr MEEN kah REE yoh) is one worker who did just that. He left his home town of Huaynamota (wy nah MOH tah), Mexico. There were no more jobs at home, and his parents needed food and medical care. Carrillo moved to a town in Oregon. Now he works in a fish processing plant. He sends most of the money he earns home to his parents. Carrillo hopes one day to become an American citizen.

Other immigrants are different. An **immigrant** is a person who has moved into one country from another. These immigrants want to return home after earning some money to help their families.

Building a Better Life Many Mexicans and Central Americans, like Fermin Carrillo, have left the region in search of a better life. Many more have followed Elvia Alvarado's example. You read about Alvarado's work with community groups in Honduras. She helps poor farmers get seeds, farm machinery, and more land. Like Alvarado, many Middle Americans have stayed at home and begun to build a better life for themselves and their neighbors.

A modern Tarahumara Indian of Mexico wearing traditional clothing

✔ **Reading Check** Why do many Mexicans move to the United States?

Section 1 Assessment

Key Terms
Review the key terms at the beginning of this section. Use each term in a sentence that explains its meaning.

Target Reading Skill
What are three effects of the Spanish colonization of Middle America?

Comprehension and Critical Thinking
1. (a) Identify What are the main languages and religions of the people of Middle America?

(b) Identify Cause and Effect How do the languages and religions of Middle America reflect the region's history?
(c) Predict How might this diversity lead to challenges for the region?
2. (a) Recall Describe life in the countryside and in the city.
(b) Identify Causes What is one reason that rural people in Mexico and Central America are moving to the cities?
(c) Predict What impact might the emigration of many Mexicans have on their country?

Writing Activity
Write a journal entry from the point of view of one of the people you read about in this section. Think about what life is like for that person. Include his or her hopes, dreams, and experiences.

Go Online
PHSchool.com

For: An activity on indigenous peoples
Visit: PHSchool.com
Web Code: lfd-1301

Distinguishing Fact and Opinion

Kate was excited. She was going to Papantla, Mexico. Lila had just been there. "The bus ride is very long and boring," she told Kate. "The town is not interesting. You should skip that trip!"

Kate's guidebook said that Papantla is near the ruins of an ancient Indian city and that traditional dances are still performed there. The bus schedule said it was a three-hour ride. Her map showed that the bus traveled through the mountains.

Kate hurried off to buy a ticket. She relied on facts rather than opinions. That the bus ride is three hours long is a **fact**. Lila's statement that the bus ride "is very long and boring" is an **opinion**.

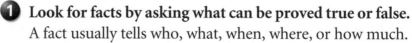

Billete / Ticket
Billete / Ticket
Papantla, México

Distinguishing fact from opinion is something you need to do almost every day. You do it as you—like Kate—reach your own decisions.

Learn the Skill

To distinguish fact from opinion, use the following steps.

1 **Look for facts by asking what can be proved true or false.** A fact usually tells who, what, when, where, or how much.

2 **Ask how you could check whether each fact is true.** Could you do your own test by measuring or counting? Could you find information in an encyclopedia?

3 **Look for opinions by identifying personal beliefs or value judgments.** Look for words that signal personal feelings, such as *I think*. Look for words that judge, such as *beautiful* and *ugly* or *should* and *ought to*. An opinion cannot be proved true *or* false.

4 **Ask whether each opinion is supported by facts or good reasons.** A well-supported opinion can help you make up your own mind—as long as you recognize it as an opinion and not a fact.

Practice the Skill

Read the paragraph in the box at the right until you are sure that you understand its meaning. Then read for facts and opinions.

 Identify facts in the paragraph that tell how much, what, where, or when.

 Explain how each fact you identified could be proven true or false.

3 (a) Identify two words that judge. Could the statements containing these words be proved true or false? (b) Identify one example of words that signal personal feelings. Could this statement be proved true or false?

4 The second sentence of the paragraph expresses an opinion. Is the opinion well supported with facts and reasons?

> Urbanization takes place when people move from rural areas to urban areas. I believe that urbanization in Mexico is bad. First, the cities are already too crowded. There are thousands of homeless people in urban areas. Many people can't find jobs. Second, the city streets were not designed for so many cars. Traffic jams are a huge headache. Finally, the water and electrical systems do not have the capacity to serve more people. I think the time has come for the government to stop urbanization.

Relaxing Beaches

Exotic Animals

Beautiful Rain Forests

Amazing Volcanoes

Visit **Costa Rica!**

Costa Rica is the most beautiful country in Latin America! It has rain forests and beaches. It even has volcanoes! And the weather is perfect all year long.

Apply the Skill

Look at the travel brochure above. List three facts and two opinions from the brochure. Are the opinions well supported? How useful would this brochure be if you were planning a trip? Explain your answer.

The Cultures of the Caribbean

Prepare to Read

Objectives

In this section you will
1. Find out what ethnic groups make up the people of the Caribbean.
2. Learn how the different cultures of the region blended to create Caribbean food, music, and celebrations.

Taking Notes

As you read the section, look for the main ideas and details about Caribbean culture. Copy the format below and use it to outline the section.

> I. The people of the Caribbean
>   A. The first people of the Caribbean
>   1.
>   2.
>   3.
>   B. People in the Caribbean today

Target Reading Skill

Recognize Multiple Causes A cause makes something happen. An effect is what happens. Sometimes an effect can have more than one cause. For example, the distinctive quality of Caribbean food is an effect with several causes, including local fishing and farming as well as the cultural heritage of the West Indian people. As you read this section, identify multiple causes for other characteristics of Caribbean culture.

Key Terms

- **West Indies** (west IN deez) *n.* the Caribbean islands
- **ethnic group** (ETH nik groop) *n.* a group of people who share the same ancestry, language, religion, or cultural traditions
- **Carnival** (KAHR nuh vul) *n.* a lively annual celebration just before Lent in Latin America

The Caribbean islands are spread across more than 2,000 miles (3,219 kilometers), from Florida to the northeast coast of South America. There are more than a dozen different nations in the Caribbean region. As you might expect, a variety of peoples with many different cultures live within this large area.

This watercolor showing the Arawaks was painted in the 1800s.

The People of the Caribbean

The Caribbean islands are also called the **West Indies** because Christopher Columbus, when he first arrived there, thought he had reached the Indies in Asia. That's why he called the people of the islands *Indians*.

The First People of the Caribbean Long before Columbus arrived, the first people to live on these islands were a Native American group called the Ciboney (see buh NAY). The Ciboney lived in the region for thousands of years. In about 300 B.C., they were joined by another indigenous group, the Arawaks (AH rah wahks), who came from South America. In about 1000, the Caribs (KAR ibz), another South American group, arrived.

The Caribs gave the region its name. They lived in the Caribbean for more than 400 years before the first Europeans arrived. Christopher Columbus and other Spaniards enslaved the Native Americans. Almost all of the Caribs, Arawaks, and other indigenous groups died either of overwork or of diseases the Spanish brought with them. Today, there are just a few hundred Caribs. They live on the island of Dominica.

Other Europeans followed the Spanish. They hoped to make money from the region's wealth of natural resources. In the 1600s, Dutch, French, and English colonists began claiming territory. They built large sugar plantations and brought many enslaved Africans to work on them.

Most of the Caribbean people today are descended from these Africans. Immigrants from China, India, and the Middle East have also come to the region to work.

People in the Caribbean Today Because so many people came to the Caribbean as colonists, slaves, or immigrants, the area has a rich ethnic variety. An **ethnic group** is a group of people who share the same ancestry, language, religion, or cultural traditions. The ethnic groups of the Caribbean are Native American, African, European, Asian, and Middle Eastern.

Recognize Multiple Causes
There are very few Native Americans left on the Caribbean islands. What causes of this effect are given in the paragraph at the left?

Caribbean Diversity
These teenagers are students in the French West Indies. **Generalize** *How does this group reflect the population of the Caribbean?*

V. S. Naipaul: Trinidad and Beyond When V. S. Naipaul was born in Trinidad in 1932, more than one third of the island's population was from India. Like many other Indian immigrants, Naipaul's grandparents had come to Trinidad to work on sugar plantations owned by Europeans. Naipaul grew up knowing people from Africa, China, South America, and Europe. For him, the culture of Trinidad was a mix of languages, religions, and customs. When he was 18, Naipaul won a scholarship to study in England, where he still lives. Naipaul has written about life in Trinidad, about England, and about his worldwide travels. In 2001, he was awarded the Nobel Prize for Literature.

Depending on their island's history, the people of a Caribbean island may speak one of several European languages. Their language may also be a mixture of European and African languages. For example, two countries and two cultures exist on the island of Hispaniola. On the eastern half is one country, the Dominican Republic. Its population is Spanish-speaking and mostly mestizo. West of the Dominican Republic is the country of Haiti. Nearly all of Haiti's people are descended from Africans. They speak French and Haitian Creole, a French-based language with some African and Spanish words.

Most West Indians are Christians, but there are also small groups of Hindus, Muslims, and Jews. Some people practice traditional African religions.

Life on the Islands Most of the Caribbean islands have very fertile soil, and many people in the region make their living farming. Dorothy Samuels is a ten-year-old from Jamaica, one of the Caribbean islands. Her family are farmers. They plant yams and other vegetables and fruits. They also plant cacao beans. Every Saturday, Dorothy's mother and grandmother take their fruits and vegetables to the market to sell. All the traders at their market are women.

Dorothy is a good student. She hopes one day to go to college in Kingston, Jamaica's capital city. Jamaican laws require that women have as much opportunity for education as men have. Equality for women is important in Jamaican culture because many Jamaican women are independent farmers and business owners.

✓ Reading Check **How are women's rights and opportunities protected in Jamaica?**

A Blend of Cultures

The rich culture of the Caribbean has a variety of sources. West Indians enjoy many kinds of music and dance, celebrations, and food. They also play a variety of sports. Baseball, soccer, and track and field are popular. On some islands, people also play cricket, which is a British game similar to baseball. Dominoes—although not a sport—is a popular game throughout the region.

Carnival Many people in the Caribbean observe the Roman Catholic tradition of Lent, which is the period of 40 days before Easter Sunday. Because Lent is a very solemn time, these people have a lively public festival called **Carnival** just before Lent.

Different countries celebrate Carnival in different ways. In Trinidad and Tobago, for example, people spend all year making costumes and floats for the celebration. Lent always starts on a Wednesday. At 5 A.M. the Monday before, people go into the streets in their costumes. Calypso bands play. Thousands of fans follow the bands through the streets, dancing and celebrating. At the stroke of midnight on Tuesday, the party stops. Lent has begun.

Explore three types of Caribbean music.

Carnival Celebration
The dancers below are Carnival performers in Port of Spain, Trinidad, while the girl on the facing page has dressed up for the celebration.
Draw Inferences *What do the costumes and props indicate about how much time and effort goes into preparing for this celebration?*

This waiter in Grenada shows a variety of Caribbean dishes.

Food Caribbean food is a mixture that represents the different cultures of the islands. It also makes use of the rich natural resources of the region. Caribbean people can enjoy many types of seafood that are not found in United States waters. For instance, the people of Barbados love to eat flying fish and sea urchin eggs. Bammy—a bread made from the cassava plant—is still made the way the African slaves made it. West Indians also cook spicy curries from India, sausages from England, and Chinese dishes. Many tropical fruits grow on the islands. The fruits are used to make many juices and other drinks that are not readily available in the United States.

Music Caribbean music, which has both African and European sources, is famous around the world. Calypso is a form of song that uses humorous lyrics and has a distinctive beat. Reggae (REHG ay) music and ska come from Jamaica. Reggae songs have a strong rhythm with a "chunking" sound at the end of each measure. The lyrics of traditional reggae songs often have political messages.

Another distinctive Caribbean musical sound is that made by steel drums. These instruments are made from recycled oil drums. A steel drum can be tuned so that different parts of it play different notes. Players strike the instruments with rubberized drumsticks.

✓ **Reading Check** Describe two types of Caribbean music.

Section 2 Assessment

Key Terms
Review the key terms at the beginning of this section. Use each term in a sentence that explains its meaning.

Target Reading Skill
What are three reasons, or causes, for the diversity of ethnic groups and cultures in the Caribbean?

Comprehension and Critical Thinking
1. (a) **Identify** Who were the first inhabitants of the Caribbean islands?

(b) **Explain** What happened to those people? Why?
(c) **Identify Causes** Why do West Indians speak a variety of languages today?
2. (a) **Recall** What kinds of activities do Caribbean people enjoy?
(b) **Categorize** Which traditions have these activities come from?
(c) **Draw Conclusions** Why is there more of a cultural blend in the Caribbean than in Middle America?

Writing Activity
Select one aspect of Caribbean culture, such as food, music, or celebrations. Write a paragraph comparing and contrasting that aspect of Caribbean culture with the cultural practices where you live.

> **Writing Tip** Before you begin, decide how you will organize your paragraph. One way is to cover all the similarities first and then all the differences.

Section 3
The Cultures of South America

Prepare to Read

Objectives

In this section you will
1. Find out what ethnic groups are represented in the different cultural regions of South America.
2. Learn what life is like in the countryside and the cities of South America.

Taking Notes

As you read this section, look for information about the cultural regions of South America. Copy the table below and record your findings in it.

Location of Region	Countries	Characteristics
Caribbean Coast		

Target Reading Skill

Understand Effects An effect is what happens as the result of a specific cause or factor. For example, you can see in the paragraph below that the geography of the Lake Titicaca region has had several effects on the way the Native Americans there live. This section discusses the effects of geography and colonization on different regions of South America. As you read, note the effects of each of these factors on the way South Americans live today.

Key Terms

- **gauchos** (GOW chohz) *n.* cowboys of the pampas of Argentina
- **subsistence farming** (sub SIS tuns FAHR ming) *n.* growing only enough food to meet the needs of the farmer's family
- **cash crop** (kash krahp) *n.* a crop grown mostly for sale rather than for the farmer's own use

Between Peru and Bolivia is the deep lake called Lake Titicaca. It lies high in the Andes Mountains. This area is cool and dry. There are few trees. Native Americans here make their living from totora reeds, a kind of thick, hollow grass that grows on the lakeshore. They use these reeds to make houses, mats, hats, ropes, sails, toys, roofs, and floors. They eat the reeds, feed them to livestock, and brew them into tea. Totora reeds can even be made into medicine.

Long ago, a number of Native American groups built floating islands with totora reeds. They used the islands to hide from the Incas. Today, some Native Americans still live on floating islands on Lake Titicaca.

Native Americans who live on Lake Titicaca make their boats out of totora reeds.

Understand Effects
What two effects of Spanish colonization are described in the paragraph at the right?

An Ancient Way of Life
Toco Indians in Peru wear traditional clothing and herd llamas much as their ancestors did. **Conclude** *Look at the setting of the photo. How do you think geography has contributed to these people keeping their traditional way of life?*

The People of South America

Most South Americans today are descended from Native Americans, Africans, or Europeans. In this way, they are like the people of Mexico and Central America. Like its neighbors to the north, South America, too, was colonized mainly by Spain. Today, many South Americans speak Spanish and are Catholic, yet different regions within South America have their own unique cultures.

Caribbean South America There are four cultural regions in South America. The first region includes Colombia, Venezuela, Guyana, Suriname, and French Guiana. These countries are in northern South America, on or near the Caribbean Sea. Their cultures are similar to those of the Caribbean islands.

Local history has also influenced the cultures of each nation. Colombia and Venezuela were Spanish colonies, and their people are mainly mestizo. Their official language is Spanish, and most of the people are Roman Catholic. On the other hand, Guyana, Suriname, and French Guiana were colonized by different European nations. Guyana was once an English colony, and its official language is English. Suriname was a Dutch colony until 1975, and the people there still speak Dutch. In both countries, many people are Muslim or Hindu. French Guiana is not an independent nation; it is an overseas department of France. While its official language is French, many of its people are of mixed African and European descent.

The Andean Countries and the South To the south and west, the culture is very different. Peru, Ecuador, and Bolivia are Andean countries. Many Native Americans live high in the Andes Mountains. In Bolivia, there are more indigenous people than mestizos. The Quechua and Aymara (eye muh RAH) peoples speak their own languages and follow the traditional ways of their ancestors.

The third cultural region consists of Chile, Argentina, Paraguay, and Uruguay. The long, narrow country of Chile has mountains, beaches, deserts, forests, and even glaciers. Although its geography is diverse, its people are not. Most people in Chile are mestizos. In Argentina and Uruguay, however, the big cities are very diverse. Many different ethnic groups live there.

Another culture exists on Argentina's pampas, or plains. The pampas are the traditional home of the **gauchos** (GOW chohz), the Argentinean cowboys. While cattle raising is still important, wheat fields are beginning to replace grazing lands on the pampas, and the day of the gaucho may be coming to an end.

Brazil South America's largest country was once a colony of Portugal, and today its people speak Portuguese. However, Brazil is culturally diverse. Many Native Americans live in Brazil, as do people of African and European descent. Some Brazilians are of mixed descent. Many people have moved to Brazil from other countries. Brazil's largest city, São Paulo (sow PAW loh), is home to more Japanese than any other place in the world except Japan.

Cityscapes
This avenue in Buenos Aires, Argentina (left photo) is said to be the widest boulevard in the world. Signs in São Paulo, Brazil, (right photo) are in Portuguese and Japanese. **Draw Conclusions** *What can you conclude about South America's cities and culture from these two photos?*

Mothers of the "Disappeared"

In 1976, a military government took control of Argentina and began arresting people who opposed their regime. Other opponents of the government simply "disappeared"—kidnapped by unidentified armed men. Fourteen mothers of these "disappeared" demanded information about their children. When the government did not respond, the women began to march in front of the presidential palace every Thursday at 3:30 P.M. They became know as the Mothers of Plaza de Mayo (PLAH zuh day MY oh). Their peaceful protests brought worldwide attention to their cause. As one observer put it, "These are women who moved from being housewives in Argentina to being global leaders for justice."

South American Literature   South America has produced many famous writers. Gabriela Mistral (gah bree AY lah mees TRAHL), a poet from Chile, was the first Latin American to win the Nobel Prize for Literature. Her poetry reflects her love of children, and so does her second career as a teacher. When she was a school principal, she encouraged the young Chilean poet Pablo Neruda (PAH bloh neh ROO duh). He went on to win the Nobel Prize in 1971. When he was a young man, Neruda composed complex poems. Toward the end of his life, however, he wrote about simple, everyday objects, such as onions and socks.

Another South American winner of the Nobel Prize for Literature was the Colombian novelist Gabriel García Márquez (gah bree EL gahr SEE ah MAHR kes). He is best known for novels in the style of magic realism, which mixes fantasy with historical facts and realistic stories. Isabel Allende (EES uh bel ah YEN day), a novelist from Chile, also uses magic realism in many of her novels and stories. She is also known for her "letters" to members of her family, which were published as books.

The Role of Women   In some ways, women do not yet play a role equal to that of men in South America. Women in South America are more likely than men to be poor. They also do not attend school for as many years as men do.

More and more women in South America today are fighting to make a living for themselves and their children. They are demanding equal rights. Women are struggling for the rights to go to school, to work in all types of jobs, to have good health care, and to have a voice in government. Some women are getting bank loans to start small businesses. These businesses are sometimes based on traditional skills such as sewing, weaving, or preparing food.

✓ **Reading Check**   What rights are women fighting for?

Country and City Life

South America has cities with millions of people, but it also has vast areas with almost no people at all. Many South Americans still live in the countryside, but others are leaving farms and moving to cities.

Farming in South America Outside of Argentina, Chile, and Uruguay, most rural people with land of their own do **subsistence farming.** That means they grow only enough food to meet their families' needs. They have only small plots of land. These farmers plant corn, beans, potatoes, and rice.

Very large farms grow crops to export to other countries. The main export cash crops of South America are coffee, sugar, cacao, and bananas. **Cash crops** are crops grown mostly for sale rather than for the farmer's own use. Export farming uses so much land for cash crops that South America has to import food for its own people to eat.

South America's Cities The cities of South America illustrate the region's mix of cultures. Many major cities—Lima, Peru, and Buenos Aires, Argentina, for example—were founded by Spanish colonists more than 400 years ago. Much of their architecture is Spanish in style. Some buildings in even older cities follow Native American designs.

Two Ways to Farm
The top photo shows a banana processing plant on a plantation in Ecuador. Below is a small family-owned coffee farm in Colombia.
Infer *Why might plantation owners not be interested in farming the area in the lower photo? How easy do you think it is to make a living there?*

City of Contrasts
This view of Buenos Aires shows poor neighborhoods in the foreground while the modern downtown rises in the distance. **Infer** *What city services do the people in the foreground seem to lack?*

In contrast, modern office blocks and apartment buildings of concrete, steel, and glass tower above the downtown areas of many South American cities. One or two cities were built quite recently. Brasília, the Brazilian capital, was constructed in the 1950s. It was a completely planned city, designed to draw people to the country's interior.

On the other hand, the slums of many South American cities have certainly been unplanned. They are called *favelas* (fuh VEH lus) in Brazil and *ranchos* in Venezuela. The population of South America is booming. Like Mexicans and Central Americans, South Americans cannot find enough jobs in rural areas. Every day, thousands of rural people move to the cities looking for work. Usually they end up in poor neighborhoods. City governments try to provide electricity and running water to everyone. But people move into cities so quickly that it is hard for city governments to keep up.

✓ **Reading Check** What types of buildings are found in South American cities?

Section 3 Assessment

Key Terms
Review the key terms at the beginning of this section. Use each term in a sentence that explains its meaning.

Target Reading Skill
What are two effects of the fact that many Native Americans still live high in the Andes Mountains?

Comprehension and Critical Thinking
1. (a) Recall Describe two cultural regions of South America.
(b) Identify Cause and Effect Explain two ways in which the geography of South America has shaped how people live.
2. (a) Identify Describe two different kinds of farms in South America.
(b) Compare and Contrast How are city life and rural life similar and different?
(c) Analyze Information How does the movement of people from the countryside to urban areas put pressure on cities?

Writing Activity
Suppose you were a newspaper reporter visiting Argentina in 1976. Write a short article about the Mothers of Plaza de Mayo for your American readers.

Go Online
PHSchool.com
For: An activity on South America
Visit: PHSchool.com
Web Code: lfd-1303

Review and Assessment

◆ Chapter Summary

Section 1: The Cultures of Middle America

- Many different cultural groups live in Middle America, and the languages and arts of the region reflect this diversity.
- Population growth and lack of jobs have caused many rural Middle Americans to move to the cities or to emigrate to the United States.

Section 2: The Cultures of the Caribbean

- The people of the Caribbean are made up of many ethnic groups, including descendants of Africans and Europeans.
- West Indian sports, food, music, and celebrations reflect the blend of cultures in the Caribbean.

Section 3: The Cultures of South America

- Life in the different cultural regions of South America is influenced by geography and by the ethnic groups that settled there.
- South America has both large farms that export their crops and small subsistence farms.
- South American cities are overcrowded with poor rural people coming to look for work.

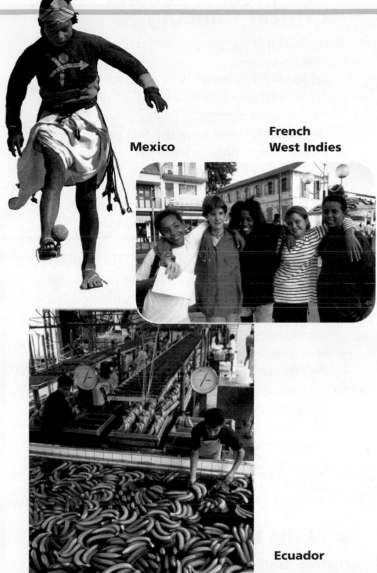

Mexico

French West Indies

Ecuador

◆ Key Terms

Match the definitions in Column I with the key terms in Column II.

Column I

1. a group of people who share ancestry, language, religion, or cultural traditions
2. descendants of the people who first lived in a region
3. growing only enough food to meet the needs of their families
4. a person who has moved from one country to settle in another
5. a poor farmer who owns little or no land

Column II

A   indigenous people

B   campesino

C   immigrant

D   ethnic group

E   subsistence farming

Review and Assessment (continued)

◆ Comprehension and Critical Thinking

6. (a) Recall Describe population growth in Middle America.
(b) Identify Effects How has population growth affected the movement of people in that region?

7. (a) Identify Who were the first people to inhabit the Caribbean islands?
(b) Identify Cause and Effect What happened to those people, and why?
(c) Draw Conclusions Why is there such cultural diversity in the Caribbean today?

8. (a) Define What is Carnival?
(b) Identify Cause and Effect How does Carnival reflect both West Indian culture and Roman Catholic traditions?

9. (a) Describe What language is spoken in Brazil?
(b) Identify Effects Why are Brazil's culture and language different from the rest of South America's?

10. (a) Define What are *ranchos* and *favelas*?
(b) Identify Causes Why are they growing?
(c) Draw Conclusions How do conditions in the countryside affect these city neighborhoods?

11. (a) Define What are cash crops?
(b) Conclude Why does export farming cause problems for some South American countries?

◆ Skills Practice

Distinguishing Fact and Opinion In the Skills for Life activity in this chapter, you learned how to distinguish facts from opinions. You also learned how to use facts and well-supported opinions to help you make decisions.

Read the paragraph below. List the facts and the opinions. Explain how this paragraph could help you decide whether to try the Carib Heaven Restaurant.

Caribbean food is the best in the world. There is so much variety from the different cultures of the area. There are also lots of tropical fruits and juices. A lot of the food is quite spicy—just the way I like it! The Carib Heaven Restaurant will give you a chance to try this great cuisine.

◆ Writing Activity: Geography

Suppose you are a writer for a travel magazine. Write an article about one of the places you "visited" in this chapter. Include descriptions of the landforms, waterways, climate, and vegetation. Explain how geography has affected the way people live in that place.

Refer to the maps in the Regional Overview and in Chapter 1 as well as to the information in this chapter. You can also do additional research if you wish.

MAP★MASTER™
Skills Activity

Latin America

Place Location For each place listed below, write the letter from the map that shows its location.

1. Trinidad and Tobago
2. Bolivia
3. Jamaica
4. Guatemala
5. Honduras
6. Hispaniola

Go Online
PHSchool.com Use Web Code lfp-1323 for an **interactive map**.

Standardized Test Prep

Test-Taking Tips

Some questions on standardized tests ask you to analyze graphs and charts. Look at the circle graph at the right. Then follow the tips to answer the sample question.

Think It Through Because only one percent of Mexicans are Protestant, you can eliminate answer D. You can also eliminate A easily, because England had little influence on Mexico. You know from the text that the Aztec influence was important, but you can see from the graph that the Aztec religion does not play a large role in Mexico today. That leaves the Roman Catholic country of Spain, which makes sense when you consider Mexico's history. Therefore, the correct answer is B.

TIP Draw your own conclusions about the graph before you look at the answer choices.

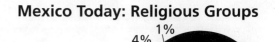

Mexico Today: Religious Groups

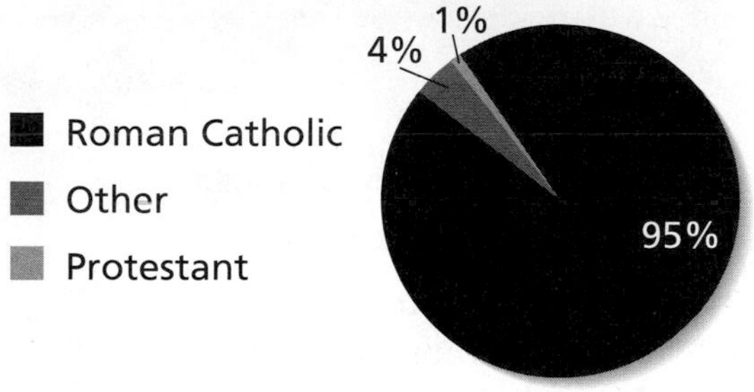

■ Roman Catholic
■ Other
■ Protestant

95%
4%
1%

Pick the letter that best answers the question.

The information in the graph could be used to show the influence of

A England on the development of modern Mexico.
B Spain on the development of modern Mexico.
C Ancient Aztecs on the development of modern Mexico.
D Protestantism on the development of modern Mexico.

TIP Look for the BEST answer, as more than one answer choice may seem to fit.

Practice Questions

Choose the letter of the best answer.

1. Most of the people of Mexico and Central America are
   A indigenous or of mixed ancestry.
   B European or Spanish.
   C indigenous or European.
   D Spanish or of mixed ancestry.

2. Rapid population growth in Mexico and Central America has caused all of the following EXCEPT
   A migration to cities.
   B emigration to other countries.
   C fewer jobs for everyone.
   D better living conditions in the cities.

3. The Andean countries of South America include
   A Bolivia, Peru, and Ecuador.
   B Peru, Brazil, and Bolivia.
   C Brazil, Argentina, and Chile.
   D Bolivia, Ecuador, and Argentina.

Study the circle graphs and answer the question that follows.

Venezuela Population: 1950

Rural 47% Urban 53%

Venezuela Population: 2002

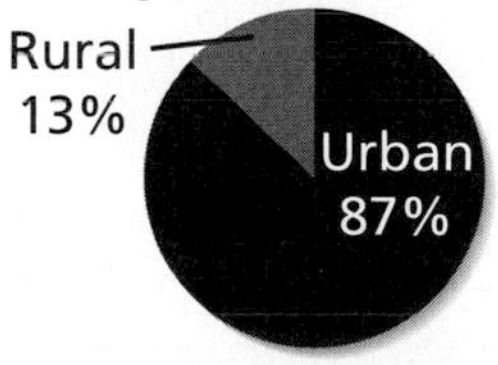

Rural 13% Urban 87%

4. Which sentence best describes the population trend in Venezuela?
   A The rural population has steadily increased.
   B The urban and rural populations have remained the same.
   C The urban population has steadily increased.
   D The urban population has steadily decreased.

Go Online
PHSchool.com

Use Web Code lfa-1301
for a **Chapter 3 self-test.**

Mexico and Central America

Chapter Preview

This chapter will introduce you to the northernmost region of Latin America: Mexico and Central America.

Country Databank
The Country Databank provides data and descriptions of each of the countries in the region: Belize, Costa Rica, El Salvador, Guatemala, Honduras, Mexico, Nicaragua, and Panama.

Section 1
Mexico
Moving to the City

Section 2
Guatemala
Descendants of an Ancient People

Section 3
Panama
An Important Crossroads

Target Reading Skill

Context In this chapter you will focus on using context to help you understand unfamiliar words. Context includes the words, phrases, and sentences surrounding the word.

▶ **A Guatemalan woman walking home from a rural market**

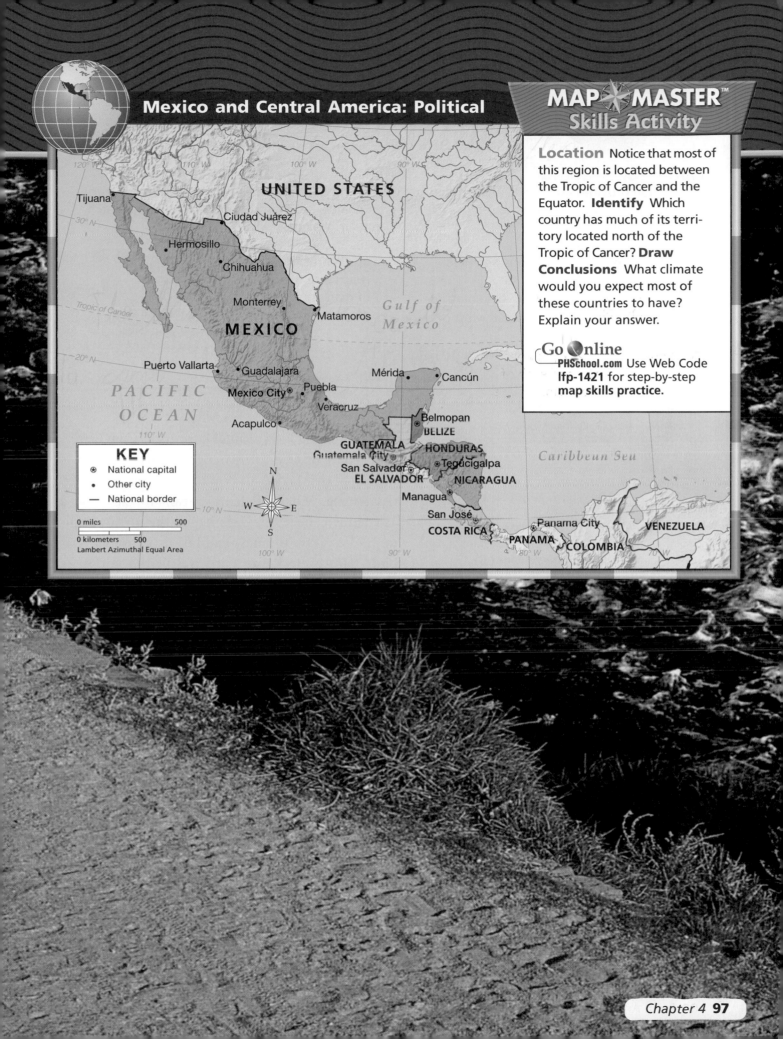

Mexico and Central America: Political

Location Notice that most of this region is located between the Tropic of Cancer and the Equator. **Identify** Which country has much of its territory located north of the Tropic of Cancer? **Draw Conclusions** What climate would you expect most of these countries to have? Explain your answer.

Go Online
PHSchool.com Use Web Code **lfp-1421** for step-by-step **map skills practice.**

UNITED STATES

Tijuana

Ciudad Juárez

Hermosillo

Chihuahua

Monterrey

Matamoros

MEXICO

Gulf of Mexico

Puerto Vallarta

Guadalajara

Mérida

Cancún

Mexico City

Puebla

Veracruz

PACIFIC OCEAN

Acapulco

Belmopan

BELIZE

GUATEMALA

HONDURAS

Caribbean Sea

Guatemala City

Tegucigalpa

San Salvador

EL SALVADOR

NICARAGUA

Managua

San José

Panama City

VENEZUELA

COSTA RICA

PANAMA

COLOMBIA

Tropic of Cancer

KEY
- ⊛ National capital
- • Other city
- — National border

0 miles 500

0 kilometers 500

Lambert Azimuthal Equal Area

N
W E
S

Guide for Reading

This section provides an introduction to the eight countries that make up the region of Mexico and Central America.

- Look at the map on the previous page and then read the paragraphs below to learn about each nation.
- Analyze the data to compare the countries.
- What are the characteristics that most of the countries share?
- What are some key differences among the countries?

Viewing the Video Overview

View the World Studies Video Overview to learn more about each of the countries. As you watch, answer this question:

- Seven countries make up Central America. How were the borders of many countries determined?

Explore the geography of Mexico and Central America.

Belize

Capital	Belmopan
Land Area	8,805 sq mi; 22,806 sq km
Population	262,999
Ethnic Group(s)	mestizo, Creole, Maya, Garifuna
Religion(s)	Roman Catholic, Protestant
Government	parliamentary democracy
Currency	Belizean dollar
Leading Exports	sugar, bananas, citrus, clothing, fish products, molasses, wood
Language(s)	English (official), English Creole, Spanish, Mayan, Garifuna (Carib)

Belize (buh LEEZ) is a small country on the Caribbean coast of Central America. It is bordered on the north by Mexico and on the south and west by Guatemala. Much of Belize is rain forest. After a 1961 hurricane severely damaged the former capital, Belize City, the new capital of Belmopan was built. However, Belize City is still the country's largest and most important city. Formerly known as British Honduras, Belize was the last British colony in North America. It didn't become independent until 1981. Today, its government is based on the British model.

Jaguar in Belize

Costa Rica

Capital	San José
Land Area	19,560 sq mi; 50,660 sq km
Population	3.8 million
Ethnic Group(s)	white, mestizo, black, indigenous Indian, East Asian
Religion(s)	Roman Catholic, Protestant
Government	democratic republic
Currency	Costa Rican colón
Leading Exports	coffee, bananas, sugar, pineapples, textiles, electronics
Language(s)	Spanish (official), English Creole, Bribri, Cabecar

Costa Rica (KAHS tah REE kuh) is a narrow country located between the Pacific Ocean and the Caribbean Sea. It is bordered by Nicaragua and Panama. Even though its name means "rich coast," few riches were found there, and the Spanish colony grew slowly. Costa Rica gained its independence in 1838. Today it is known for its stable government, democratic traditions, and the fact that its army was abolished in 1948. Wealth is more evenly divided in Costa Rica than in other countries in the region, and more government resources go to education and public welfare.

El Salvador

Capital	San Salvador
Land Area	8,000 sq mi; 20,720 sq km
Population	6.4 million
Ethnic Group(s)	mestizo, indigenous Indian, white
Religion(s)	Roman Catholic, Protestant
Government	republic
Currency	Salvadoran colón, U.S. dollar
Leading Exports	offshore assembly exports, coffee, sugar, shrimp, textiles, chemicals, electricity
Language(s)	Spanish (official)

Small and densely populated, El Salvador (el SAL vuh dawr) is one of the poorest countries in the region. It is bordered by Guatemala, Honduras, and the Pacific Ocean. A row of volcanoes runs through El Salvador. In 2001, violent earthquakes killed many people and shattered the economy. El Salvador also suffered from political unrest and a bloody civil war from 1979 to 1992. For much of its history, El Salvador's economy depended on coffee, but manufacturing increased in the 1960s when El Salvador joined the Central American Common Market.

Guatemala

Capital	Guatemala City
Land Area	41,865 sq mi; 108,430 sq km
Population	13.3 million
Ethnic Group(s)	mestizo, indigenous Indian, white
Religion(s)	Roman Catholic, Protestant, traditional beliefs
Government	constitutional democratic republic
Currency	quetzal
Leading Exports	coffee, sugar, bananas, fruits and vegetables, cardamom, meat, apparel, petroleum, electricity
Language(s)	Spanish (official), Quiché, Cakchiquel, Kekchi

One third of the people in Central America live in Guatemala (gwaht uh MAH luh), and Guatemala City is the largest city in Central America. Guatemala is bordered by Mexico, Belize, Honduras, and El Salvador as well as the Caribbean Sea and the Pacific Ocean. Earthquakes, volcanic eruptions, and hurricanes have caused repeated disasters. Guatemala was once home to the ancient Mayan civilization. More recently, it has suffered from harsh military dictatorships, civil war, and discrimination against its large indigenous population.

Introducing Mexico and Central America

Honduras

Capital	Tegucigalpa
Land Area	43,201 sq mi; 111,890 sq km
Population	6.6 million
Ethnic Group(s)	mestizo, indigenous Indian, black, white
Religion(s)	Roman Catholic, Protestant
Government	democratic constitutional republic
Currency	Lempira
Leading Exports	coffee, bananas, shrimp, lobster, meat, zinc, lumber
Language(s)	Spanish (official), Black Carib, English Creole

Honduras (hahn DOOR us) stretches from the Caribbean Sea to the Pacific Ocean. It is also bordered by Guatemala, El Salvador, and Nicaragua. Much of the country is mountainous, and the Mosquito Coast on the Caribbean has few people. Most of the population lives in the central highlands. During the early 1900s, foreign-owned banana plantations dominated the economy, and Honduras was ruled by a series of military governments. There was a return to democracy in 1984, and diversification of the economy began. In 2005, the country was devastated by Hurricane Stan, and it is still recovering from this disaster.

Mayan statue at Copán in Honduras

***The Flower Carrier* (1935) by Mexican artist Diego Rivera**

Mexico

Capital	Mexico City
Land Area	742,486 sq mi; 1,923,040 sq km
Population	103.4 million
Ethnic Group(s)	mestizo, Amerindian, European
Religion(s)	Roman Catholic, Protestant
Government	federal republic
Currency	Mexican peso
Leading Exports	manufactured goods, oil and oil products, silver, fruits, vegetables, coffee, cotton
Language(s)	Spanish (official), Nahuatl, Mayan, Zapotec, Mixtec

Mexico (MEK sih koh) is located south of the United States and northwest of Central America. It stretches from the Pacific Ocean to the Gulf of Mexico and the Caribbean Sea. Like the United States, Mexico is a federal republic. It has 31 states. The election of President Vicente Fox in 2000 and subsequent elections reflected a move toward greater democracy and the growth of a multiparty system. Mexico is a major oil producer, but also has considerable foreign debt.

Nicaragua

Capital	Managua
Land Area	46,430 sq mi; 120,254 sq km
Population	5.2 million
Ethnic Group(s)	mestizo, white, black, indigenous Indian
Religion(s)	Roman Catholic, Protestant
Government	republic
Currency	Córdoba oro
Leading Exports	coffee, shrimp and lobster, cotton, tobacco, beef, sugar, bananas, gold
Language(s)	Spanish (official), English Creole, Miskito

Nicaragua (nik uh RAH gwuh) stretches across Central America from the Caribbean Sea to the Pacific Ocean. It is bordered on the north by Honduras and on the south by Costa Rica. Like its neighbors, Nicaragua has a row of volcanoes and has experienced many eruptions and earthquakes. After the overthrow of a 40-year dictatorship in 1979, Nicaragua was plunged into civil war, which ended in 1990. In 2005, the country was devastated by Hurricane Stan and is still recovering from the aftermath of the hurricane and the years of civil war.

Panama

Capital	Panama City
Land Area	29,340 sq mi; 75,990 sq km
Population	2.9 million
Ethnic Group(s)	mestizo, mixed black and indigenous Indian, white, indigenous Indian
Religion(s)	Roman Catholic, Protestant
Government	constitutional democracy
Currency	Balboa
Leading Exports	bananas, shrimp, sugar, coffee, clothing
Language(s)	Spanish (official), English Creole, indigenous Indian languages

The narrow country of Panama (PAN uh mah) has been both a barrier and a bridge between the Atlantic and Pacific oceans. It is bordered on the west by Costa Rica and on the east by the South American nation of Colombia. At first, Panama's rough terrain and rain forests hindered travel across the isthmus. The Panama Canal, which opened in 1914, made Panama a main shipping route and led to its economic growth. Most Panamanians live near the canal. Panama City is located at the canal's Pacific entrance. Another major city, Colón, is found near the Caribbean entrance to the canal.

SOURCES: DK World Desk Reference Online; *CIA World Factbook*; *The World Almanac*, 2003

Assessment

Comprehension and Critical Thinking

1. Compare and Contrast Compare the physical size and the population size of Honduras and Guatemala.

2. Draw Conclusions What are the characteristics that most of the countries share?

3. Compare and Contrast What are some key differences among the countries?

4. Categorize What kinds of products are the major exports of this region?

5. Infer What can you infer about a country if many of its exports are made in factories?

6. Make a Bar Graph Create a bar graph showing the population of the countries in the region.

Keeping Current

Access the **DK World Desk Reference Online** at **PHSchool.com** for up-to-date information about all eight countries in this chapter.

Go Online
PHSchool.com

Web Code: lfe-1410

Mexico
Moving to the City

Prepare to Read

Objectives

In this section you will
1. Learn what life is like for people in rural Mexico.
2. Find out why many Mexicans have been moving from the countryside to the cities.
3. Understand why the growth of Mexico City presents challenges for people and the environment.

Taking Notes

As you read this section, look for ways that life is similar and different in rural and in urban Mexico. Copy the Venn diagram below and record your findings in it.

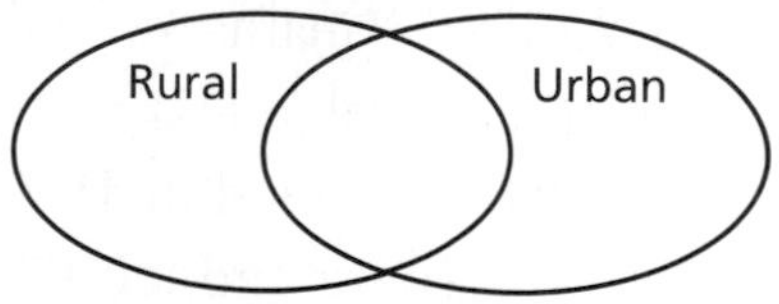

Life in Mexico

Rural   Urban

Target Reading Skill

Use Context Clues When you come across an unfamiliar word, you can often figure out its meaning from clues in the context. The context refers to the surrounding words, phrases, and sentences. Sometimes the context will define the word. In this example, the phrase in italics explains what smog is: "Smog, *a low-lying layer of polluted air,* hung over the city."

Key Terms

- **migrant worker** (MY grunt WUR kur) *n.* a laborer who travels from one area to another, picking crops that are in season
- **plaza** (PLAH zuh) *n.* a public square at the center of a village, a town, or a city
- **squatter** (SKWAHT ur) *n.* a person who settles on someone else's land without permission

Using oxen to plow a field

Most farm families in Mexico are poor. Many are campesinos. Some work their own small farms. They often plow the land and harvest their crops by hand because they cannot afford expensive farm machinery. Other campesinos do not own land. They work on large farms owned by rich landowners. These **migrant workers** travel from one area to another, picking the crops that are in season.

Mexico's population has risen dramatically over the last 30 years. The country's population is growing at one of the highest rates in the world. There is not enough farm work for so many people. A large family cannot support itself on a small farm. And there are not enough jobs for all the migrant workers.

Many rural Mexicans are moving from the countryside to Mexico City. Why are they making this move? How does moving to the city change their lives? How is this trend changing the country of Mexico?

Life in Rural Mexico

Find the Plateau of Mexico on the map titled *Physical Latin America* on page 4. The southern part of the plateau has Mexico's best farmland. Throughout much of this region, life has changed little over many years.

Rural Villages Nearly every village in the Mexican countryside has a church and a market. At the center of most villages is a public square called a **plaza.** Farm families grow their own food. If they have extra food, they sell it at the market in the plaza. Rural people buy nearly everything they need—clothing, food, toys, and housewares—at the market rather than in stores.

Farm Work Ramiro Avila (rah MEE roh ah VEE luh) grew up in the state of Guanajuato (gwah nah HWAH toh), in central Mexico. In his small village, Ramiro knew everyone and everyone knew him.

Ramiro's family were campesinos who owned no land. Even as a young child, Ramiro had to work to help support his family. He and his father had jobs as farm laborers. They worked on someone else's farm. They made less than a dollar a day. When Ramiro was 13, his parents decided to move to Mexico City. They joined many other Mexicans who were making this move.

✓ **Reading Check** What is life like in rural Mexican villages?

A Village Market in Mexico
Like many Mexican markets, this one sells a wide variety of goods.
Infer *Why do you think markets like this one become the center of village life?*

Mexico

As Mexico's population has expanded, large numbers of Mexicans have been moving to the cities to find jobs. Some of the jobs available in the cities are industrial, or jobs in which people produce manufactured goods. Most of Mexico's industry takes place in Mexico City and other large cities. Mexico exports most of the manufactured goods it produces. Study the map and graphs to learn about Mexico's exports and trade partners. Think about how the country's economy shapes the lives of ordinary Mexicans.

Mexico: Resources and Manufacturing

KEY

- National border
- National capital
- Other city
- Car manufacture
- Chemicals
- Electronics
- Textiles
- Oil deposits
- Gas deposits
- Industrial area

0 miles 600
0 kilometers 600
Lambert Azimuthal Equal Area

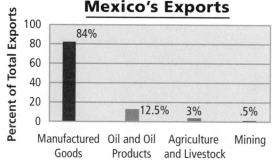

Mexico's Exports

Percent of Total Exports

- Manufactured Goods: 84%
- Oil and Oil Products: 12.5%
- Agriculture and Livestock: 3%
- Mining: .5%

SOURCE: National Institute of Statistics; *Geography and Informatics 2005*

Mexico's Trading Partners

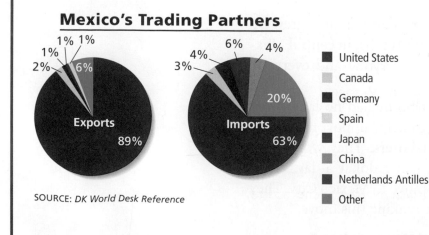

Exports: 89%, 6%, 2%, 1%, 1%, 1%

Imports: 63%, 20%, 6%, 4%, 4%, 3%

- United States
- Canada
- Germany
- Spain
- Japan
- China
- Netherlands Antilles
- Other

SOURCE: *DK World Desk Reference*

Map and Chart Skills

1. **Identify** Where are most of Mexico's manufacturing jobs located?

2. **Infer** To what country does Mexico export the most goods? What role might geography play in this trade partnership?

3. **Synthesize** How can a country's economy and trade partners affect where its people live?

Go Online
PHSchool.com

Use Web Code Ife-1411 for DK World Desk Reference Online.

Life in the City
New arrivals to Mexico City often live in temporary houses (left). But the children still have a chance to attend school (right). **Infer** *Using clues from the photos, describe what life is like for the family shown washing clothes outdoors.*

Moving to Mexico City

Many rural people move to the cities because they cannot find work in the countryside. They hope they can make a better living in urban areas such as Mexico City. They also hope that their children will get a better education in city schools. Although city life will be very different from life in the countryside, these families leave their familiar villages behind to make a new start in the city.

Housing in the City Like thousands of other campesino families coming to the city, Ramiro's family did not have much money. When they arrived in Mexico City, they could not afford a house. They went to live in Colonia Zapata, one of many neighborhoods where poor people become squatters. A **squatter** is a person who settles on someone else's land without permission.

Many small houses built by squatters cling to the sides of a steep hill in the Colonia. The older houses near the bottom of the hill are built of concrete. However, most people cannot afford to make sturdy houses when they first arrive. Therefore many of the newer houses higher up the hill are constructed of scrap metal. Most squatter families hope that they will soon be able to buy land from the government. Then they can build their own permanent houses and even have a garden and a patio.

Work and School Once they settle in Mexico City, many families discover that it is still difficult to find work. Sometimes the men of the family look for jobs across the border, in the United States. They often work as farm laborers in states near the Mexican border, such as Texas and California. These men leave their families behind in Mexico, but many of them send money home every month.

DISCOVERY CHANNEL SCHOOL Video

Learn how natural hazards affect life in Mexico.

Children in these families not only have to get used to city life. They must also adjust to being without their fathers for months at a time. The older children have many new responsibilities. Sometimes they care for the younger children. Or they may work at low-paying jobs in the daytime to help support their families and then go to school at night.

✔ **Reading Check** What new responsibilities might older children face when they move to Mexico City?

Opportunities and Challenges

Large cities in Mexico—and around the world—share many problems as well as many advantages. Even so, each city is unique. Take a closer look at Mexico City.

Mexico's Capital City Mexico City was built on the site of the Aztec capital, Tenochtitlán. During colonial times, it was the capital of New Spain. Today, it is the capital of the modern nation of Mexico.

Much of Mexico's urban population lives in Mexico City. If you count the people in outlying areas, Mexico City has nearly 20 million people. It is one of the largest cities in the world.

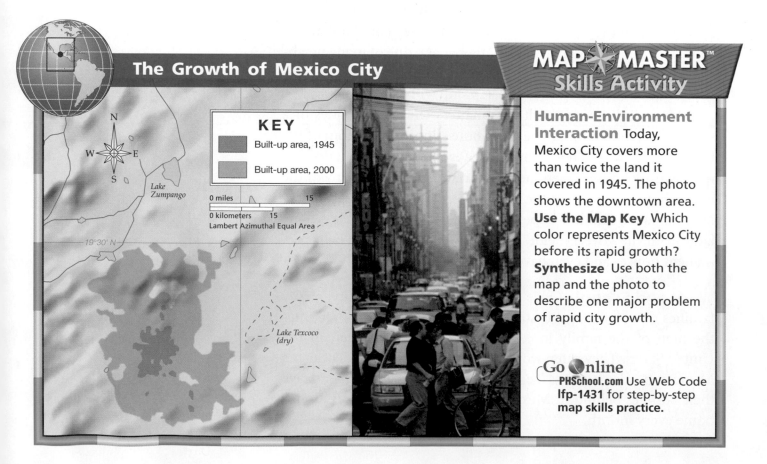

The Growth of Mexico City

KEY

■ Built-up area, 1945
■ Built-up area, 2000

0 miles 15
0 kilometers 15
Lambert Azimuthal Equal Area

19°30' N

Lake Zumpango

Lake Texcoco (dry)

MAP MASTER™ Skills Activity

Human-Environment Interaction Today, Mexico City covers more than twice the land it covered in 1945. The photo shows the downtown area. **Use the Map Key** Which color represents Mexico City before its rapid growth? **Synthesize** Use both the map and the photo to describe one major problem of rapid city growth.

Go Online
PHSchool.com Use Web Code lfp-1431 for step-by-step map skills practice.

Smog in Mexico City

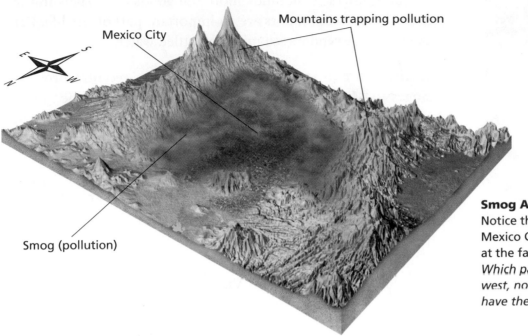

Mexico City

Mountains trapping pollution

Smog (pollution)

Smog Alert
Notice the mountains surrounding Mexico City, and study the compass at the far left. **Analyze Images** *Which part of Mexico City—east, west, north, or south—seems to have the least smog? Explain why.*

Old and New, Rich and Poor Mexico City has both modern skyscrapers and older, historic areas with two- and three-story buildings. Wide avenues and highways along with narrower side streets can barely handle the traffic of this sprawling city. The subway, the underground railroad system, carries more than four million people each day.

Small neighborhoods of very wealthy people are tucked away from the rest of the city. But most of Mexico City's residents are not wealthy. The poorest live on the outskirts of the city. Some of them must travel several hours a day just to get to their jobs.

Pollution and Geography Because of their rapid population growth, many of Mexico's large cities face problems of traffic, pollution, and water shortages. In Mexico City, millions of cars and trucks jam the streets. They compete with taxis, trolleys, and buses. The exhaust fumes from these vehicles pollute the air. Mexico City has also outgrown its fresh water supply. The city must now pump in water from sources as far as 100 miles away.

Mexico City's geography makes its pollution problem worse. The city spreads across a bowl-shaped valley. The surrounding mountains trap automobile exhaust, factory smoke, and other kinds of pollution near the city. The resulting smog cannot blow away, and it hangs over Mexico City as a brown cloud.

Use Context Clues
If you do not know what a subway is, look in the surrounding words for a context clue. Here, the phrase following *subway* is a definition of the term. What is a subway?

Making a Living In spite of all their problems, large cities offer many ways to make a living. Millions of people work in factories and offices. Thousands more sell goods from stalls in the street. These street vendors are an important part of city life. For example, some vendors sell juice or bottled water.

Looking to the Future Two events have recently brought changes to Mexico. One of these was the signing of the North American Free Trade Agreement (NAFTA) in 1994. As you read in Chapter 2, the purpose of NAFTA was to improve trade among Canada, the United States, and Mexico.

In Mexico, manufacturing and exports did increase. So did foreign investment. But some say that poor Mexican farmers and factory workers did not benefit from NAFTA. Their incomes actually went down. What's more, new industrial development has increased pollution in Mexico's cities.

In 2000, Mexicans elected Vicente Fox president. Until Fox's election, one political party, the Institutional Revolutionary Party (PRI), had ruled Mexico for 71 years. During his six years as president, Fox focused on improving the economy and strengthening Mexico's relationship with the United States. Elections in 2006 revealed a deep divide within the country, and for months, the results of the close presidential election remained contested.

The 2000 election of President Vicente Fox, of the National Action Party, was a historic change in Mexico.

✓ **Reading Check** What changes has Mexico recently gone through?

Section 1 Assessment

Key Terms
Review the key terms at the beginning of this section. Use each term in a sentence that explains its meaning.

Target Reading Skill
Find the word *sprawling* on page 107. Use context to figure out its meaning. What clue helped you figure out its meaning?

Comprehension and Critical Thinking
1. (a) Recall Describe life in a Mexican village.

(b) Identify Causes Why do so many rural Mexicans move to the cities?

2. (a) Describe How do poor people live in Mexico City?

(b) Synthesize What new problems do rural Mexicans face when they move to the city?

3. (a) Describe What is Mexico City like?

(b) Identify Causes What factors cause pollution in Mexico City?

(c) Evaluate Information Identify the benefits and drawbacks of moving to Mexico City.

Writing Activity
Write an entry in your journal comparing Mexico City with your hometown. How are the two places similar and how are they different? How would your life be different if you lived in a place like Mexico City?

Go Online
PHSchool.com

For: An activity on Mexico City
Visit: PHSchool.com
Web Code: lfd-1401

Guatemala
Descendants of an Ancient People

Prepare to Read

Objectives

In this section you will
1. Learn why there is a struggle for land in Guatemala.
2. Find out how the Mayas lost their land.
3. Discover how groups are working to improve the lives of Guatemala's indigenous people.

Taking Notes

As you read this section, look for details about the Mayas' struggle for their rights. Copy the chart below, and record your findings in it.

```
               Struggle for Mayan Rights

   Under            During         Since 1996
Spanish Rule       Civil War
   •                 •                •
   •                 •                •
```

Target Reading Skill

Use Context Clues
Context, the words and phrases surrounding a word, can help you understand a new word. One context clue is contrast, a word or words that have the opposite meaning of the unfamiliar word. In this example, the contrast with the newly arrived Spanish helps explain the word *indigenous:* "The struggle of the indigenous people of Guatemala to keep their land began when the Spanish first arrived."

Key Terms

- **ladino** (luh DEE noh) *n.* a mestizo, or person of mixed Spanish and Native American ancestry in Guatemala
- **land reform** (land ree FAWRM) *n.* the effort to distribute land more equally and fairly
- **political movement** (puh LIT ih kul MOOV munt) *n.* a large group of people who work together for political change
- **strike** (stryk) *n.* a refusal to work until certain demands of workers are met

In Guatemala, Native Americans make up the majority of the population. They form 23 ethnic groups. Even though the indigenous groups of Guatemala are related to one another, each group is different. Each one has its own language and customs. The largest group is the Quiché Maya.

Mayan families are often poor. They raise corn on tiny plots of land, but can barely earn enough money to survive. Children often work to help support their families. Mayan girls do weaving to bring in extra money. One Mayan girl described her childhood as similar to the childhoods of "all Indian girls, at the side of my mother, making tortillas and learning to weave and embroider."

Like many other indigenous people, the Mayas have found it difficult to get an education and escape poverty. They have also struggled to preserve their traditional culture as they become part of modern Guatemala.

Modern Mayan women weave much as their ancestors did.

Farming in the Mountains
This small Mayan farm clings to a Guatemalan hillside. **Analyze Images** *Look carefully at the buildings and the fields. What do these details tell you about making a living on this farm?*

The Struggle for Land

Land is a valuable resource in Guatemala, as it is in all of Latin America. Fair distribution of the land is a serious problem throughout the region.

The People and the Land Much of the land in Guatemala belongs to a few rich families. The rich landowners of Guatemala are **ladinos** (luh DEE nohz), mestizos who are descended from Native Americans and Spaniards. Native Americans who follow European ways are also considered to be ladinos.

For many years, most Mayas have lived in the mountains because it was the only land available to Native Americans. Although Mayan families work hard on their farms, they often fail to produce good crops. The soil of the Guatemalan highlands is not very good. Soil erosion makes farming even more difficult.

Use Context Clues If you do not remember what *hacienda* means, consider these context clues. A hacienda is "where crops are grown to sell abroad." Haciendas are also contrasted with small farms. Therefore a hacienda is _____.

Land Distribution In many Latin American countries, the best land is used for haciendas where crops are grown to sell abroad. Guatemalan haciendas produce coffee, cotton, sugar cane, and bananas. In contrast, campesinos grow maize, beans, and squash on small farms in the highlands. These crops are often sold in village markets and provide food for the local population.

Since the 1930s, **land reform,** the effort to distribute land more equally, has been a major goal of many reform and political groups. The wealthy landowners, who have the greatest political power in many Latin American countries, have often resisted these reforms. Clashes between those in favor of reform and those against it have even led to violence and civil war. You will read about the Guatemalan civil war later in this section.

✓ **Reading Check** How is land distributed in many Latin American countries?

The Mayas Lose Their Land

In order to get enough land to make a living—or even to keep the land they have—the Mayas of Guatemala have faced many challenges. One challenge relates to their culture. Indigenous people do not always think of themselves as citizens of the country in which they live. A Mayan woman is more likely to think of herself as a Maya than as a Guatemalan.

Learn about growing coffee in Guatemala.

COUNTRY PROFILE

Focus on Culture

Guatemala

Guatemala today has two distinct cultures: indigenous and ladino. Ladinos speak Spanish, the country's official language, and live mainly in the cities. The majority of Guatemala's population, however, are Mayas. Most Mayas live in villages and towns in the country's highlands. From town to town, Mayan groups speak slightly different languages and create unique art. Their art includes distinctive fabric patterns woven by each group. Study the map and charts to learn more about Guatemalan culture.

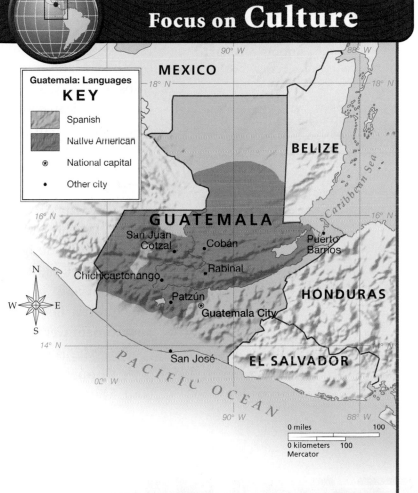

Guatemala: Languages
KEY
- Spanish
- Native American
- ⊛ National capital
- • Other city

Ethnic Groups

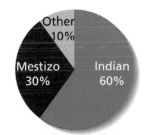

Other 10%
Mestizo 30%
Indian 60%

SOURCE: *DK World Desk Reference*

Mayan Towns

Town Name	Language	Sample Fabric
Patzún	Cakchiquel	
Cobán	Kekchí	
Chichicastenango	Quiché	
San Juan Cotzal	Ixil	
Rabinal	Pokomchi	

Map and Chart Skills

1. **Identify** In what parts of the country is Spanish spoken? What language would you expect the people in Rabinal to speak?
2. **Infer** What advantages and disadvantages result from having so many languages in one country?

Go Online PHSchool.com
Use Web Code lfe-1412 for **DK World Desk Reference Online.**

Justina Tzoc: A Voice for Change

For many years, Justina Tzoc (hoo STEE nah tsohk) has worked to help Mayan women in remote areas of Guatemala. She calls her effort "the kind of work that has no beginning and no end." During the Guatemalan civil war, Tzoc faced many dangers as she helped these women organize to fight for their rights. Although the civil war is over, Tzoc's work goes on. According to Tzoc, the indigenous women of Guatemala will continue to work "so that we are recognized—have a voice and a vote."

In addition, the majority of Native Americans in Guatemala cannot read or write. For these two reasons, most Mayas have not filed any papers with the government showing that they own land. Even after they have worked hard for many years to grow crops on a piece of land, a Mayan family often has no way to prove that their land belongs to them.

A 500-Year-Old Struggle The indigenous people of Guatemala have fought to keep both their land and their culture for more than 500 years. This struggle began when the Spanish first arrived in the Americas.

The Spanish conquistadors conquered the Native Americans by force. Many were killed. Others died of hunger or the hardships of slavery. Still others died from European diseases. In many Latin American countries, there are few indigenous people left. In contrast, Guatemala is largely Native American. However, the Native Americans have little political power or land.

Civil War Beginning around 1960, a civil war raged in Guatemala for more than 30 years. First, an elected leader who favored land reform was overthrown by the military. Then government military forces fought rebel groups that were living in the highlands. Armed fighters were not the only ones killed in the fighting. Thousands of civilians were also killed, and many others fled the country. Those who fought for human rights or opposed the government were treated harshly by a series of military rulers.

The Mayas suffered during the civil war. In hundreds of villages throughout Guatemala, soldiers came to claim the Mayas' land. Many Mayas lost all of their belongings and were forced out of their villages. Some had to move to other countries to live.

✓ **Reading Check** What happened to the Mayas during the civil war?

Working for a Better Life

Some Mayas remained in Guatemala during the civil war. They started **political movements,** which are large groups of people who work together for political change. One such movement, called Nukuj Akpop (nooh KOO ahk POHP), still works to fight poverty and bring human rights to Mayas.

A political demonstration in Guatemala City

Defending Campesino Rights Today, Mayan political movements seek to defend campesino rights. They help villages plan ways to protect themselves. They teach people the history of their land and how to read. They also help organize meetings, protests, and strikes. A **strike** is a refusal to work until certain demands of workers are met. Above all, these political movements defend Native American land rights.

Changes Come to Guatemala These efforts brought change in Guatemala. For the first time, Mayas gained a voice in their government. Mayan priests were appointed to advise government officials about Mayan culture. Radio programs were broadcast in Mayan languages, and Mayan-language books and newspapers also appeared.

In 1996, agreements were signed ending the civil war. Among these was a promise that indigenous communities would be rebuilt. However, not all of these agreements have been carried out. Violations of human rights by the government increased again in 2000, and many Guatemalans protested in the streets. The fight for the rights of the Mayas—and for all the ordinary people of Guatemala— continues.

Some political movements in Guatemala are geared toward helping indigenous people, such as the man above.

✔ **Reading Check** How do political movements try to help the Mayas?

Section 2 Assessment

Key Terms
Review the key terms at the beginning of this section. Use each term in a sentence that explains its meaning.

Target Reading Skill
Find the word *civilians* on page 112. Look for a contrast near the word. How does this contrast help you define *civilians*?

Comprehension and Critical Thinking
1. (a) **Describe** How is land used in Guatemala?
(b) **Identify Causes** Why do the Mayas often fail to earn a living from their land?

2. (a) **Recall** What are two reasons the Mayas lost their land?
(b) **Synthesize** Explain how the Mayas have been at a disadvantage in their struggle against their rulers.
3. (a) **Identify** What are two ways that political movements work to help the Mayas?
(b) **Summarize** What kinds of changes have these groups brought about?
(c) **Predict** Do you think life will improve for the Mayas in the decades ahead? Explain.

Writing Activity
Suppose you are a reporter for a radio news program. Write a report on the situation of the Mayas in Guatemala. Present background information about Mayan culture and history. Then tell your listeners about current conditions. Be sure that your report can be read in two to three minutes.

Writing Tip Introduce your report with a "hook," an interesting event or observation that will make your listeners stay tuned.

When Mr. Macintosh walked into the classroom, Tina watched him carefully.

"Uh-oh," she said quietly. "Looks like a pop quiz." Tina started flipping through the pages of last night's homework assignment.

Miguel heard Tina. "Why do you think there's going to be a quiz?" he whispered to Tina.

"For starters, it's Friday. He tends to give quizzes at the end of the week. And do you see that blue notebook he's got in his hand?" Miguel saw it. "He always writes test questions in it. Whenever he pulls it out, we have a test."

Just then Mr. Macintosh said, "Good morning, class. Please close your books for a pop quiz."

Tina was correct that the class would have a pop quiz. You can understand why. She drew good inferences and a strong conclusion.

An inference is an educated guess based on facts or evidence. A conclusion is a judgment. Conclusions are often based on several inferences.

Learn the Skill

Use the steps below to draw logical inferences and a strong conclusion.

1 **Identify what you know or assume to be true.** Tina stated these facts: First, it was Friday. Mr. Macintosh tends to give quizzes at the end of the week. Second, he was carrying his blue notebook in which he writes test questions.

2 **Use the facts to draw inferences.** Inferences can usually be stated as an "if . . . then" sentence. The "if" part is the facts you know. The "then" part is an educated guess that follows logically from the facts.

3 **Use two or more inferences to draw a reasoned judgment or conclusion.** From her two inferences, Tina was able to draw this conclusion: The class was about to have a pop quiz.

A protest by Mayas in Guatemala City

Practice the Skill

Read the passage titled Working for a Better Life on pages 112 and 113. Then use the steps below to draw inferences and a conclusion about the situation of the Mayas in Guatemala.

Smog in Mexico City

1. Answer these questions in order to help you find facts: What have political movements done to improve life for Guatemalans? What changes have occurred in Guatemala?

2. Use the facts to create at least two inferences, or educated guesses. State your inferences as "if . . . then" sentences. For example: If Mayas learn to read, then they will be more successful at defending their rights.

3. Using the inferences you have written, what conclusion can you draw about the Mayas in Guatemala?

Apply the Skill

Turn to Section 1 of Chapter 4 and reread the passage titled Opportunities and Challenges on pages 106 and 107. Use the steps of this skill to draw inferences and a conclusion about some aspect of life in Mexico City, such as traffic or pollution.

Prepare to Read

Objectives
In this section you will
1. Find out why people wanted to build a canal across the Isthmus of Panama.
2. Learn how the Panama Canal was built.
3. Understand how the canal has affected the nation of Panama.

Taking Notes
As you read this section, look for the problems the builders of the Panama Canal faced and how they solved those problems. Copy the table below, and record your findings in it.

Building the Panama Canal

Problem	Solution

 Target Reading Skill

Use Context Clues
Sometimes you come across a word you know that is being used in an unfamiliar way. You can use context clues and your own general knowledge to understand the new use of the word. For example, you may know that *vessel* often means "ship," and that a cargo ship carries cargo. Therefore, a water vessel is probably a container that holds, or carries, water.

Key Terms
- **Panama Canal** (PAN uh mah kuh NAL) *n.* a shipping canal across the Isthmus of Panama, linking the Atlantic Ocean to the Pacific Ocean
- **lock** (lahk) *n.* a section of waterway in which ships are raised or lowered by adjusting the water level
- **Canal Zone** (kuh NAL zohn) *n.* a 10-mile strip of land along the Panama Canal, once governed by the United States
- **ecotourism** (ek oh TOOR iz um) *n.* travel to unspoiled areas in order to learn about the environment

Ever since Christopher Columbus first explored the Isthmus of Panama, the Spanish had been looking for a water route through it. They wanted to be able to sail west from Spain all the way to Asia. The Spanish were also looking for gold. In 1513, the conquistador Vasco Nuñez de Balboa heard of "a mighty sea beyond the mountains" of what is now Panama. He also heard that the streams flowing into that sea were filled with gold.

Balboa organized an expedition of Spaniards and Indians. They struggled across the isthmus, through very difficult country, for over a month. Finally Balboa waded into the Pacific Ocean, which he claimed for Spain. Balboa went on to explore the Pacific coast and found gold and other treasure there.

Balboa still hoped that a water route could be found through the isthmus. But if not, he said, "it might not be impossible to make one." The effort to create this waterway has shaped the history of the isthmus and led to the creation of the nation of Panama. Even today, geography has a major effect on Panama.

Statue of Vasco Nuñez de Balboa in Panama City, Panama

Why Build a Canal?

The **Panama Canal,** a manmade waterway across the Isthmus of Panama, is a shortcut through the Western Hemisphere. It is the only way to get from the Pacific Ocean to the Atlantic Ocean by ship without going all the way around South America. Sailors had dreamed of a canal through Central America since the 1500s. A canal could shorten the trip from the Atlantic to the Pacific by 7,800 miles (12,553 kilometers), saving both time and money. But it was not until the 1900s that engineers had the technology to make such a canal.

Crossing the Isthmus By 1534, the Spanish had built a seven-foot-wide stone road across the isthmus. It was used to carry treasure to the Atlantic coast for shipment to Spain. More than 300 years later, during the California Gold Rush, prospectors wanted to get from the east coast of the United States to California as quickly as possible. However, there was not yet a transcontinental railroad in the United States, and travel by horse and wagon was slow and difficult. Instead, many prospectors traveled by boat to Panama, trekked across the isthmus, and took another boat to California.

Passing Through the Canal
Special Panama Canal pilots steer ships through the canal. Here, the captain and first mate of a ship consult with a pilot. **Infer** *Why do you think the passage of ships through the canal is controlled so carefully?*

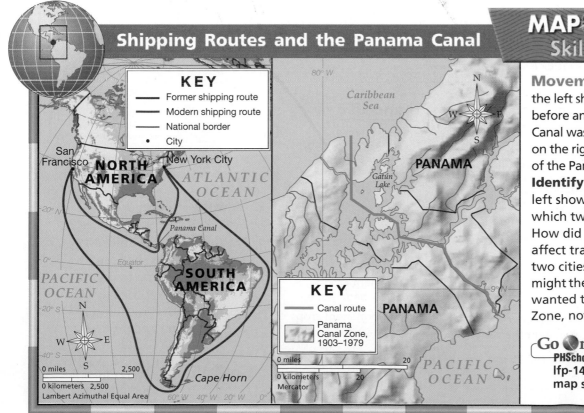

Shipping Routes and the Panama Canal

MAP★MASTER
Skills Activity

KEY
— Former shipping route
— Modern shipping route
— National border
• City

San Francisco
NORTH AMERICA
New York City
ATLANTIC OCEAN
Panama Canal
PACIFIC OCEAN
Equator
SOUTH AMERICA
Cape Horn

0 miles 2,500
0 kilometers 2,500
Lambert Azimuthal Equal Area

Caribbean Sea
PANAMA
Gatún Lake
80° W
9° N

KEY
— Canal route
▢ Panama Canal Zone, 1903–1979

PANAMA
PACIFIC OCEAN

0 miles 20
0 kilometers 20
Mercator

Movement The map at the left shows shipping routes before and after the Panama Canal was built. The map on the right is a close-up of the Pamama Canal. **Identify** The map at the left shows routes between which two American cities? How did building the canal affect travel between those two cities? **Infer** Why might the United States have wanted to control the Canal Zone, not just the canal?

Go Online
PHSchool.com Use Web Code **lfp-1413** for step-by-step map skills practice.

The French Begin a Canal In 1881, when Panama was part of Colombia, a French company gained the rights to build a canal through Panama. However, the builders had to struggle with mud slides, a mountain range, and a dense tropical forest. Tropical diseases killed many workers. After several years of digging and blasting, the French company went bankrupt. Work on the canal stopped.

In 1902, the United States government bought the French company's equipment. Then, the United States began negotiating with Colombia for the rights to continue building a canal.

COUNTRY PROFILE   Focus on Geography

Panama

Panama's geography has created some challenges for its people. Growing food, for example, is difficult in a country heavily covered by rain forest. Panama's location between two oceans, however, has given the country other economic opportunities. The nation has developed many services and industries that support the canal or the companies that use the canal. Study the map and charts to learn more about how Panama's geography shapes its economy.

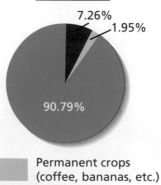

Panama: Vegetation
KEY
- Tropical rain forest
- Mixed forest
- Tropical savanna
- National border
- ⊛ Capital city
- • Other city

Panama Canal Facts

Length of Panama Canal	44 miles
Highest elevation above sea level	85 feet
Number of ships that have used the Panama Canal	Approximately 1 milllion ships have used the canal since 1914.
Workforce	About 9,000 employees operate and maintain the canal.
Highest toll ever paid	$226,194.25 in 2003

Land Use

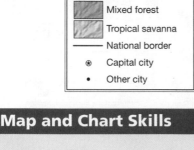

7.26%
1.95%
90.79%

- Permanent crops (coffee, bananas, etc.)
- Non-permanent crops (corn, rice, etc.)
- Other (forest, roads, etc.)

Map and Chart Skills

1. **Identify** How much of Panama is covered by forest?
2. **Predict** Loss of rain forest causes the lakes that support the Panama Canal to dry up, making it harder for ships to pass through. How might that affect Panama's economy?

Use Web Code Ife-1413 for DK World Desk Reference Online.

The New Nation of Panama Colombia refused to grant the United States rights to build a canal. But business people in Panama thought a canal would benefit the local economy. Also, many Panamanians wanted to be free of Colombia's rule. They saw the canal as an opportunity to win independence.

At the same time, President Theodore Roosevelt felt that the canal was important for the United States. It would speed trade between the Atlantic and Pacific coasts. It would also allow the American navy to move back and forth in case of war. Roosevelt did not wait for events to unfold. He took action. In November 1903, the United States helped Panama revolt against Colombia. Two weeks after Panama declared its independence, the United States received the rights to build the canal.

Learn about Panama's changing landscape.

✓ **Reading Check** Why did Panamanians want a canal?

Building the Canal: A Heroic Effort

The Americans faced the same challenges of moving earth and rock that the French had faced. In addition, the project called for a dam to be built to form a lake. There were locks to design and build. A **lock** is a section of waterway in which ships are raised or lowered by adjusting the water level.

While the work on the canal was difficult and slow, by far the biggest problem was disease. Some 20,000 workers had died of malaria and yellow fever while the French worked on the canal. Scientists did not know what caused these diseases, so they could do little to prevent them.

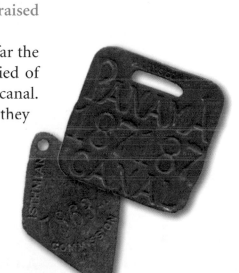

Digging the Canal
Canal workers wore the badges shown above. In the photo at the left, they use steam shovels and trains to build the Panama Canal.
Draw Conclusions *From what you see in the photo, how were trains used in the construction?*

Use Context Clues
You know that *standing* often refers to a person "staying still in an upright position." Use part of that definition to help you understand *standing water*. Ask yourself, can water stand still? What does *standing* mean in this context? What is *standing water*?

In the early 1900s, doctors discovered that malaria and yellow fever were both carried by mosquitoes. The mosquitoes bred in standing water. In 1904, the Panama Canal Company hired a doctor and a large crew to deal with the mosquito problem. It took more than a year to complete the job. Workers burned sulfur in every house to kill mosquitoes. They covered every water vessel with mesh to keep mosquitoes out. They filled in swampy breeding grounds with dirt. Without these efforts, the Panama Canal probably could not have been built.

It took eight years and more than 70,000 workers, mostly Caribbean islanders, to build the Panama Canal. It remains one of the greatest engineering feats of modern times.

✓ **Reading Check** How did workers fight the mosquitoes?

Panama and Its Canal

When the United States gained the rights to build a canal, it signed a treaty with Panama. The treaty gave the United States the right to build the Panama Canal and to control it forever.

The Canal Zone The United States also controlled an area called the Canal Zone. The **Canal Zone** was an area containing the canal, the land on either side of the canal, the ports, the port cities, and the railroad. The treaty allowed the United States to govern the Canal Zone according to its laws and gave the United States the right to invade Panama to protect the canal. The United States built 14 military bases in the Canal Zone and stationed thousands of soldiers there.

Many Panamanians felt the United States had too much power in Panama. For years, Panama held talks with the United States about transferring control of the canal to Panama. In the 1960s and 1970s, angry Panamanians rioted to protest American control.

A Change of Ownership In 1977, after years of talks, President Jimmy Carter signed two new treaties with Panama's government. These treaties gave Panama more control over the canal. In 1999, Panama finally gained full control of the Panama Canal.

Panama Today The Panama Canal dominated life in Panama for much of the 1900s, and it continues to be extremely important today. Because of the canal, Panama has become an international crossroads for trade. The ships that pass through the Panama Canal each day pay tolls according to their weight. International trade is very important to Panama's economy. The canal has made Panama a leading banking and finance center.

Panama City at night

The Panama Canal

Every day, an average of 33 ships pass through the Panama Canal. It takes each ship around nine hours to cross from one ocean to the other. The Panama Canal is like a water elevator with lakes. Ships are raised and lowered in the locks as they travel from one ocean to the other.

Gatún Locks

The construction of the canal's locks was a massive task involving a total workforce of more than 70,000 people. As shown above, the railroad was used to haul earth and other materials through the central channel of the canal.

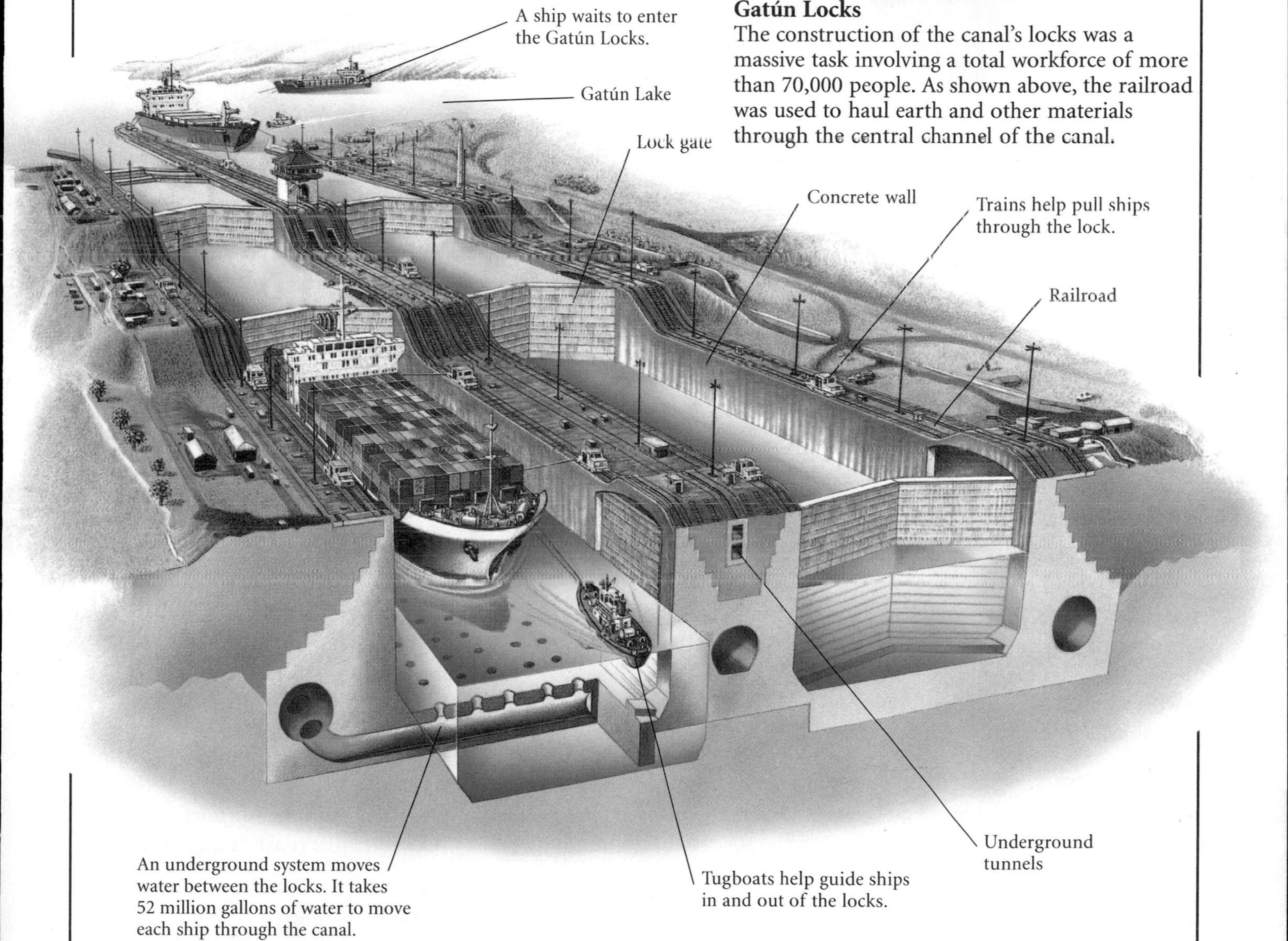

A ship waits to enter the Gatún Locks.

Gatún Lake

Lock gate

Concrete wall

Trains help pull ships through the lock.

Railroad

An underground system moves water between the locks. It takes 52 million gallons of water to move each ship through the canal.

Tugboats help guide ships in and out of the locks.

Underground tunnels

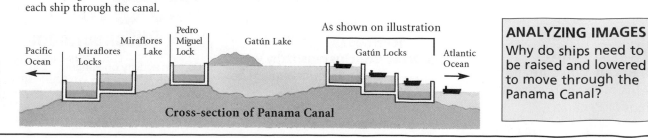

Pacific Ocean — Miraflores Locks — Miraflores Lake — Pedro Miguel Lock — Gatún Lake — As shown on illustration — Gatún Locks — Atlantic Ocean

Cross-section of Panama Canal

ANALYZING IMAGES
Why do ships need to be raised and lowered to move through the Panama Canal?

An ecotourist riding through Panama's rain forest

New Industries Traffic through the canal has also encouraged warehousing and manufacturing. Many factories in Panama are similar to the maquiladoras in Mexico. They assemble parts imported from abroad and then export the finished products. Materials for these factories come from Hong Kong, the United States, and Japan as well as other countries. Most finished products are shipped to Latin American nations or are sold within Panama itself.

Panama is also a communications hub. International fiber-optic networks cross through Panama. Fiber-optic networks are used for long-distance telephone lines and computer networks.

Tourism Another important industry in Panama is tourism. Many tourists come to travel through the canal. They also visit Panama's rain forests. Look at the map in the Country Profile on page 118 to see how much of Panama is covered by rain forests. Tourism in unspoiled areas to observe wildlife and learn about the environment is called **ecotourism**. Ecotourists come to see the wide variety of plants and animals in the rain forest. These include howler monkeys, sloths, harpy eagles, and capybaras—huge rodents that look like guinea pigs. Panama's government has recently invested millions of dollars to promote ecotourism in its rain forests.

✓ **Reading Check** Why is the canal important to Panama today?

Section 3 Assessment

Key Terms
Review the key terms at the beginning of this section. Use each term in a sentence that explains its meaning.

Target Reading Skill
Find the word *unfold* on page 119. Use your own knowledge and the surrounding words and phrases to explain what *unfold* means in this context.

Comprehension and Critical Thinking
1. (a) Recall What are the benefits of a canal across the Isthmus of Panama?

(b) Sequence List three events, in order, that led to the building of the canal.

2. (a) Describe What kinds of difficulties did the builders of the canal face?

(b) Identify Cause and Effect How did advances in medicine lead to the successful completion of the Panama Canal?

3. (a) Define What was the Canal Zone?

(b) Explain How was the Canal Zone governed?

(c) Draw Conclusions Why was it so important to Panamanians to gain control of the canal?

Writing Activity
Suppose you are an American newspaper editor in the 1970s. Write an editorial either for or against giving control of the Panama Canal and the Canal Zone to Panama. State your position clearly. Be sure to support your position with reasons and facts.

Go Online
PHSchool.com

For: An activity on Panama
Visit: PHSchool.com
Web Code: lfd-1403

Review and Assessment

◆ Chapter Summary

Section 1: Mexico

- Many farmers in Mexico are poor, and jobs in the countryside are scarce.
- Many rural Mexicans move to the cities to look for work, but they find that city life is hard and very different from life in the countryside.
- Mexico City is a huge city that is facing overcrowding and pollution problems.

Section 2: Guatemala

- Most of the land in Guatemala is owned by only a few wealthy ladino families who grow crops for export.
- The Mayas lost much of their land to their Spanish conquerors and later they lost more land during the civil war.
- Today, political movements are working to improve life for the Mayas.

Section 3: Panama

- The Panama Canal shortens sea travel between the Atlantic Ocean and the Pacific Ocean.
- After the French could not complete the canal, the United States overcame engineering challenges and disease to build it.
- The Panama Canal is a key water route today and is important to Panama's economy.

Mexico

Guatemala

Panama

◆ Key Terms

Each of the statements below contains a key term from the chapter. If the statement is true, write *true.* If it is false, rewrite the statement to make it true.

1. A migrant worker is a person who settles on someone else's land without permission.

2. A plaza is an open field in the countryside.

3. A canal uses a series of locks to raise and lower ships by adjusting the water level.

4. Land reform is a new and better way of farming the land.

5. When people strike, they stop working in order to achieve a goal.

6. Ecotourism can involve visiting the rain forest to learn about its environment.

7. A ladino is any person from Latin America.

8. The Panama Canal shortens the route ships must travel between the Atlantic Ocean and the Pacific Ocean.

◆ Comprehension and Critical Thinking

9. (a) Identify Name two places many rural Mexicans go when they leave the countryside.
(b) Generalize Why do so many people make these moves?

10. (a) Recall Describe population growth in Mexico.
(b) Identify Effects How does population growth affect Mexico's cities?

11. (a) Summarize What happened to the Mayas during the Guatemalan civil war?
(b) Synthesize Why have so many Mayas been forced from their land?

12. (a) Identify What groups are working to improve life for the Mayas?
(b) Identify Cause and Effect What are two methods these groups use, and how might these methods bring about change?

13. (a) Identify What country first tried to build a canal across Panama?
(b) Identify Causes Why did that country fail to complete the canal?
(c) Draw Conclusions How does the whole world benefit from the Panama Canal?

14. (a) Summarize How did Panama become an independent nation?
(b) Identify Causes Why did Panama want the United States to build the Panama Canal?
(c) Identify Effects What benefits has the Panama Canal brought to Panama?

◆ Skills Practice

Drawing Inferences and Conclusions In the Skills for Life activity in this chapter, you learned how to draw inferences. You also learned how to draw a conclusion, or make a reasoned judgment, using two or more inferences.

Review the steps you followed to learn this skill. Then reread The New Nation of Panama on page 119. List several inferences you can draw about the events described there. Finally, use your inferences to draw a conclusion about those events.

◆ Writing Activity: Science

Suppose you were the science reporter for a newspaper covering the building of the Panama Canal. Write a brief report about how advances in science contributed to the successful completion of the Panama Canal.

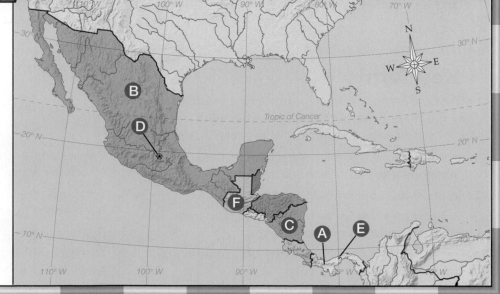

MAP◆MASTER™ Skills Activity

Mexico and Central America

Place Location For each place listed below, write the letter from the map that shows its location.
1. Mexico
2. Guatemala
3. Panama
4. Nicaragua
5. Mexico City
6. Panama Canal

Go Online
PHSchool.com Use Web Code **lfp-1423** for an **interactive map.**

Standardized Test Prep

Test-Taking Tips

Some questions on standardized tests ask you to analyze a reading selection. Study the passage below. Then follow the tips to help you answer the sample question.

> Many people have moved to Mexico City to find jobs in factories. Cars and buses clog the city streets. In addition, the city is located in a valley surrounded by mountains, and pollution gets trapped there. <u>Because</u> of its geography and heavy traffic, Mexico City has one of the worst cases of air pollution in the world.

TIP Look for words that signal causes or reasons, such as the word *because* in the last sentence.

Pick the letter that best completes the statement.

Mexico City's air pollution problem is made worse by

A ~~smog from South America.~~

B its location.

C its textile factories.

D ~~its lack of rain.~~

TIP First cross out answers that you know are wrong. Then consider each remaining choice before selecting the best answer.

Think It Through Look at the remaining answer choices. Answer C might be correct, but the passage does not mention textile factories. Remember the signal word *because*. The sentence beginning with *because* gives geography as one reason for Mexico City's pollution. Geography includes location, so B is the correct answer.

Practice Questions

Use the tips above and other tips in this book to help you answer the following questions.

1. Which of the following was not a problem for the builders of the Panama Canal?

   A disease carried by mosquitoes

   B mudslides

   C blizzards

   D a mountain range blocking the route

2. In Guatemala, most of the land is owned by

   A Native Americans.

   B Spanish conquerors.

   C a few wealthy ladino families.

   D the Mayas.

3. What is one result of rapid population growth in Mexico?

   A Farms are getting overcrowded.

   B The economy is improving because there are more people to buy things.

   C Rural people are moving to the cities to find work.

   D Factories are shutting down.

Use the circle graph below to answer Question 4. Choose the letter of the best answer to the question.

Population of Guatemala

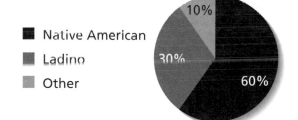

- Native American
- Ladino
- Other

10%

30%

60%

4. According to the circle graph, which of the following statements is true?

   A Most people in Guatemala are descended from Europeans and Native Americans.

   B Half of Guatemala's population is ladino.

   C Most Guatemalans are Native American.

   D There are more Spaniards than ladinos in Guatemala.

Go Online
PHSchool.com

Use Web Code lfa-1401 for a **Chapter 4 self-test.**

Chapter Preview

This chapter will introduce you to 13 island nations and one commonwealth of the Caribbean.

Country Databank
The Country Databank provides data and descriptions of the commonwealth and each of the countries in the region: Antigua and Barbuda, The Bahamas, Barbados, Cuba, Dominica, Dominican Republic, Grenada, Haiti, Jamaica, Saint Kitts and Nevis, Saint Lucia, Saint Vincent and the Grenadines, and Trinidad and Tobago.

Target Reading Skill

Main Idea In this chapter you will focus on finding and remembering the main idea, or the most important point, of sections and paragraphs.

► Rowboats on a Curaçao beach

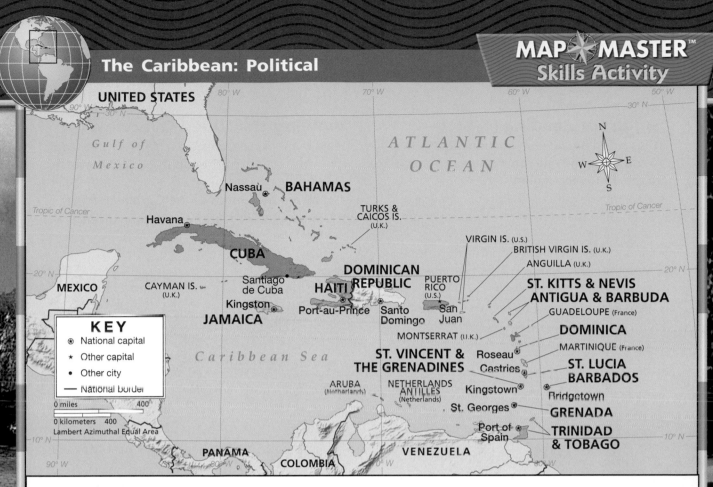

MAP MASTER™
Skills Activity

UNITED STATES

Gulf of Mexico

ATLANTIC OCEAN

Tropic of Cancer

Nassau ⊛ BAHAMAS

Havana ⊛

CUBA

TURKS & CAICOS IS. (U.K.)

VIRGIN IS. (U.S.)
BRITISH VIRGIN IS. (U.K.)
ANGUILLA (U.K.)

MEXICO

CAYMAN IS. (U.K.)

Santiago de Cuba

Kingston ⊛

JAMAICA

DOMINICAN REPUBLIC

HAITI

Port-au-Prince

Santo Domingo

PUERTO RICO (U.S.)

San Juan

ST. KITTS & NEVIS
ANTIGUA & BARBUDA

GUADELOUPE (France)

DOMINICA

MONTSERRAT (U.K.)

MARTINIQUE (France)

Caribbean Sea

KEY
⊛ National capital
★ Other capital
• Other city
— National border

0 miles 400
0 kilometers 400
Lambert Azimuthal Equal Area

ST. VINCENT & THE GRENADINES

Roseau ⊛
Castries ⊛

ST. LUCIA
BARBADOS

ARUBA (Netherlands)

NETHERLANDS ANTILLES (Netherlands)

Kingstown ⊛

Bridgetown

St. Georges ⊛

GRENADA

Port of Spain ⊛

TRINIDAD & TOBAGO

PANAMA

COLOMBIA

VENEZUELA

N W E S

Tropic of Cancer

30° N
20° N
10° N

90° W 80° W 70° W 60° W 50° W

Movement Notice that this region is made up of islands. This affected how people and ideas moved from one place to another. **Infer** Before the invention of radio and airplanes, how do you think people in Jamaica communicated with people in Puerto Rico? **Conclude** How might the sea have affected the economies of the Caribbean islands?

Go Online
PHSchool.com Use Web Code lfp-1521 for step-by-step map skills practice.

Introducing
The Caribbean

Guide for Reading

This section provides an introduction to the 13 countries and one commonwealth that make up the Caribbean region.

- Look at the map on the previous page and then read the paragraphs to learn about each nation.
- Analyze the data to compare countries.
- What are the characteristics that most of these countries share?
- What are some key differences among the countries?

Viewing the Video Overview

View the World Studies Video Overview to learn more about each of the countries. As you watch, answer these questions:

- How did the islands of the Caribbean form?
- What factors influence the cultural diversity of these islands?

Explore the lands and cultures of the Caribbean.

Antigua and Barbuda

Capital	Saint John's
Land Area	171 sq mi; 442 sq km
Population	67,448
Ethnic Group(s)	black, white, Southwest Asian
Religion(s)	Protestant, Roman Catholic, traditional beliefs
Government	constitutional monarchy
Currency	East Caribbean dollar
Leading Exports	petroleum products, manufactured goods, machinery and transport equipment, food and live animals
Language(s)	English (official), English Creole

The tiny nation of Antigua and Barbuda (an TIG wuh and bahr BOO dah) is made up of three islands located in the eastern Caribbean Sea. Christopher Columbus landed on the main island, Antigua, in 1493. English settlers began arriving there in the 1630s. They raised tobacco and then sugar cane. Enslaved Africans were imported to work on the plantations. However, slavery was abolished in the British colony in 1834. In 1981, Antigua joined with neighboring Barbuda and with Redonda, a nearby uninhabited island, to become an independent nation. Today, tourism is the nation's main source of income.

English Harbor, Antigua

The Bahamas

Capital	Nassau
Land Area	3,888 sq mi; 10,070 sq km
Population	308,529
Ethnic Group(s)	black, white, Asian, Hispanic
Religion(s)	Anglican, Baptist, Roman Catholic, Methodist, Church of God
Government	constitutional parliamentary democracy
Currency	Bahamian dollar
Leading Exports	fish and crawfish, rum, salt, chemicals, fruits and vegetables
Language(s)	English (official), English Creole, French Creole

More than 700 islands make up the nation called The Bahamas (buh HAH muz), but fewer than 30 of them are inhabited. The island chain stretches southward off the east coast of Florida to within 50 miles (80.5 kilometers) of Cuba. It is thought that Christopher Columbus first landed in the Americas on the Bahamian island of San Salvador. The Bahamas are generally flat, with a mild climate and beautiful beaches, so it is not surprising that tourism is a major industry. Banking has also become important. Once a British colony, The Bahamas now has a government based on the British parliamentary model.

Barbados

Capital	Bridgetown
Land Area	166 sq mi; 431 sq km
Population	276,607
Ethnic Group(s)	black, white, mixed white and black
Religion(s)	Protestant, Roman Catholic
Government	parliamentary democracy
Currency	Barbados dollar
Leading Exports	sugar and molasses, rum, other foods and beverages, chemicals, electrical components, clothing
Language(s)	English (official), Bajan

Barbados (bahr BAY dohs) is a triangular-shaped island in the eastern Caribbean Sea. It was settled by the British in the 1600s and gained its independence in 1966. Today, both the culture and the government of Barbados reflect its British colonial heritage. In the past, much of Barbados was used for sugar plantations. Today, the government promotes smaller farms that grow food for the local population. The government spends approximately 20 percent of its budget on education, and 98 percent of the people can read and write.

Cuba

Capital	Havana
Land Area	42,803 sq mi; 110,860 sq km
Population	11.2 million
Ethnic Group(s)	mixed white and black, white, black, East Asian
Religion(s)	Roman Catholic, Protestant
Government	communist state
Currency	Cuban peso
Leading Exports	sugar, nickel, tobacco, fish, medical products, citrus, coffee
Language(s)	Spanish

Cuba (KYOO buh) is the largest country in the Caribbean region. Its main island lies south of Florida in the Caribbean Sea near the Gulf of Mexico. The island has many beaches, bays, and harbors. In 1903, the United States leased Guantánamo Bay from Cuba for use as a naval base, and it is still under American control today. The rest of the island is a communist state headed by Fidel Castro, who has governed Cuba since the revolution of 1959. Cuban culture reflects its Spanish colonial past and African influences.

Introducing The Caribbean

Dominica

Capital	Roseau
Land Area	291 sq mi; 754 sq km
Population	73,000
Ethnic Group(s)	black, mixed white and black, white, Southwest Asian, Carib
Religion(s)	Roman Catholic, Protestant
Government	parliamentary democracy
Currency	East Caribbean dollar
Leading Exports	bananas, soap, bay oil, vegetables, grapefruit, oranges
Language(s)	English (official), French Creole

Dominica (dahm uh NEE kuh) lies between Guadeloupe and Martinique in the Caribbean Sea. The island was formed by volcanic activity. Hot springs, such as those that feed Boiling Lake, are still active. In spite of its rich soil and pleasant climate, Dominica is very poor. Hurricanes often destroy crops. Tourism is hampered by poor transportation and lack of hotels. Dominica is one of the few Caribbean islands on which Carib Indians still live and continue to practice the cultural traditions of their ancestors.

Dominican Republic

Capital	Santo Domingo
Land Area	18,679 sq mi; 48,380 sq km
Population	8.7 million
Ethnic Group(s)	mixed white and black, white, black
Religion(s)	Roman Catholic
Government	representative democracy
Currency	Dominican Republic peso
Leading Exports	ferronickel, sugar, gold, silver, coffee, cocoa, tobacco, meats, consumer goods
Language(s)	Spanish (official), French Creole

The Dominican Republic (doh MIN ih kun rih PUB lik) occupies the eastern two thirds of Hispaniola. The island was first colonized by Spain. In 1697, France acquired the western third of Hispaniola. That part of the island became the independent country of Haiti in 1804. The remaining portion—which later became the Dominican Republic—was controlled by France, Spain, and Haiti at various times. It also suffered many revolutions and dictatorships. Today, its government is stable. Agriculture and tourism are important to the economy of the Dominican Republic.

Grenada

Capital	Saint George's
Land Area	133 sq mi; 344 sq km
Population	89,211
Ethnic Group(s)	black, mixed white and black, white, South Asian, Carib
Religion(s)	Roman Catholic, Protestant
Government	constitutional monarchy
Currency	East Caribbean dollar
Leading Exports	bananas, cocoa, nutmeg, fruits and vegetables, clothing, mace
Language(s)	English (official), English Creole

Nutmeg, Grenada

Grenada (gruh NAY duh) is an oval-shaped island in the eastern Caribbean Sea. It has forested mountains as well as highlands with many rivers and streams. Bays, natural harbors, and beaches dot the southern coast. Grenada is sometimes called the Isle of Spice because of its production of nutmeg, cinnamon, cloves, ginger, and vanilla. Agricultural exports and tourism support the economy. Once governed by France and later by Great Britain, Grenada is now an independent nation.

Haiti

Capital	Port-au-Prince
Land Area	10,641 sq mi; 27,560 sq km
Population	7.1 million
Ethnic Group(s)	black, mixed white and black, white
Religion(s)	Roman Catholic, Protestant, traditional beliefs
Government	elected government
Currency	gourde
Leading Exports	manufactured goods, coffee, oils, cocoa
Language(s)	French (official), French Creole (official)

Occupying the western third of the island of Hispaniola, Haiti (HAY tee) was once heavily forested. Today, there are few woodlands left, and much of the land is no longer able to support farming due to soil erosion. Even so, most of Haiti's people are farmers, although they have little modern machinery or fertilizers. Haiti is one of the most densely populated nations in the world and the poorest in the Western Hemisphere. Numerous revolutions and dictatorships have plagued Haiti since its hopeful beginning as the first independent nation in Latin America.

Jamaica

Capital	Kingston
Land Area	4,182 sq mi; 10,831 sq km
Population	2.7 million
Ethnic Group(s)	black, mixed white and black, South Asian, white, East Asian
Religion(s)	Protestant, Roman Catholic, traditional beliefs
Government	constitutional parliamentary democracy
Currency	Jamaican dollar
Leading Exports	alumina, bauxite, sugar, bananas, rum
Language(s)	English (official), English Creole

Jamaica (juh MAY kuh) is a mountainous island located 90 miles (145 kilometers) south of Cuba in the Caribbean Sea. Tourism is vital to the economy of this beautiful island. Most of the population lives on the coastal plains, and more than half of Jamaicans live in cities. The island was first colonized by the Spanish and then by the British. Enslaved Africans were brought to Jamaica to work on the sugar and coffee plantations. Today, Jamaica's population is diverse, including Asian and Arab immigrants as well as people of European and African descent.

Puerto Rico

Capital	San Juan
Land Area	3,459 sq mi; 8,959 sq km
Population	4.0 million
Ethnic Group(s)	white, black, indigenous Indian, Asian, mixed white and black
Religion(s)	Roman Catholic, Protestant
Government	commonwealth
Currency	U.S. dollar
Leading Exports	pharmaceuticals, electronics, apparel, canned tuna, beverage concentrates, medical equipment
Language(s)	Spanish and English (official)

The self-governing commonwealth of Puerto Rico (PWEHR tuh REE koh) lies approximately 50 miles (80 kilometers) east of the Dominican Republic in the Caribbean Sea. The northern shore of the main island faces the Atlantic Ocean. Several smaller islands are also part of the commonwealth. The island's economy originally depended on sugar. In the mid-1900s, however, industry and trade became more important. Today, Puerto Rico has a more diverse economy than any of the other Caribbean islands.

Introducing **The Caribbean**

St. Kitts and Nevis

Capital	Basseterre
Land Area	101 sq mi; 261 sq km
Population	38,736
Ethnic Group(s)	black, white, Southwest Asian
Religion(s)	Roman Catholic, Protestant
Government	constitutional monarchy
Currency	East Caribbean dollar
Leading Exports	machinery, food, electronics, beverages, tobacco
Language(s)	English (official), English Creole

Two small islands located in the eastern Caribbean Sea make up the Federation of St. Kitts and Nevis (saynt kits and NEE vis). They gained their independence from Great Britain in 1983, and are now part of the British Commonwealth. The islands are of volcanic origin, and a dormant volcano is the highest point on St. Kitts. The beaches of that island have black, volcanic sands. Nevis is known for its hot and cold springs, and is surrounded by coral reefs. St. Kitts and Nevis have become popular tourist destinations.

St. Lucia

Capital	Castries
Land Area	234 sq mi; 606 sq km
Population	160,145
Ethnic Group(s)	black, mixed white and black, South Asian, white
Religion(s)	Roman Catholic, Protestant
Government	parliamentary democracy
Currency	East Caribbean dollar
Leading Exports	bananas, clothing, cocoa, vegetables, fruits, coconut oil
Language(s)	English (official), French Creole

The island nation of St. Lucia (saynt LOO shuh) is located in the eastern Caribbean Sea. Its geography is marked by wooded mountains and fertile valleys as well as by two huge pyramids of rock, called the Twin Pitons, which rise more than 2,400 feet (731.5 kilometers) from the sea. In the crater of a dormant volcano are boiling sulphur springs, which attract many tourists. St. Lucia's rain forests are also a major tourist attraction. Sugar cane was the most important crop on the island until 1964, when most of the land was converted to raising bananas.

St. Vincent and the Grenadines

Capital	Kingstown
Land Area	150 sq mi; 389 sq km
Population	116,394
Ethnic Group(s)	black, mixed white and black, South Asian, Carib
Religion(s)	Protestant, Roman Catholic, Hindu
Government	parliamentary democracy
Currency	East Caribbean dollar
Leading Exports	bananas, eddoes and dasheen, arrowroot starch, tennis racquets
Language(s)	English (official), English Creole

The nation of St. Vincent and the Grenadines (saynt VIN sunt and thuh GREN uh deenz) is made up of the island of St. Vincent and a string of islands called the Grenadines. They are located in the eastern Caribbean Sea, between St. Lucia and Grenada. St. Vincent has forested volcanic mountains. Its tallest volcano, Soufrière, last erupted in 1979, causing extensive damage. However, the volcanic ash has also made the soil fertile. The Grenadines are made up of coral reefs and have fine beaches. Therefore, it is not surprising that agriculture and tourism play important roles in the nation's economy.

Trinidad and Tobago

Capital	Port-of-Spain
Land Area	1,980 sq mi; 5,128 sq km
Population	1.2 million
Ethnic Group(s)	black, South Asian, mixed white and black, white, East Asian
Religion(s)	Roman Catholic, Hindu, Muslim, Protestant
Government	parliamentary democracy
Currency	Trinidad and Tobago dollar
Leading Exports	petroleum and petroleum products, chemicals, steel products, fertilizer, sugar, cocoa, coffee, citrus, flowers
Language(s)	Engllsh (official), English Creole, Hindi, French, Spanish

SOURCES: DK World Desk Reference Online; *CIA World Fact-book*, 2002, *World Almanac*, 2003

Trinidad and Tobago (TRIN ih dad and toh BAY goh) are located close to the South American coast, northeast of Venezuela. Trinidad, the larger island, has mountains with spectacular waterfalls as well as swampy areas. Tobago is surrounded by coral reefs. The reefs have rich marine life, and are popular tourist attractions. The bird sanctuary at Caroni Swamp also attracts tourists. Trinidad has a very diverse population, with Spanish, French, African, English, East Indian, and Chinese influences, and many languages are spoken there. Trinidad is known for its calypso and steel-drum music.

Green honeycreeper, Trinidad and Tobago

Assessment

Comprehension and Critical Thinking

1. Compare and Contrast Compare the physical size and population of Cuba to those of the Dominican Republic.

2. Draw Conclusions What are the characteristics that most Caribbean countries share?

3. Compare and Contrast What are some key differences among the countries?

4. Categorize Which countries rely on agricultural products as their major exports? Which rely on other products?

5. Infer How has geography influenced the economies of the Caribbean countries?

6. Make a Bar Graph Use your answer to Question 1 to make a bar graph. What does the graph reveal about the population densities of Cuba and the Dominican Republic?

Keeping Current

Access the **DK World Desk Reference Online** at PHSchool.com for up-to-date information about all the countries in this chapter.

Go Online
PHSchool.com

Web Code: lfe-1510

Cuba
Clinging to Communism

Prepare to Read

Objectives

In this section you will

1. Find out how Cuba's history led to thousands of Cubans leaving their homeland.
2. Discover how Cuban exiles feel about their lives in the United States and about their homeland.
3. Learn about recent changes in Cuba.

Taking Notes

As you read this section, look for details about life in communist Cuba. Copy the web diagram below, and record your findings in it.

Life in Communist Cuba

Target Reading Skill

Identify Main Ideas It is impossible to remember every detail that you read. Good readers identify the main idea in every section or paragraph. The main idea is the most important point—the one that includes all the other points. For example, the first sentence under the red heading Cuban Exiles, on page 137, states the main idea of that portion of text.

Key Terms

- **Fidel Castro** (fih DEL KAS troh) *n.* the leader of Cuba's government
- **communism** (KAHM yoo niz um) *n.* an economic system in which the government owns all large businesses and most of the country's land
- **illiterate** (ih LIT ur ut) *adj.* unable to read and write
- **ally** (AL eye) *n.* a country joined to another country for a special purpose
- **exile** (EK syl) *n.* a person who leaves his or her homeland for another country, often for political reasons

Cubans in a makeshift raft set out for the United States.

In the summer of 1994, more than 20,000 Cubans took to the sea. They sailed on anything that would float—rubber tires, old boats, and homemade rafts. One hope kept them going. It was the thought of making it to the United States. They wanted desperately to live in the United States as immigrants.

These Cubans left their homeland for two main reasons. One reason was Cuba's struggling economy. People often did not have enough to eat. Clothing, medicine, and other basic necessities were also hard to get. A desire for freedom was even more important to many Cubans. Cuba's leader, **Fidel Castro** (fih DEL KAS troh), was a dictator. He did not allow Cubans to speak out against government policies they disagreed with.

Political and economic changes in Cuba caused many of its citizens to leave their country. How and why did these changes occur? How has Cuba changed since then?

Cuba's History

Cuba's government and economy had once been very different than they were in 1994. Although it is a small country, Cuba has many advantages. It has fertile farmland. It is located at the entrance to the Gulf of Mexico, and has excellent harbors. The map titled The Caribbean: Political, at the beginning of this chapter, shows why Cuba's location makes it a good place for trade with the United States and other parts of the Caribbean.

Cuban Independence When the United States won the Spanish-American War in 1898, Cuba gained its independence from Spain. In the years that followed, Cuba became the richest country in the Caribbean. Sugar planters made money selling to people in the United States. Hotels were built, and tourists came to Cuba to enjoy its beautiful beaches and wonderful climate. Many Cubans became businesspeople, teachers, doctors, and lawyers.

Not all Cubans shared in the country's wealth, however. Most farm and factory workers earned low wages. Cuba also had many harsh leaders who ruled as dictators. In the 1950s, Fulgencio Batista (fool HEN see oh bah TEE stah) ruled Cuba. Rebel groups began forming. They wanted to remove the corrupt Batista regime and change the country.

Communism in Cuba A young lawyer named Fidel Castro led one of these small rebel groups. After two attempts to overthrow the government, he was finally successful in 1959.

Fidel Castro still holds power in Cuba today. Castro's government is communist. Under **communism,** the government owns all large businesses and most of the country's land. After Castro took power, the Cuban government nationalized, or took over, private businesses and land. Further, Castro said that newspapers and books could print only information supporting his government. Anyone who disagreed with government policy was put in jail. Huge numbers of Cubans fled the island. Many settled in Miami, Florida, in a neighborhood that came to be called Little Havana, named after the capital of Cuba.

An Important Vote
Fulgencio Batista, "strong man" of Cuba, casts his vote in the 1940 presidential election. **Infer** *Why do you think dictators hold "elections"?*

Learn about baseball in Cuba.

The Cold War Heats Up
The photograph above shows Fidel Castro (left) and Nikita Khrushchev (right), the Soviet premier. At the right, an American patrol plane flies over a Soviet freighter during the Cuban Missile Crisis. **Infer** *What kind of relationship did Cuba and the Soviet Union have in the 1960s?*

Identify Main Ideas
What sentence states the main idea of the text headed Cold War Crisis?

At the same time, Castro's government brought some improvements to Cuba. In the 1960s and 1970s, many Cubans were **illiterate**, or unable to read and write. Castro sent teachers into the countryside, and literacy improved dramatically. Today, about 97 percent of Cubans can read and write. The government also provides basic health care for all.

As a communist country, Cuba became an ally of the Soviet Union. An **ally** is a country joined with another country for a special purpose. The Soviet Union was the most powerful communist nation in the world. It wanted to spread communism worldwide. The Soviets sent money and supplies to Cuba. Relations between Cuba and the United States grew worse when the United States openly welcomed the people who fled from Cuba.

Cold War Crisis The United States viewed communist Cuba as a threat to American interests in the region. This was a period of tension between the United States and the Soviet Union and their allies. It was called the Cold War as the conflict did not involve "hot," or military, action. It lasted from 1945 to 1991.

In the 1960s, the Soviets began sending military support to Cuba. Then, in 1962, photographs taken by American aircraft revealed the construction of Soviet atomic-missile sites in Cuba. Those missiles, if fired, would be able to reach the United States.

U.S. President John F. Kennedy demanded the missiles be removed, and sent the American navy to prevent Soviet ships from going to Cuba. He said that an attack from Cuba would be viewed as an attack by the Soviet Union. After a week of tension called the Cuban Missile Crisis, Soviet Premier Nikita Khrushchev agreed to remove the missiles if the United States promised not to invade Cuba. A "hot" war was prevented, but the Cold War continued.

✓ **Reading Check** What was the Cuban Missile Crisis?

Cuban Exiles

Cubans have been leaving their country ever since Castro took power. They have become exiles. An **exile** is a person who leaves his or her homeland for another country, usually for political reasons. A large number of Cuban exiles have come to the United States to live.

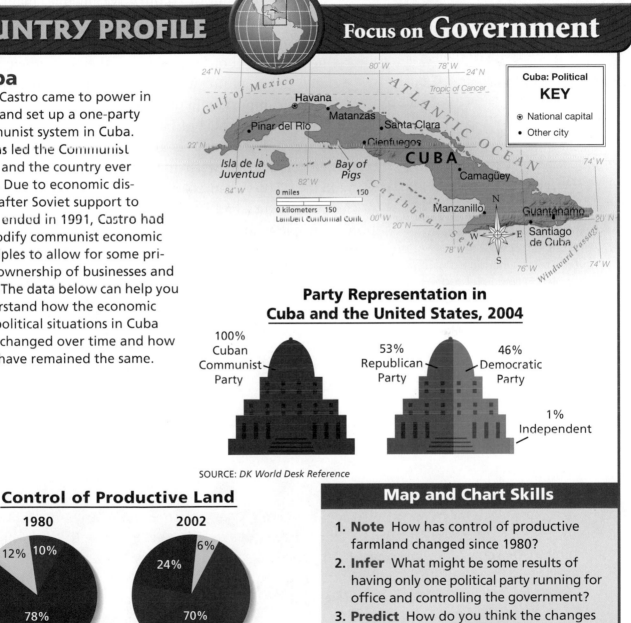

COUNTRY PROFILE   Focus on **Government**

Cuba

Fidel Castro came to power in 1959 and set up a one-party communist system in Cuba. He has led the Communist Party and the country ever since. Due to economic distress after Soviet support to Cuba ended in 1991, Castro had to modify communist economic principles to allow for some private ownership of businesses and land. The data below can help you understand how the economic and political situations in Cuba have changed over time and how they have remained the same.

Cuba: Political KEY
- ⊛ National capital
- • Other city

Party Representation in Cuba and the United States, 2004

100% Cuban Communist Party

53% Republican Party

46% Democratic Party

1% Independent

SOURCE: *DK World Desk Reference*

Control of Productive Land

1980
- 12%
- 10%
- 78%

2002
- 6%
- 24%
- 70%

- ■ In cooperatives*
- ■ Privately held
- ■ Under government control

SOURCE: Economic Commission for Latin America and the Caribbean

* A cooperative is an organization owned by and operated for the benefit of its members.

Map and Chart Skills

1. **Note** How has control of productive farmland changed since 1980?
2. **Infer** What might be some results of having only one political party running for office and controlling the government?
3. **Predict** How do you think the changes in land ownership might affect other areas of Cuban life in the future? Explain your answer.

Go Online PHSchool.com

Use Web Code lfe-1511 for **DK World Desk Reference Online.**

Links Across The World

The Baseball Connection

You've probably heard that baseball is "America's pastime," but did you know that it is also the national pastime of Cuba? Baseball has been played on the island since the 1860s, and major league teams used Cuba for spring training until Castro took power. Cubans also played in the major leagues. Today, however, the Cuban government regards baseball stars who leave the country as traitors. Nevertheless, many Cuban players have defected, or come to the United States. Orlando Hernandez, called El Duque (el DOO kay), or "The Duke," fled Cuba by boat in 1997. He became a starring pitcher for the New York Yankees as shown above.

A New Life Lydia Martin left Cuba in 1970 when she was only six years old. Her mother had grown tired of the limits on freedom and lack of opportunity in communist Cuba. She wanted to take Lydia to the United States. Lydia's father begged them to stay. He asked them, "Have you stopped to think you may never see me again?"

Like Lydia, many Cuban exiles left family members behind. They dream of returning to Cuba—once it is no longer a communist country. Meanwhile, many Cubans have made successful new lives in the United States. A large number have settled in Miami, Florida. In the Cuban neighborhood of Little Havana, they keep their language and their culture alive. At the same time, they have become important in the economic, cultural, and political life of Miami and the state of Florida. They own successful businesses, serve as elected officials, and influence government policy.

When relations between the United States and Cuba grew worse in the 1970s, Cuban exiles suffered. They could not even write to the families they had left behind. Castro's government might punish people who got a letter from the United States. What's more, the United States did not allow Americans to visit Cuba.

Cuban exiles playing dominoes in Little Havana, Miami, Florida

138 Latin America

Another Wave of Exiles In 1991, the government of the Soviet Union collapsed and could no longer help Cuba. Food, medicine, tools, and other necessities became even more scarce in Cuba. Many families had little more than rice to eat.

As the situation in Cuba worsened, more people wanted to leave the island. Vanesa Alonso (vah NES uh ah LOHN soh) was one of them. In 1994, Vanesa and her family left Cuba on a rickety raft. Today, Vanesa lives in Miami, just a few miles from the ocean, but she hardly ever goes to the beach. The blue waves and roaring surf remind her of her terrifying trip from Cuba to the United States. That memory still gives her bad dreams.

✓ **Reading Check** What caused another wave of exiles?

Changes Come to Cuba

In the 1990s, when Cuba's economy was near collapse, Castro began allowing private ownership of some businesses. In addition, the Cuban government began encouraging tourism. The United States also loosened some restrictions on travel to Cuba. American businesspeople and farmers have begun to visit Cuba, hoping to sell their products there. The Cuban economy is improving. Castro has ruled Cuba for more than 40 years. Many Cuban exiles hope that the regime that follows Castro's will encourage better relations with the United States. They hope that they will be able to return home or to visit there in freedom.

✓ **Reading Check** What changes did Castro make in the 1990s?

New Visitors
Tourism increased in Cuba during the 1990s. **Analyze Images** *Judging from this photo of Havana, why might tourists want to visit Cuba?*

Section 1 Assessment

Key Terms
Review the key terms at the beginning of this section. Use each term in a sentence that explains its meaning.

🎯 Target Reading Skills
One important main idea of this section is stated on the first page. What is it?

Comprehension and Critical Thinking
1. (a) Describe How did Castro come to power in Cuba?

(b) Identify Effects How did life for Cubans change—for better and for worse—under Castro's rule?
(c) Synthesize What role did the Soviet Union play in Cuba?
2. (a) Define What is Little Havana?
(b) Find Main Ideas How have many Cubans adapted to life in the United States?
3. (a) Recall What do Cuban exiles hope will happen in Cuba in the near future?
(b) Predict What changes do you think are in store for Cuba? Explain your answer.

Writing Activity
Write a letter to a relative in Cuba from the point of view of a Cuban exile in the United States. Have another student write a response from the point of view of the Cuban relative. The relatives should exchange information about their daily lives and their hopes for the future.

Writing Tip Before you begin, decide on the age, gender, and personality of the person writing the letter.

"Come to the Caribbean," say the TV ads. But which Caribbean will you choose: an island with a Spanish culture or one with Native American, African, British, or French heritage? Do you want a luxury resort or a small village?

To plan your trip, you'd have to think about what you want to see and do and about which islands have these characteristics.

Then you would use the skill of comparing and contrasting to decide which country to visit.

To compare and contrast means to look for similarities and differences. It is a skill you use often, but you can learn to use it even more effectively by following the steps below.

Learn the Skill

Follow the steps below to learn the skill of comparing and contrasting.

1 **Identify a topic and purpose.** What do you want to compare, and why? Some examples of a purpose are to make a choice, to understand a topic, and to discover patterns.

2 **Select some categories for comparison.** For example, if you wanted to choose between two cars, your categories might be model, cost, and power seats.

3 **Make notes or a chart about the categories you're comparing.** A category such as power seats calls for a *yes* or a *no*. For other categories, such as model or cost, you need to note specific details.

4 **Identify the similarities and differences.** For each category, are the things you are comparing the same or different? What are the differences? Which differences are most important for your purpose?

5 **Draw conclusions.** Use the similarities and differences you found to answer an important question about your topic or to make a choice.

Practice the Skill

Suppose you are planning a January vacation. Use the postcards above to help you decide between two possible vacation spots: one in the Caribbean and one in the northern United States. Follow the steps on the previous page to compare and contrast the two choices.

1 In this example, the purpose is provided for you: to make a choice. What is the topic?

2 Ask yourself, "What aspects of these two places could I compare based on the postcards?" Jot down ideas. These ideas will be your categories.

3 Use your categories to jot down notes about each place.

4 For each category, decide whether the two vacation spots are similar or different. In what ways are they different?

5 Draw a conclusion. Are the two vacation spots basically similar or different? Which differences are important to your decision? Write a conclusion stating where you want to spend your vacation and why.

A Jamaican family

Apply the Skill

Turn to the Country Databank at the beginning of Chapter 4 or 5. Choose two countries, each from a different region. Compare and contrast the two countries and draw a conclusion about them.

Haiti
A Struggle for Democracy

Prepare to Read

Objectives

In this section you will

1. Find out how democracy has been threatened in Haiti.
2. Learn what life is like for the people of Haiti, both in the countryside and in the cities.

Taking Notes

As you read this section, look for the events in Haiti's struggle for democracy. Copy the timeline below, and record the events in the appropriate places on it.

1750

Target Reading Skill

Identify Supporting Details The main idea of a paragraph or section is supported by details that give further information about it. These details may explain the main idea or give examples or reasons. The main idea of the portion of text titled The Boat People is "The Haitians who fled by sea became known as the Haitian boat people." As you read, notice how the example that follows helps explain who the boat people were and why they fled.

Key Terms

- **Jean-Bertrand Aristide** (zhan behr TRAHN ah rees TEED) *n.* former president of Haiti
- **refugee** (ref yoo JEE) *n.* someone who leaves his or her homeland to protect personal safety and escape persecution
- **Creole** (KREE ohl) *n.* a person of mixed African and European descent; in Haiti, a language that mixes French and African languages

In 2004, armed rebels (left) forced Haitian president Jean-Bertrand Aristide to leave office.

Over the years, Haiti's military and its wealthy elite have used violence to block the country's attempts at democracy and economic improvement. One percent of Haiti's population controls nearly 50 percent of the country's wealth. This small, wealthy group is prepared to use violence when its control is challenged.

In 2006, though, with the support of the country's poor majority, René Préval was elected Haiti's president. Préval was already an important Haitian leader. In the 1970s, he had helped get rid of Haiti's military dictator. In the 1990s, he also worked closely with Jean-Bertrand Aristide (zhan behr TRAHN ah rees TEED), who ruled at various times. They both wanted to fight poverty in Haiti. However, in 2004, armed groups overthrew Aristide and took control. The year 2006 marked the first presidential election since that time.

Democracy in Danger

Haiti's problems in 2004 were not unusual. The country has a long history of tensions between rich and poor, political instability, and violence. For example, Aristide was first elected president in 1990 but was forced out after only seven months in office.

The Boat People Thousands of Aristide's supporters had to flee Haiti's capital, Port-au-Prince (pawrt oh PRANS). Many of them fled by sea. They became known as the Haitian boat people. Because they left their homeland to protect their own personal safety and escape persecution, they are called **refugees.** Many Haitian boat people headed for the United States.

The Beaubrun (boh BRUN) family was among those refugees. Bazelais (bah zuh LAY) Beaubrun had spoken out against the military government in Haiti. After soldiers threatened him, he knew his life was in danger if he stayed. First Bazelais went into hiding. Then he took his family onto a crowded boat that was headed for the United States.

The U. S. Coast Guard stopped the boat and took the Haitians to an American military base. If Bazelais was really in danger for his political beliefs, he and his family could immigrate to the United States. After three months, the Beaubruns were allowed to enter the United States. Some families were not so lucky. U. S. officials sent them back to Haiti.

Refugees
The Beaubrun family escaped from Haiti and now live in Brooklyn, New York. **Infer** *Why would it be particularly difficult for a family like the Beaubruns, with young children, to make the journey described here?*

The Birth of Haiti The overthrow of the elected government in 2004 does not mean that most Haitians did not want democracy. Their country was born out of a desperate struggle for freedom. Haiti is the only nation in the Americas formed from a successful revolt of enslaved Africans.

As you can see on the map of Haiti on the next page, Haiti lies on the western third of the island of Hispaniola. It was once a colony of France. Europeans brought enslaved Africans to Haiti to work on sugar cane and coffee plantations. In the 1790s, slave revolts began. The Haitian leader Toussaint L'Ouverture helped banish slavery from Haiti in 1801. He also offered Haitians a new way of life, based on the idea that all people could live as equals.

DISCOVERY CHANNEL **SCHOOL** Video
Learn about everyday life in Haiti.

Haiti

Haiti has a stormy history of colonization, revolution, and dictatorships. The nation's European and African roots can still be seen in its vibrant Creole language and heritage. Yet Haiti's history has shaped the country in other ways as well. Today, Haiti is the poorest country in Latin America. Years of political and economic unrest have caused many Haitians to leave the country. Study the map, time-line, and charts. Think about how Haiti's history affects the life of an ordinary Haitian.

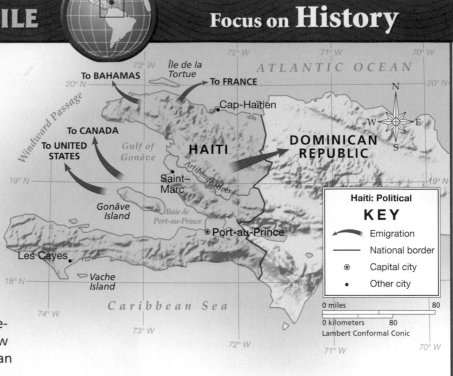

Haiti: Political
KEY

Emigration
National border
⊛ Capital city
• Other city

0 miles 80
0 kilometers 80
Lambert Conformal Conic

Foreign Influence in Haiti Since Independence

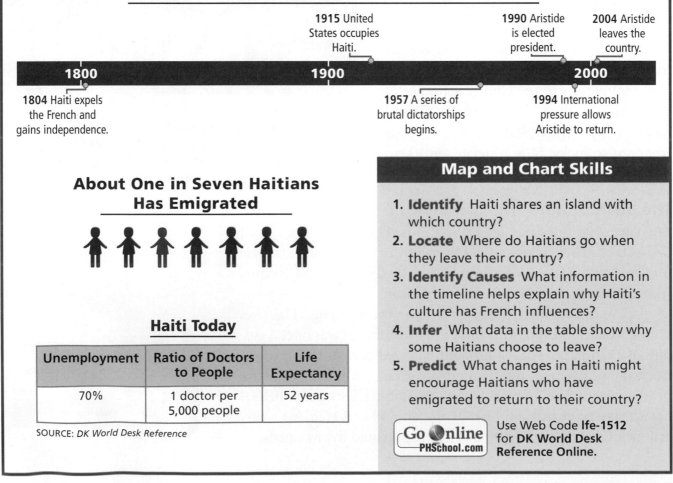

1915 United States occupies Haiti.

1990 Aristide is elected president.

2004 Aristide leaves the country.

1800   **1900**   **2000**

1804 Haiti expels the French and gains independence.

1957 A series of brutal dictatorships begins.

1994 International pressure allows Aristide to return.

About One in Seven Haitians Has Emigrated

Haiti Today

Unemployment	Ratio of Doctors to People	Life Expectancy
70%	1 doctor per 5,000 people	52 years

SOURCE: *DK World Desk Reference*

Map and Chart Skills

1. **Identify** Haiti shares an island with which country?
2. **Locate** Where do Haitians go when they leave their country?
3. **Identify Causes** What information in the timeline helps explain why Haiti's culture has French influences?
4. **Infer** What data in the table show why some Haitians choose to leave?
5. **Predict** What changes in Haiti might encourage Haitians who have emigrated to return to their country?

Go Online
PHSchool.com

Use Web Code lfe-1512 for **DK World Desk Reference Online.**

Years of Dictatorship In the years that followed, Toussaint L'Ouverture's goal of freedom and equality was never fully realized. Most of Haiti's presidents became dictators once they got into power. One of the worst was François Duvalier (frahn SWAH doo vahl YAY), who took power in 1957. Because Duvalier had been a country doctor, Haitians called him "Papa Doc." Papa Doc was followed by his son, Jean-Claude Duvalier (zhan KLAWD doo vahl YAY), or "Baby Doc." Both were cruel leaders who stole government funds and used violence to keep power.

In 1986, rebels forced Baby Doc to leave the country. Many Haitians thought a period of freedom and prosperity was about to begin. Instead, Haiti was ruled by one military dictator after another.

A Brief Period of Hope Aristide's election in 1990 briefly brought hope to Haitians. However, these hopes were dashed when yet another military uprising forced Aristide to flee the country. The United States and other nations pressured the military to give power back to Aristide. In 1994, Aristide returned to Haiti, restoring democratic government. Haitians rejoiced, believing that peace and progress would follow.

In national elections held in 2000, it seemed that Aristide's supporters had won control of the legislature, and Aristide again assumed the presidency. But the election results were challenged. Armed rebels began to attack government offices. In early 2004, after rebel groups gained control of much of Haiti, Aristide left the country. Democracy in Haiti was threatened again. It took two years to organize new elections. Finally in 2006, René Préval was elected president.

✓ **Reading Check** What were the results of the 2000 elections?

Loune Viaud: Winner of Human Rights Award
Loune Viaud (loon vee OH) has been fighting injustice for a long time. During "Baby Doc's" regime, she courageously spoke out for human rights. Today she fights for all Haitians to have the right to healthcare—no matter how poor or sick they are. Viaud runs a clinic and works to ensure safe drinking water. When she received the 2002 Robert F. Kennedy Human Rights Award, Viaud called herself "a humble foot soldier in the struggle for health and human rights."

The dictator Jean-Claude "Baby Doc" Duvalier ruled Haiti from 1971 to 1986.

Identify Supporting Details

What details in the paragraph at the right are examples that support this idea: Haitian culture blends African, French, and West Indian traditions?

The People of Haiti

The Haitian people have suffered a great deal. Nevertheless, Haitian refugees remember many good things about their homeland: the warm weather, children playing soccer with their friends, dressing up for church, and many festivals. Haitian culture blends African, French, and West Indian traditions. Nearly all of Haiti's people are descended from the enslaved Africans who were brought to Haiti during colonial times. Haitians of mixed African and European ancestry are referred to as **Creole.** They are a minority in Haiti, but they have much of the wealth and power. Creole also refers to the language spoken in Haiti, which is based on both French and African languages.

Rural Life Today, Haiti is the poorest country in the Western Hemisphere. About two thirds of the people struggle to make a living farming small plots of land. But the land has been overused. Most trees have been cut. Rains wash the topsoil into the sea. When farmer Pierre Joseph stands on his small farm, he can see the calm waters of the Caribbean. When he looks down, he sees the dry, cracked earth of his one-acre field. Joseph is thin because he rarely gets enough to eat. "The land just doesn't yield enough," he says. He points to the few rows of corn and beans that he can grow on his one acre.

Fishing and Farming
A rural fisherman casts his net (above). The homes in the photo at the right have adobe walls and thatched roofs.
Synthesize *What can you learn about rural life in Haiti from these photos?*

City Life Because of rural poverty, many people have left the countryside for the cities. They come to Port-au-Prince looking for work. Most poor people from the country cannot afford decent housing. They live in the poorest neighborhoods. These areas are dirty and crowded. The streets are not paved, so the rain turns them to mud. Many of the tiny homes are made of crumbling concrete. At the same time, the wealthy live in large wooden houses on the hills overlooking the city. There is also a small middle class of doctors, lawyers, teachers, and owners of small businesses. These people live fairly well. But the overwhelming majority of Haitians—in the city as well as in the countryside—are poor.

What Lies Ahead Recent election disputes and political violence have put Haitian democracy at risk once again. And these conditions have hurt the economy as well. Most people in Haiti are still poor. Many live in cities where violence is common. And many still try to leave their homeland, in search of a better life.

✔ **Reading Check** **Describe the poor neighborhoods of Port-au-Prince.**

Colorful Culture
Haitians often decorate buses and trucks in bright colors. **Analyze Images** *What can you learn about city life in Haiti from this photo of Port-au-Prince?*

Section 2 Assessment

Key Terms
Review the key terms at the beginning of this section. Use each term in a sentence that explains its meaning.

Target Reading Skills
State the details that support the main idea on page 145: *Toussaint L'Ouverture's goal of freedom and equality was never fully realized.*

Comprehension and Critical Thinking
1. (a) Define Who are the Haitian boat people?

(b) Sequence List the major events of Haiti's history in the order they occurred.
(c) Identify Cause and Effect How did the events of Haiti's history lead to the migration of the boat people?
2. (a) Describe What is rural life like for many Haitians?
(b) Compare and Contrast How is life in the city similar to and different from life on a farm?
(c) Find Main Ideas What are the major problems facing Haiti today?

Writing Activity
Suppose you were an American newspaper reporter in Haiti in 2004. Write an article about conditions in Haiti immediately after President Aristide was forced from power. Include the experiences of individual Haitians.

Go Online
PHSchool.com

For: An activity on Haiti
Visit: PHSchool.com
Web Code: lfd-1502

Prepare to Read

Objectives

In this section you will

1. Understand why the people of Puerto Rico are both American and Puerto Rican.
2. Find out what life is like on the island of Puerto Rico.
3. Learn about the three kinds of political status Puerto Ricans are considering for their future.

Taking Notes

As you read this section, look for ways that life is similar and different in Puerto Rico and on the mainland United States. Copy the Venn diagram below, and record your findings in it.

Puerto Rican Life

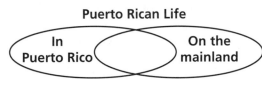

In Puerto Rico   On the mainland

Target Reading Skill

Identify Implied Main Ideas Identifying main ideas can help you remember the most important points you read. Sometimes the main idea is not stated directly. All the details in that portion of text add up to a main idea, but you must state the main idea yourself. For example, you could state the main idea of the text headed A Mix of Cultures this way: *Puerto Rico shows influences of Spanish, African, Caribbean, and United States mainland culture.*

Key Terms

- **constitution** (kahn stuh TOO shun) *n.* a statement of a country's basic laws and values
- **citizen** (SIT uh zun) *n.* a person with certain rights and responsibilities under a particular government
- **commonwealth** (KAHM un welth) *n.* a self-governing political unit that has strong ties to a particular country

A government building in Puerto Rico

Puerto Rico was once a Spanish colony. When the United States defeated Spain in the Spanish-American War, Spain ceded, or gave, Puerto Rico to the United States. The United States slowly granted Puerto Rico more control of its own government and affairs. In 1951, Puerto Ricans voted to adopt their own constitution. A **constitution** is a statement of a country's basic laws and values. This gave Puerto Rico its own lawmakers. But it was still connected to the United States.

What is the nature of Puerto Rico's connection to the United States? How does that relationship affect life in Puerto Rico? And why do some Puerto Ricans want to change the nature of their island's relationship to the United States?

Puerto Ricans in the Mainland United States, 2000

Population	
Total	3,406,178
Northeast	2,074,574
South	759,305
Midwest	325,363
West	246,936

Distribution by Region

7.2%
9.6%
22.3%
60.9%

- Northeast
- South
- Midwest
- West

SOURCE: United States Census Bureau

Puerto Rican and American

People move from Puerto Rico to the United States mainland and back again very easily because Puerto Rico is part of the United States. Puerto Ricans are American citizens. **Citizens** are individuals with certain rights and responsibilities under a particular government. But Puerto Rico is not a state of the Union. It has a different status.

The Commonwealth of Puerto Rico Today, Puerto Rico is a commonwealth of the United States. A **commonwealth** is a self-governing political unit that has strong ties to a particular country. Although Puerto Ricans are American citizens, they cannot vote in presidential elections. They do not pay United States taxes. And they have only a nonvoting representative in the United States Congress. However, Puerto Ricans do serve in the armed forces of the United States.

Puerto Ricans on the Mainland Many Puerto Ricans have moved to the mainland United States. Most settle in cities in the Northeast. Life is very different there. While Puerto Rico has a warm Caribbean climate, winters in Northern cities can be cold and harsh. And cities like New York are much bigger than any city in Puerto Rico. The language of the mainland is English, while people speak Spanish in Puerto Rico. There is a lot to get used to.

◾| Chart Skills

This market is in an area of New York City called Spanish Harlem, where many Puerto Ricans have settled. **Identify** According to the graph, which region has the largest Puerto Rican population? The smallest? **Infer** *Why do you think that people tend to settle in areas where there are already many people from their former homes?*

Esmeralda Santiago

Coming to New York City Esmeralda Santiago (ez mehr AHL dah sahn tee AH goh) moved from Puerto Rico to New York City when she was 13 years old. At first, she found life on the mainland strange and confusing. One problem was that to succeed in school, she had to improve her English. She also found that Puerto Ricans living in New York were different from her friends on the island. Instead of the salsa and merengue music she loved, they preferred rock music. Most of the time they spoke neither pure Spanish nor English, but a mixture of the two that they called "Spanglish." Although they were Puerto Rican, Esmeralda felt different from them. Eventually, she learned their ways. She became more like them and thought less about her old life on the island.

✓ **Reading Check** When Puerto Ricans move to New York City, what kinds of differences do they find?

Life on the Island

Many people travel back and forth between the mainland and Puerto Rico. They live for a while in each place. Many Puerto Ricans moved to the mainland during the 1950s. However, since 1965, just as many Puerto Ricans have been moving back to their island as are leaving it.

Returning Home Julia de Jesus Chaparro (HOO lee ah day HAY soos chah PAH roh) moved back to a small mountain village in Puerto Rico after spending more than 14 years in Boston, Massachusetts. To explain why, she takes visitors to her back porch. From there, she can see a row of steep mountains. Peeking between them is the bright blue of the Caribbean Sea. The mountain slopes steeply down from Julia's back porch, but she has managed to clear some land. Her garden of mangoes, coconuts, grapefruit, and lemons thrives in the sun. Behind a nearby tree, a hen and six chickens are pecking in the dirt.

Puerto Rican Hillside
This hilly region is in the Central Mountains of Puerto Rico. **Draw Conclusions** *What can you learn about the geography, climate, and land use of this region from the photograph?*

Much of Puerto Rico is made up of hills and mountains—the kind of landscape you would see from Julia's back porch. In the hills, Puerto Rican cowhands, called *jíbaros* (HEE bahr ohs), raise cattle. They also hunt, fish, and raise chickens and pigs. On other parts of the island, farmers ride horses through fields of tall sugar cane. To the southwest, where the land is lower, fishing villages dot the coast.

Discovery CHANNEL SCHOOL Video

Learn about Puerto Rico, past and present.

COUNTRY PROFILE Focus on Government

Puerto Rico

Since becoming a United States Territory in 1898, Puerto Rico has been slowly gaining self-government. In 1917, the people of Puerto Rico were given American citizenship. In 1948, they elected their own governor, and in 1951, they adopted their own constitution. Today, Puerto Rico is a commonwealth of the United States with one nonvoting commissioner in the House of Representatives. As you study the charts below, think about how Puerto Rico's commonwealth status affects the lives of its people.

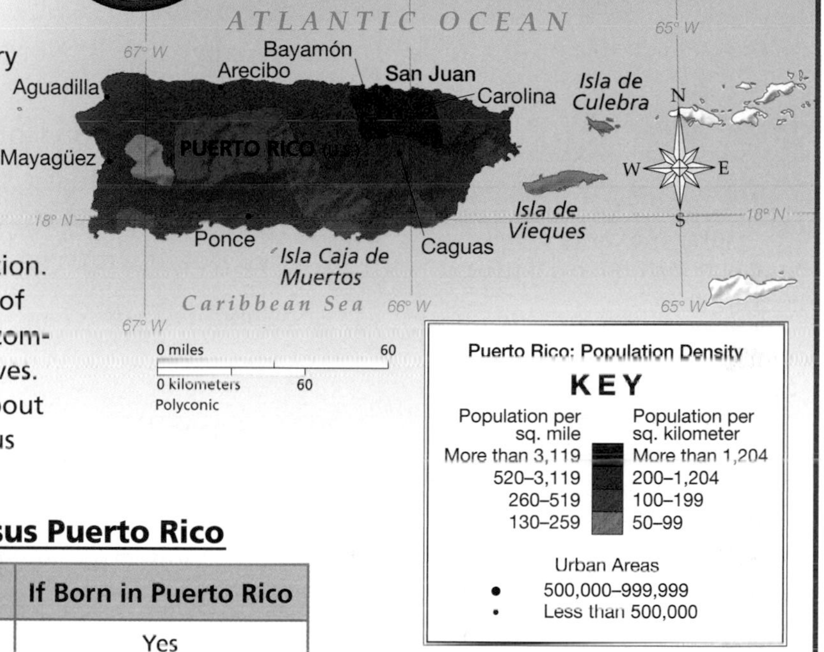

Map labels: ATLANTIC OCEAN, Aguadilla, Bayamón, Arecibo, San Juan, Carolina, Isla de Culebra, Mayagüez, PUERTO RICO, Ponce, Isla Caja de Muertos, Caguas, Isla de Vieques, Caribbean Sea

0 miles 60 / 0 kilometers 60 / Polyconic

Puerto Rico: Population Density
KEY

Population per sq. mile	Population per sq. kilometer
More than 3,119	More than 1,204
520–3,119	200–1,204
260–519	100–199
130–259	50–99

Urban Areas
- 500,000–999,999
- Less than 500,000

Citizen Status in Iowa versus Puerto Rico

	If Born in Iowa	If Born in Puerto Rico
Citizen of United States	Yes	Yes
Vote for U.S. president	Yes	No
Pay income taxes	Yes	No
Serve in military	Yes	Yes
Representatives in U.S. Congress	Five	One (with no vote)
Senators in U.S. Congress	Two	None

2004 Puerto Rico Election Results

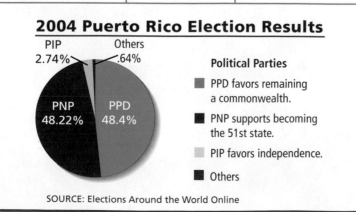

PIP 2.74% / Others .64% / PNP 48.22% / PPD 48.4%

Political Parties
- PPD favors remaining a commonwealth.
- PNP supports becoming the 51st state.
- PIP favors independence.
- Others

SOURCE: Elections Around the World Online

Map and Chart Skills

1. **Identify** What two rights and responsibilities do people born in Iowa have that someone born in Puerto Rico does not have?

2. **Analyze** What do the results of the 2004 elections tell you about how Puerto Ricans feel about their relationship with the United States?

3. **Draw Conclusions** Why do you think political opinion is divided the way it is?

Go Online PHSchool.com
Use Web Code Ife-1513 for DK World Desk Reference Online.

This guitar maker is playing a cuatro, Puerto Rico's national instrument.

A Mix of Cultures As people travel back and forth, they bring customs and products with them. If you visited Puerto Rico, you would see many influences from the United States mainland. You would also see that in Puerto Rico, there is a strong cultural connection to the Caribbean. Most people are a mix of Spanish and African ancestry.

Puerto Rican cities show influences of Spanish, Caribbean, and United States mainland culture. About 75 percent of Puerto Ricans live in cities. Many city people work in factories. Others work in the hotels and restaurants that draw many tourists. Puerto Rico's capital, San Juan (san HWAHN), has a large waterfront area known as the Condado (kohn DAH do). It is packed with luxury hotels. Not far away, modern skyscrapers pierce the brilliant sky.

In the old section of San Juan, Spanish-style buildings are everywhere. A 450-year-old Catholic church built by the Spanish has been carefully restored. Not far from the church sit ancient houses graced with iron balconies in lacy Spanish style.

✓ **Reading Check** Compare old and new San Juan.

Old and New
The San Geronimo Fortress, built in the 1500s by the Spanish, stands in sharp contrast to the modern hotels of San Juan. **Infer** *How do you think the fortress might contribute to the current economy of San Juan?*

Seeking a New Direction

Puerto Rico is bound by many United States laws, and Puerto Ricans have many questions about this situation. Is it good for Puerto Rico? Should Puerto Rico become independent? Or should it become a state of the United States?

Commonwealth or Statehood?   Puerto Ricans have many disagreements over what the status of their island should be. Many feel that having "one foot" in Puerto Rico and "one foot" in the United States can lead to problems. Others point out how the relationship with the United States has helped Puerto Rico. American businesses on the island have raised the standard of living. Each year, the United States government sends millions of dollars to the island to help people in need.

Some people still feel that Puerto Rico is at a disadvantage because Puerto Ricans cannot vote in United States elections. They say Puerto Rico should try to become a state. But if it does, it will become the poorest state in the union. Puerto Ricans earn more money than people in other Caribbean countries. However, they earn less than people on the United States mainland. Also, if Puerto Rico becomes a state, Puerto Ricans will have to pay United States taxes. This could lower the earnings of many people who have little to spare. For these reasons, in 1993 and again in 1998, Puerto Ricans voted not to become the 51st state of the United States.

Statehood Now!
These people are rallying for Puerto Rican statehood in a 1996 demonstration. **Transfer Information** *What arguments in favor of statehood might these demonstrators give?*

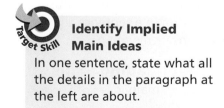

Identify Implied Main Ideas
In one sentence, state what all the details in the paragraph at the left are about.

Rally for Independence
This rally of the Independenista Party was held in 1980. **Predict** *Do you think these demonstrators or those on the previous page will ever get their wish for Puerto Rico? Explain your answer.*

The Question of Independence Some people who voted against statehood have even bigger dreams for Puerto Rico. They want it to become a separate nation. If it does not, they fear that Puerto Ricans will become confused about their identity. They stress Puerto Rico's connection to other Caribbean nations. They want to make sure that Puerto Ricans always identify with the Spanish language and Spanish culture. But for now, Puerto Rico will keep its links to the mainland. Many Puerto Ricans hope that their relationship with the United States will lead to a profitable and peaceful future.

✓ **Reading Check** **Why do some people favor Puerto Rican independence?**

Section 3 Assessment

Key Terms
Review the key terms at the beginning of this section. Use each term in a sentence that explains its meaning.

Target Reading Skills
State two main ideas of Section 3.

Comprehension and Critical Thinking
1. (a) Explain What is Puerto Rico's relationship to the United States?
(b) Sequence How did Puerto Rico gain more control over its own affairs?

2. (a) Describe List three different regions of Puerto Rico, and tell how people earn a living in each one.
(b) Synthesize How does Puerto Rican culture show Spanish, Caribbean, and mainland influences?
3. (a) List What are the three options Puerto Ricans consider for the future of their relationship with the United States?
(b) Analyze What are the benefits and drawbacks of each option?

Writing Activity
Write a journal entry from the point of view of either Julia or Esmeralda. Discuss your feelings about life on the mainland and in Puerto Rico. Explain where you would prefer to live and why.

Go Online
PHSchool.com

For: An activity on San Juan
Visit: PHSchool.com
Web Code: lfd-1503

Review and Assessment

◆ Chapter Summary

Section 1: Cuba

- Cuba became a communist country under Fidel Castro and then became an ally of the Soviet Union.
- During the Cold War, relations between Cuba and the United States worsened.
- Many Cubans have fled Cuba for the United States, where they have made successful new lives, but some dream of returning to a free and democratic Cuba.
- Recently Castro has allowed some private ownership of businesses and is encouraging tourism and trade.

Cuba

Section 2: Haiti

- Haiti has struggled for democracy since independence, but has enjoyed only short periods of elected government.
- The election of President Aristide brought a brief period of hope, but then a military take-over caused many Haitians to flee their country.
- The people of Haiti are poor. Farmers struggle on land that has been overused, crowded city slums do not have basic services, and political violence is a fact of life.

Section 3: Puerto Rico

- Puerto Rico is a commonwealth of the United States. Puerto Ricans are American citizens, and many of them move to the United States mainland.
- Life in Puerto Rico blends Caribbean and mainland influences.
- Puerto Ricans disagree over whether they should become a state, become independent, or remain a commonwealth.

◆ Key Terms

Match the definitions in Column I with the key terms in Column II.

Column I

1. a statement of a country's basic laws and values
2. a country joined to another country for a special purpose
3. a place that has its own government but also has strong ties to another country
4. those who leave their homeland for their own personal safety and to escape persecution
5. individuals with certain rights and responsibilities under a particular government

Column II

A citizens
B ally
C commonwealth
D constitution
E refugees

Review and Assessment (continued)

◆ Comprehension and Critical Thinking

6. (a) Name What are two advantages Cuba has because of its geography?
(b) Identify Cause and Effect How did these advantages lead to Cuba's prosperity?
(c) Synthesize Information How did Cuba change from a prosperous country to a poor one?

7. (a) Recall Why did revolutionary leaders like Fidel Castro gain support in Cuba?
(b) Describe What is life like under Castro's communist government of Cuba?
(c) Identify Effects What happened in Cuba when the communist regime of the Soviet Union collapsed? Explain why.

8. (a) Name Haiti was a colony of which European country?
(b) Synthesize Describe Toussaint L'Ouverture's ideals for Haiti, and explain whether or not the rule of the Duvaliers fulfilled those ideals.

9. (a) Identify Who is Jean-Bertrand Aristide?
(b) Sequence What are the main events of Aristide's struggle for power?
(c) Draw Conclusions How did what happened to Aristide affect ordinary people who supported him? Explain why.

10. (a) List What rights and responsibilities of United States citizenship do Puerto Ricans have?
(b) Find Main Ideas Explain why so many Puerto Ricans move back and forth between their island and the mainland.
(c) Compare What are the advantages and disadvantages of commonwealth status for Puerto Rico?

◆ Skills Practice

Comparing and Contrasting In the Skills for Life activity in this chapter, you learned how to compare and contrast. Review the steps of this skill.

Now look again at the first two sections of this chapter. As you recall, people from both Cuba and Haiti have fled their countries to come to the United States. What kinds of countries did they leave behind? How are Cuba and Haiti similar and different? Use a chart to compare the two countries. Then write a conclusion sentence on the topic.

◆ Writing Activity: Math

Review the charts in Country Profile: Haiti on page 144. Also consider the current population of Haiti, which is approximately 8 million. Use this information and your math skills to write a paragraph about Haiti's loss of population. You may wish to convert numbers into percentages or explain ratios in your paragraph.

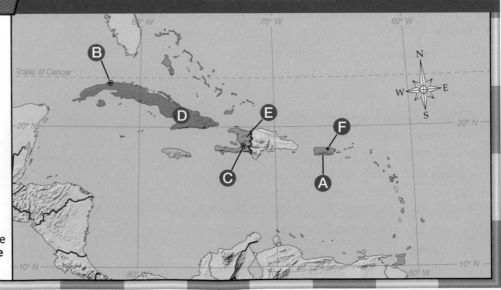

MAP MASTER™
Skills Activity

Place Location For each place listed below, write the letter from the map that shows its location.
1. Havana
2. Cuba
3. San Juan
4. Haiti
5. Puerto Rico
6. Port-au-Prince

Go Online
PHSchool.com Use Web Code **lfp-1523** for an interactive map.

The Caribbean

Standardized Test Prep

Test-Taking Tips

Some questions on standardized tests ask you to sequence information. Study the timeline below. Then follow the tips to answer the sample question.

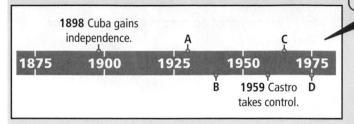

1898 Cuba gains independence.

1875 1900 1925 1950 1975

A   C
B   1959 Castro   D
takes control.

TIP Notice that the leader lines connect events to their dates on the timeline. See which dates are closest to each answer choice.

Pick the letter that best answers the question.

At which point on the timeline did large numbers of Cuban exiles <u>begin</u> going to the United States?

- **A** point A
- **B** point B
- **C** point C
- **D** point D

TIP Preview the question first. Look for information relating to the question as you examine the timeline.

Think It Through Notice the key word *begin* in the question. You know that many Cubans left Cuba for the United States because they opposed Castro's government. Therefore, they must have *started* leaving after Castro came to power. So you can rule out choices A and B. Although exiles may still have been leaving Cuba in 1975, the exile movement most likely *began* shortly after Castro's new government was formed. So the correct answer is C.

Practice Questions

Choose the letter of the best answer.

1. Before Cuba gained independence, it was a colony of
   - **A** France.
   - **B** Spain.
   - **C** the United States.
   - **D** Portugal.

2. Which of the following nations was formed from a revolt of enslaved Africans?
   - **A** Haiti
   - **B** Cuba
   - **C** Puerto Rico
   - **D** Hispaniola

3. Which of the following statements best describes Puerto Rico's relationship with the United States?
   - **A** It is a colony of the United States.
   - **B** It is a state of the United States.
   - **C** It is a country with special ties to the United States.
   - **D** It is a commonwealth of the United States.

Study the timeline below and answer the question that follows.

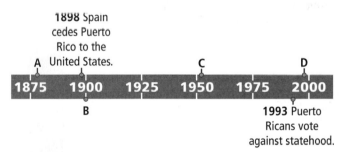

1898 Spain cedes Puerto Rico to the United States.

A   C   D
1875 1900 1925 1950 1975 2000
     B   1993 Puerto Ricans vote against statehood.

4. At which point on the timeline did Puerto Rico become a commonwealth?
   - **A** point A
   - **B** point B
   - **C** point C
   - **D** point D

Go Online
PHSchool.com
Use Web Code lfa-1501 for a **Chapter 5 self-test.**

Chapter 6

South America

Chapter Preview

This chapter will introduce you to the countries of the continent of South America.

Country Databank

The Country Databank provides data and descriptions of each of the countries in the region: Argentina, Bolivia, Brazil, Chile, Colombia, Ecuador, Guyana, Paraguay, Peru, Suriname, Uruguay, and Venezuela.

Section 1

Brazil
Geography Shapes a Nation

Section 2

Peru
An Ancient Land Looks to the Future

Section 3

Chile
Land of Contrasts

Section 4

Venezuela
Oil Powers the Economy

Target Reading Skill

Comparison and Contrast In this chapter you will focus on using comparison and contrast to help you sort out and analyze information.

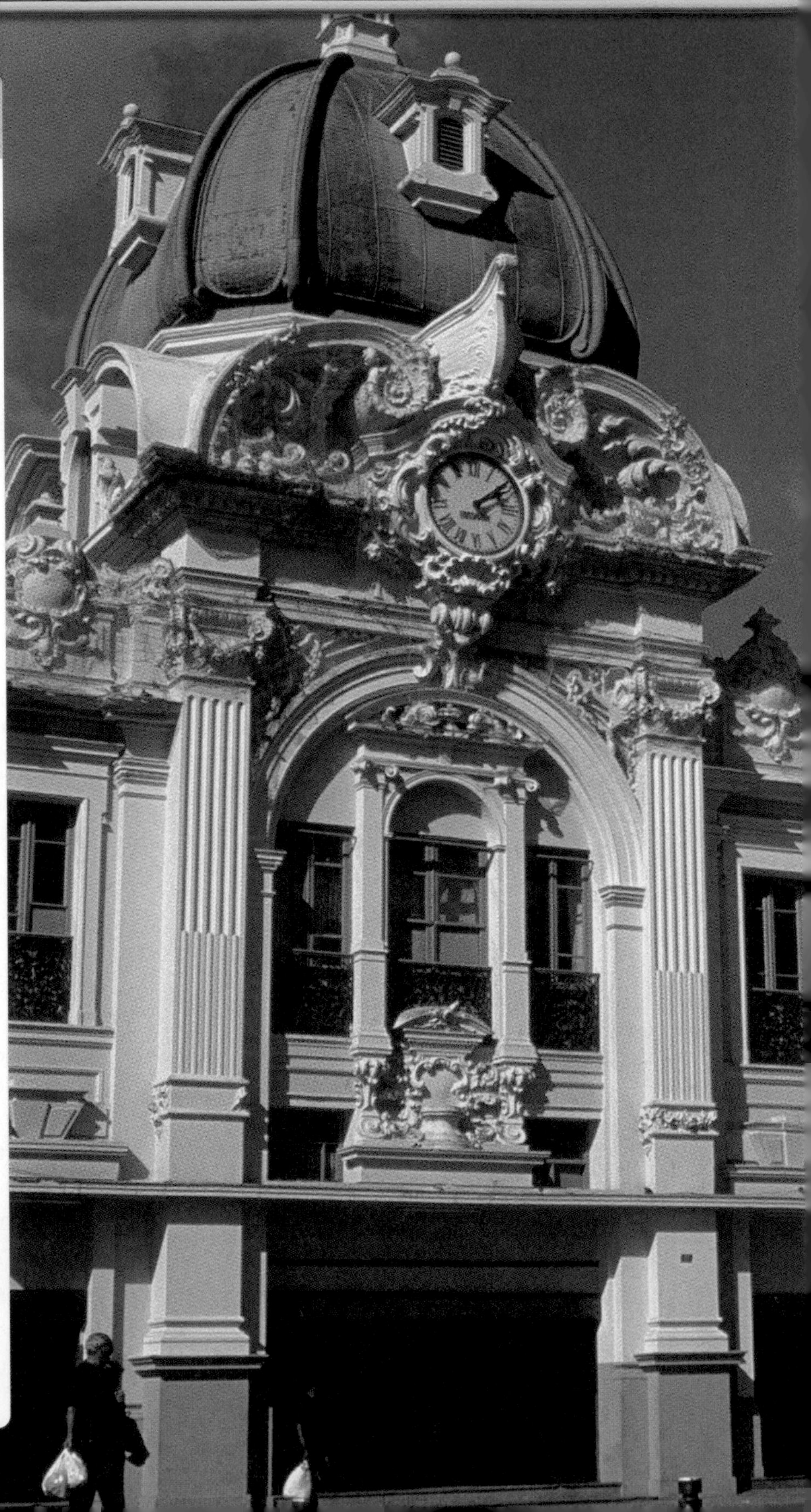

▶ **A plaza in Rio de Janeiro, Brazil**

South America: Political

Caribbean Sea

ATLANTIC OCEAN

Barranquilla
Maracaibo
Caracas
GUYANA
SURINAME
VENEZUELA
Medellín
Georgetown
Paramaribo
Cayenne
Bogotá
FRENCH GUIANA (France)
GALÁPAGOS ISLANDS (Ecuador)
Cali
COLOMBIA
Equator
Equator
0°
ECUADOR
Quito
Belém
Manaus
Amazon River
Guayaquil
Fortaleza

PACIFIC OCEAN

B R A Z I L

Recife

PERU
Lima
Cuzco
Salvador
Arequipa
La Paz
Brasília
BOLIVIA
Sucre
20° S
Belo Horizonte
20° S
Tropic of Capricorn
PARAGUAY
Río de Janeiro
São Paulo
Tropic of Capricorn
CHILE
Asunción
Curitiba
Córdoba
Porto Alegre
Santiago
Rosario
URUGUAY
Montevideo
ATLANTIC OCEAN
Buenos Aires
40° S
ARGENTINA

40° S

KEY
⊛ National capital
★ Other capital
• Other city
— National border

FALKLAND ISLANDS (U.K.)

0 miles 1,000
0 kilometers 1,000
Lambert Azimuthal Equal Area

Tierra del Fuego
SOUTH GEORGIA (U.K.)

N W E S

80° W
60° W
40° W
20° W
0°

Regions Notice that the Equator runs through South America. **Locate** Which countries are completely north of the Equator? Which ones have land both north and south of the Equator? **Identify Effects** If you were to start at the Equator and travel south, how do you think the climate would change? Explain why.

Go Online
PHSchool.com Use Web Code lfp-1621 for step-by-step map skills practice.

Introducing South America

Guide for Reading

This section provides an introduction to the 12 countries of South America.

- Look at the map on the previous page and then read the paragraphs to learn about each nation.
- Analyze the data to compare the countries.
- What characteristics do most of these countries share?
- What are some key differences among the countries?

Viewing the Video Overview

View the World Studies Video Overview to learn more about each of the countries. As you watch, answer these questions:

- What topographical feature has a major influence on the climate of South America?
- What topographical features influence the climate where you live?

Explore the varied landscape of South America.

Argentina

Capital	Buenos Aires
Land Area	1,056,636 sq mi; 2,736,690 sq km
Population	37.8 million
Ethnic Group(s)	white, mestizo, indigenous Indian
Religion(s)	Roman Catholic, Protestant, Jewish
Government	republic
Currency	Argentine peso
Leading Exports	edible oils, fuels and energy, cereals, feed, motor vehicles
Language(s)	Spanish (official), Italian, indigenous Indian languages

The second-largest country in South America, Argentina (ahr jun TEE nuh) covers more than 1 million square miles (2.7 million square kilometers). It is located in the southern part of the continent, between the Andes Mountains and the Atlantic Ocean, and extends to the southern tip of South America. The Andes slope down to a fertile plain called the pampas, where raising livestock and wheat dominates the culture and the economy. Argentina has suffered from a series of harsh military regimes. In 1983, however, the nation established a democratic government.

Albatross chicks, Diego Ramirez Islands, Chile

Bolivia

Capitals	La Paz and Sucre
Land Area	418,683 sq mi; 1,084,390 sq km
Population	8.5 million
Ethnic Group(s)	Quechua, mestizo, Aymara, white
Religion(s)	Roman Catholic, Protestant
Government	republic
Currency	boliviano
Leading Exports	soybeans, natural gas, zinc, gold, wood
Language(s)	Spanish (official), Quechua (official), Aymara (official)

Bolivia (buh LIV ee uh) is a landlocked country in central South America. Much of its population lives in the Altiplano, or high plateau region, which Bolivia shares with Peru. This plain lies between two ranges of the Andes Mountains. Mountains and rain forests isolate the Altiplano from the sea and from the rest of South America. Although Bolivia has rich mineral resources, mining is difficult at high altitudes. It is also difficult to transport the minerals to market. So, in spite of its resources, Bolivia has remained poor. More than half of Bolivians are indigenous people.

Brazil

Capital	Brasília
Land Area	3,265,059 sq mi; 8,456,510 sq km
Population	176 million
Ethnic Group(s)	white, mixed white and black, black, Asian, Arab, indigenous Indian
Religion(s)	Roman Catholic
Government	federal republic
Currency	real
Leading Exports	manufactured goods, iron ore, soybeans, footwear, coffee, autos
Language(s)	Portuguese (official), German, Italian, Spanish, Polish, Japanese, indigenous Indian languages

Brazil (bruh ZIL) is the largest country in South America. It occupies the eastern-central region of the continent, bordering the Atlantic Ocean. Brazil is known as the home of the huge Amazon rain forest and for its vibrant culture. The influence of its Portuguese colonial past can still be seen in Brazil's language, culture, and architecture. However, other groups have also made contributions to a distinctive Brazilian culture. These groups include the native Indians, Africans originally brought to Brazil as slaves, and immigrants from northern Europe and Japan.

Chile

Capital	Santiago
Land Area	289,112 sq mi; 748,800 sq km
Population	15.5 million
Ethnic Group(s)	white, mestizo, indigenous Indian
Religion(s)	Roman Catholic, Protestant
Government	republic
Currency	Chilean peso
Leading Exports	copper, fish, fruits, paper and pulp, chemicals
Language(s)	Spanish (official), indigenous Indian languages

Chile (CHIL ee) is a long, narrow country. It lies along the western coast of South America, from its northern border with Peru to the southern tip of the continent. Chile has varied landforms and climates, from deserts in the north and central fertile plains, to its rainy, stormy southern tip. Mountains, lakes, and glaciers complete the picture. Most Chileans live in the fertile valley of central Chile. About one third of Chile's people live in the vibrant capital of Santiago.

Introducing South America

Colombia

Capital	Bogotá
Land Area	401,042 sq mi; 1,038,700 sq km
Population	41 million
Ethnic Group(s)	mestizo, white, mixed white and black, mixed black and indigenous Indian, indigenous Indian
Religion(s)	Roman Catholic
Government	republic
Currency	Colombian peso
Leading Exports	petroleum, coffee, coal, apparel, bananas, cut flowers
Language(s)	Spanish (official), indigenous Indian languages

Located on the northwest corner of South America, Colombia (kuh LUM bee uh) has coastlines on both the Pacific Ocean and the Caribbean Sea. To the northwest, it is bordered by Panama, which was once part of its territory. Colombia is located at the intersection of Central and South America and near the Panama Canal. This location makes it important to transportation and communication between the regions. Three ranges of the Andes Mountains divide the country. Most of Colombia's people live in the central valley or the hot, wet western region.

Ecuador

Capital	Quito
Land Area	106,888 sq mi; 276,840 sq km
Population	13.5 million
Ethnic Group(s)	mestizo, indigenous Indian, white, black
Religion(s)	Roman Catholic
Government	republic
Currency	U.S. dollar
Leading Exports	petroleum, bananas, shrimp, coffee, cocoa, cut flowers, fish
Language(s)	Spanish (official), Quechua, other indigenous Indian languages

Once part of the Incan empire, Ecuador (EK wuh dawr) was colonized by Spain in 1533 and became independent in 1830. A small country on the Pacific Coast, Ecuador has three regions. The lowland coastal region is the industrial center as well as the farm belt of Ecuador. Subsistence farming is the main economic activity in the highlands of the Andes Mountains. This is the region where the descendants of the Incas live and struggle to maintain their languages and traditional ways of life. The inland region benefits from large deposits of oil.

Giant tortoise, Ecuador

Guyana

Capital	Georgetown
Land Area	76,004 sq mi; 196,850 sq km
Population	698,209
Ethnic Group(s)	South Asian, black, indigenous Indian, white, East Asian, mixed white and black
Religion(s)	Christian, Hindu, Muslim
Government	republic
Currency	Guyanese dollar
Leading Exports	sugar, gold, bauxite/alumina, rice, shrimp, molasses, rum, timber
Language(s)	English (official), English Creole, Hindi, Tamil, indigenous Indian languages

Guyana (gy AN uh) lies on the northeast coast of South America. It is similar to its Caribbean island neighbors. Guyana was originally colonized by the Dutch, who imported enslaved Africans to work on their plantations. It became a British colony in 1814. After slavery ended in 1838, the British brought workers from India to do farm work. The descendants of these Africans and Indians form the largest ethnic groups in Guyana today. Most of the population lives on the narrow, wet coastal plain. The interior of the country is covered with dense rain forests.

Paraguay

Capital	Asunción
Land Area	153,398 sq mi; 397,300 sq km
Population	5.9 million
Ethnic Group(s)	mestizo
Religion(s)	Roman Catholic, Protestant
Government	constitutional republic
Currency	guaraní
Leading Exports	soybeans, feed, cotton, meat, edible oils, electricity
Language(s)	Spanish (official), Guaraní (official)

A small landlocked country, Paraguay (PA ruh gway) is bordered by Brazil, Argentina, and Bolivia. The Paraguay River divides the country into two sections. Much of the population is clustered in the fertile plains and hills of the eastern region. The west is sparsely populated. Most of the people of Paraguay are descended from the Spanish and the Guaraní, an indigenous group. In the cities, both Spanish and Guaraní are spoken, but in the countryside most people speak Guaraní.

Peru

Capital	Lima
Land Area	494,208 sq mi; 1,280,000 sq km
Population	28 million
Ethnic Group(s)	indigenous Indian, mestizo, white, black, East Asian
Religion(s)	Roman Catholic
Government	constitutional republic
Currency	nuevo sol
Leading Exports	fish and fish products, gold, copper, zinc, crude petroleum and byproducts, lead, coffee, sugar, cotton
Language(s)	Spanish (official), Quechua (official), Aymara

Peru (puh ROO) lies along the Pacific coast of South America, south of Colombia and Ecuador, and north of Chile. The Andes Mountains run the length of the country. A high plateau called the Altiplano is home to descendants of the Incas and other indigenous groups. Many of them live much as their ancestors did and speak Indian languages. The economic center of Peru is Lima, on the coast. Peru has been slow to modernize and industrialize. It has also suffered from military dictatorships and government corruption, but today it has an elected democratic government.

Introducing **South America**

Suriname

Capital	Paramaribo
Land Area	62,344 sq mi; 161,470 sq km
Population	436,494
Ethnic Group(s)	South Asian, Creole, Javanese, Maroon, indigenous Indian, East Asian, white
Religion(s)	Christian, Hindu, Muslim, traditional beliefs
Government	constitutional democracy
Currency	Suriname guilder or florin
Leading Exports	alumina, crude oil, lumber, shrimp and fish, rice, bananas
Language(s)	Dutch (official), Sranan, Javanese, Sarnami Hindi, Saramaccan, Chinese, Carib

Suriname (soor ih NAHM) is a small country on the northern coast of South America. Mountains and rain forest dominate its geography. Most of the people live on a narrow coastal plain. Suriname was settled by the Dutch, who imported enslaved Africans to work their coffee and sugar cane plantations. After slavery ended, workers from India, Java, and China were brought to work in the fields. The result is an ethnically mixed population. Suriname became independent in 1975. A series of military regimes followed, but democratic rule was established in 1987.

A gaucho in Uruguay

Uruguay

Capital	Montevideo
Land Area	67,108 sq mi; 173,620 sq km
Population	3.4 million
Ethnic Group(s)	white, mestizo, black
Religion(s)	Roman Catholic, Protestant, Jewish
Government	constitutional republic
Currency	Uruguayan peso
Leading Exports	meat, rice, leather products, wool, vehicles, dairy products
Language(s)	Spanish (official)

Uruguay (YOOR uh gway) is a small country located between two large ones: Brazil to the north and Argentina to the west. The capital, Montevideo, is situated where the River Platte empties into the Atlantic Ocean, making the city an important port for international trade. Most of Uruguay is made up of grassy plains and low hills. Raising cattle and sheep are the main occupations of that region. Tourism has become important along the country's sandy coastal beaches. Banking and other service industries also contribute to the economy.

Venezuela

Capital	Caracas
Land Area	340,560 sq mi; 882,050 sq km
Population	24.3 million
Ethnic Group(s)	white, Southwest Asian, black, indigenous Indian
Religion(s)	Roman Catholic, Protestant
Government	federal republic
Currency	bolívar
Leading Exports	petroleum, bauxite and aluminum, steel, chemicals, agricultural products, basic manufactured goods
Language(s)	Spanish (official), indigenous Indian languages

SOURCES: DK World Desk Reference Online; *CIA World Factbook,* 2002 and 2006; *World Almanac,* 2003

Venezuela (ven uh ZWAY luh) is located on the northern coast of South America, along the Caribbean Sea. The government has encouraged both agriculture and industry in an effort to diversify the economy. However, Venezuela still depends largely on its huge deposits of oil. Most of Venezuela's people live in cities, primarily in the northern part of the country. Some of the country's indigenous population lives in isolated areas of rain forest. Once a Spanish colony, Venezuela freed itself from Spain in 1821 and then became part of Gran Colombia. Venezuela became an independent republic in 1830.

Caraballeda, Venezuela

Assessment

Comprehension and Critical Thinking

1. Compare and Contrast Which is the largest country in South America? Which is the smallest? What do these two countries have in common, in spite of their difference in size?

2. Categorize What characteristics do the countries south of the Equator share?

3. Contrast How have such contrasting geographic features as rolling, grassy plains and high altitudes affected the cultures and economies of the countries in which they are found?

4. Draw Conclusions Which countries have the most diverse populations? Explain how you reached that conclusion.

5. Make a Bar Graph Create a population graph of the five most populous countries of South America.

Keeping Current

Access the **DK World Desk Reference Online** at **PHSchool.com** for up-to-date information about all the countries in this chapter.

Go Online
PHSchool.com

Web Code: lfe-1433

Brazil
Geography Shapes a Nation

Prepare to Read

Objectives

In this section you will
1. Learn about the geography of Brazil.
2. Discover why the rain forests are important to Brazil and to the whole world.
3. Find out what groups make up the people of Brazil and how they live.

Taking Notes

As you read this section, look for information about the rain forest. Copy the flowchart below and record your findings in it.

Amazon Rain Forest		
Importance	**Dangers**	**Efforts to Protect It**
•	•	•
•	•	•

Target Reading Skill

Compare and Contrast
When you compare, you examine the similarities between things. When you contrast, you look at the differences. Comparing and contrasting can help you sort out and analyze information. As you read this section, look for similarities and differences in the geographic regions, cultures, and cities of Brazil.

Key Terms

- **canopy** (KAN uh pea) *n.* the dense mass of leaves and branches that form the top layer of a rain forest
- **Amazon rain forest** (AM uh zahn rayn FAWR ist) *n.* a large tropical rain forest occupying the Amazon Basin in northern South America
- **Rio de Janeiro** (REE oh day zhuh NEHR oh) *n.* a large city in Brazil
- **Brasília** (bruh ZIL yuh) *n.* Brazil's new capital city
- **savanna** (suh VAN uh) *n.* a flat, grassy region, or plain

A toucan from Brazil's rain forest

Deep in Brazil's rain forest, the light barely penetrates. At the top of the trees, the leaves form a dense mass called a **canopy.** Sun and rain beat down upon the canopy. But on the ground, it is almost chilly. The cool, moist air is filled with sounds, such as the calls of birds, monkeys, and insects.

The **Amazon rain forest** is a large area of abundant rainfall and dense vegetation in northern Brazil. It occupies the Amazon Basin, the land drained by the Amazon River and its tributaries. Find the Amazon River and the Amazon Basin on the map titled Physical Latin America on page 4. The Amazon rain forest gets more than 80 inches (200 centimeters) of rain each year and has an average temperature of 80°F (27°C). It has millions of species of plants and animals, including orchids, jaguars, and toucans.

The dense foliage makes travel through the rain forest difficult, and few people live there. Even so, the Amazon rain forest is very important to the people of Brazil. It is also important to the rest of the world. Find out what Brazil is doing to protect and develop its rain forest resources.

The Geography of Brazil

Brazil, the largest country in South America, is nearly as big as the United States. It is also one of the richest countries in the world in land and resources. Until recently, its immense rain forests remained undisturbed. Only the few indigenous groups that had lived in them for centuries ever explored them.

Rain Forest and More Brazil's rain forests take up more than a third of the country. Look at the map titled Latin America: Vegetation Regions on page 20. In the southeast, the forests give way to a large plateau divided by mountain ranges and river valleys. The plateau reaches Brazil's long coast. Many harbors lie along the coast. **Rio de Janeiro** (REE oh day zhuh NEHR oh), Brazil's former capital, is one of many Brazilian cities that grew up around these coastal harbors. Most of Brazil's people live near the coast, far from the rain forests.

Brazil's New Capital: Brasília In the 1950s, the government of Brazil wanted to develop Brazil's interior region using the resources of the rain forest. But few Brazilians wanted to move to the interior of the country. How could the government tempt Brazilians to move?

The government's solution was to build a new capital city called **Brasília** in the interior, near the rain forest. They chose a site on the vast interior plain, or **savanna,** called the Cerrado (suh RAH doh). Work started in 1957, and the government began to move to the partly-completed capital in 1960. Today, Brasília has a population of nearly 2 million people, and many of Brazil's companies and organizations have their headquarters there.

√ **Reading Check** Why was Brasília built?

Links to
Science

The Photosynthesis "Factory" What is the source of the oxygen we breathe? The food we eat? The fuels we burn? They all begin with photosynthesis. This process is carried out by green plants. They transform water, sunlight, carbon dioxide, and other minerals into energy-rich substances. Plants store these substances for their own nourishment. But animals eat the plants as food. And people eat those animals, as well as eating plants directly. At the same time, the process of photosynthesis releases oxygen into the air. The Amazon rain forest, with its wealth of green plants, is such an important source of oxygen that it is sometimes called "the lungs of Earth."

And there's more. Fuels such as coal and oil are the remains of ancient plants. So photosynthesis, in a way, powers the world.

DISCOVERY CHANNEL SCHOOL Video
Learn how Carnival is celebrated in Brazil.

The Importance of the Rain Forest

The rain forest is very important to life all over the world. Scientists estimate that rain forests produce about one third of the world's oxygen. They also calculate that the Amazon rain forest has several million different species of plants, animals, and insects—some that have not even been discovered yet. That is more species than any other region in the world.

Using Rain Forest Resources Many modern medicines have been made from rain forest plants, and scientists hope to discover even more species that have practical uses. The rain forest also holds about one fifth of the world's fresh water. But many scientists think that when people begin to use the resources of the rain forest, they upset the delicate balance of nature.

For example, in the past, Brazil made efforts at land reform by moving poor farmers to the Amazon rain forest and giving them land there. The farmers burned down trees to clear the land for their crops. After a few years, the soil in the rain forest became unfit for farming.

Graph Skills

Differences in temperature and rainfall create different environments for plants, animals, and people. **Transfer Information** Which city shown in the graphs gets more rainfall? Which has the higher temperatures? **Contrast** Use these climate differences to infer how life might be different in Brasília and Manaus.

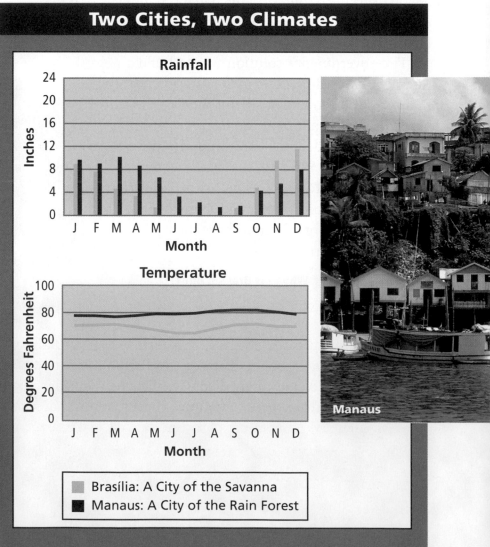

Two Cities, Two Climates

Rainfall
Inches — 0, 4, 8, 12, 16, 20, 24
Month — J F M A M J J A S O N D

Temperature
Degrees Fahrenheit — 0, 20, 40, 60, 80, 100
Month — J F M A M J J A S O N D

Brasília: A City of the Savanna
Manaus: A City of the Rain Forest

Brasília

Manaus

Threats to the Amazon Rain Forest

Today, Brazil's leaders are trying to control development of the rain forest. They want to find ways to help the economy and the farmers while protecting this important resource. They are working to protect the rain forest from the following dangers:

First, if too much timber is cut down, there will not be enough trees to absorb the carbon dioxide in the atmosphere. The buildup of carbon dioxide may trap heat near Earth's surface, altering the world's climate. When part of the forest is destroyed, the animals and plants that live there may not survive. Plants that might produce important medicines could be destroyed before they are even discovered.

Smuggling is another problem. Approximately 12 million animals are smuggled out of Brazil each year. Many are endangered, and it is illegal to capture or kill them. There are also laws to slow down the logging of mahogany, a wood used to make furniture. But these laws are being broken. Illegal logging continues to threaten the rain forest.

Pollution caused by mining is a third problem. In the late 1980s, the mercury used in gold mining polluted streams in the forest. It made people in several Native American villages sick. The government of Brazil passed strict laws about mining in the rain forest. Sometimes the government insisted that the miners leave. At times, military police had to be called in to make sure they did.

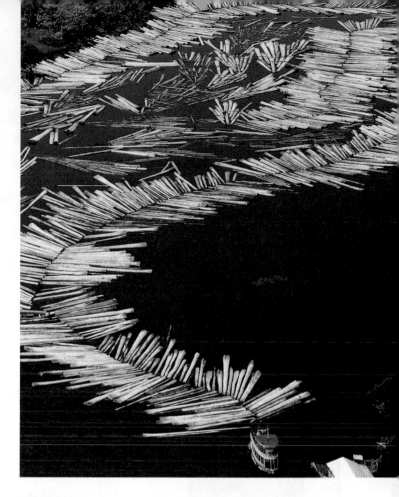

Illegal Logging
The small boat is towing a long raft of illegally cut logs down the Amazon River. **Analyze Images** *Which details in the photo suggest why logging might be difficult in the rain forest? Which details suggest why it might be easy?*

Threats to Traditional Ways of Life   Threats to the Amazon rain forest are also threats to the people who have traditionally lived there. The difficulty of traveling in the rain forest had kept many indigenous peoples isolated. They continued their ancient ways of life. Once the rain forest was opened to development, however, miners, farmers, and land speculators arrived. These newcomers brought diseases the Indians had not been exposed to before, and many died. Conflicts between the developers and the Indians were sometimes violent, and Indians were killed. And the isolated culture of the indigenous people began to change as it was brought into contact with modern ways.

Compare and Contrast What are some differences between the way the indigenous people lived before the development of the rain forest and the way they live now?

✔ **Reading Check**   **Describe three dangers threatening the rain forest.**

Brazil

Brazil's culture is vibrant and diverse. Portuguese and African influences are evident in Brazilian architecture, religion, music, and food. They also shape the culture of Brazil's cities, where 82 percent of the people live. The indigenous Indian culture, however, has remained largely separate from the rest of Brazil, isolated in the interior of the Amazon rain forest. As you study the map and charts, consider how geography and settlement patterns shape a nation's culture.

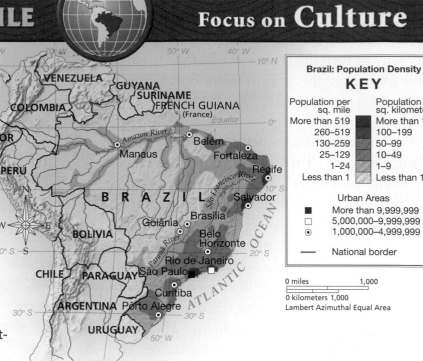

Brazil: Population Density

KEY

Population per sq. mile	Population per sq. kilometer
More than 519	More than 199
260–519	100–199
130–259	50–99
25–129	10–49
1–24	1–9
Less than 1	Less than 1

Urban Areas
■ More than 9,999,999
□ 5,000,000–9,999,999
⊙ 1,000,000–4,999,999
— National border

0 miles 1,000
0 kilometers 1,000
Lambert Azimuthal Equal Area

Cultural Regions of Brazil

The Northeast
Sugar plantations shaped the culture of the northeast. Enslaved Africans imported to work on the plantations brought their culture with them. Today, the area is rich in art and music. The dance called the samba (shown above) was born here.

SOURCE: *Encyclopedia Britannica*

The South
European immigrants shaped the culture of the south. People mainly of Portuguese descent brought cattle ranching, wheat farming, and coffee production to the region. A distinct diet based on meat products developed here.

The Rain Forests
European immigrants had little contact with Brazil's indigenous peoples. These peoples continued to lead traditional lives, isolated in Brazil's rain forests. Some 230 groups live here today. Among them are the Yanomami, who are hunter-gatherers.

The Cities
In urban centers such as Rio de Janeiro (above) and São Paulo, African and European cultures blended together. For example, the Brazilian celebration called Carnival mixes Catholic and African traditions.

Brazil's Ethnic Groups

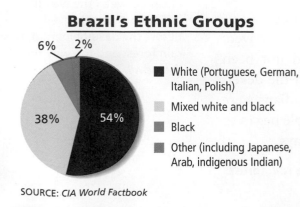

6%   2%
38%   54%

■ White (Portuguese, German, Italian, Polish)
Mixed white and black
Black
■ Other (including Japanese, Arab, indigenous Indian)

SOURCE: *CIA World Factbook*

Map and Chart Skills

1. **Identify** Where do most Brazilians live?
2. **Identify Causes** What are some of the reasons why Brazilians live where they do?
3. **Draw Conclusions** Why do you think Brazil's cities are more culturally diverse than the interior rain forest?

Go Online
PHSchool.com

Use Web Code **lfe-1611** for **DK World Desk Reference Online.**

The People of Brazil

The Native Americans living in the rain forest were some of the first people to live in Brazil. Today, many Brazilians are a mix of Native American, African, and European heritages. The Yanomami (yah noh MAH mee) are one of the larger Native American groups. They still live in traditional communities in the rain forest. As the rain forest is threatened, however, so too is the Yanomami way of life. Some Native Americans have left the rain forest for the cities.

The Different Cultures of Brazil Daniel Monteiro Costa is a writer and teacher who lives in São Paulo, Brazil. He is also known as Daniel Munduruku (mun duh ROO koo). Daniel is a Munduruku Indian. Many Munduruku still live in small villages in the rain forest. Daniel was born in the city of Belém (buh LEM), but he often visited his relatives in a nearby village. There, he heard stories the Munduruku people told about their history and culture. When he was growing up, Daniel saw that Indians were often treated with disrespect. He began studying the indigenous peoples of Brazil and became proud of his heritage. Now, Daniel works to keep Munduruku stories alive and to end discrimination against Indians in Brazil.

Native Americans are not the only cultural groups in Brazil. Many features of African culture also flourish there. The most African of Brazilian cities, Salvador, lies on the coastal plain. Most of the people who live here are descendants of the millions of Africans brought to Brazil as slaves.

Many Brazilians also have a European heritage. Some are descended from the Portuguese who colonized the area. Other more recent immigrants come from countries such as Italy. There are also Asian immigrants from Japan.

Modern and Traditional
In the top photo, Brazilian soccer star Sissi participates in the 1999 Women's World Cup competition. The photo above shows a Kaiapo Indian from the rain forest.
Synthesize *Use the text to help you describe the two very different Brazilian ways of life represented by the photos.*

Working on Farms and in Factories In Brazil, most of the land that is suitable for growing crops is owned by only a few people. Sometimes they choose not to farm their land. About one third of Brazil's farmland, approximately 300 million acres (122 million hectares), is unused.

In the 1990s, Brazil's government gave some of this unused land to poor farmers. People began starting small farms just north of Rio de Janeiro. The farms allow them to support themselves.

The plantations, or large farms, of Brazil produce crops for export. Brazil is the largest coffee producer in the world. But Brazilians know that they cannot depend on only one or two crops. The government has discouraged coffee production and tried to diversify the economy by building more factories. Today, Brazil produces iron and steel, cars, and electrical equipment. Since 1960, about 30 million people have left farms and plantations and moved into the cities to get jobs in these new industries.

A Brazilian City: Rio de Janeiro Brazilian cities are home to both the rich and the very poor. Rio de Janeiro is a good example of these contrasts. It lies on the Atlantic coast, surrounded by huge mountains that dip to the sea. If you climbed to the top of one, you could see the whole city. To the south, you would see expensive hotels and shops for tourists. In the downtown area, you would see old palaces and government buildings. Rio de Janeiro was Brazil's capital from 1822 to 1960.

But to the north, you would see clusters of small houses where factory workers live. On the slopes of the mountains are neighborhoods crowded with homes that have no electricity or running water. About 20 percent of Rio's more than 10 million people live in these *favelas*, or slums. However, most of Rio's people live in well-built houses with electricity and running water.

✔ **Reading Check** What is Rio de Janeiro like?

Rio de Janeiro

Section 1 Assessment

Key Terms
Review the key terms at the beginning of this section. Use each term in a sentence that explains its meaning.

Target Reading Skills
What are two ways Brasília and Rio de Janeiro are similar? What are two ways they are different?

Comprehension and Critical Thinking
1. (a) Name What are the main features of Brazil's geography?

(b) Infer Why do you think many people moved to Brasília?

2. (a) Identify Effects Why are Brazil's rain forests important to the whole world?

(b) Analyze Explain why it is difficult for Brazil to protect its rain forest and improve its economy at the same time.

3. (a) Identify What is the cultural heritage of Brazilians?

(b) Draw Conclusions How does unequal land distribution affect the economy and people of Brazil?

Writing Activity
Suppose you lived in a Brazilian city, such as Rio de Janeiro or Salvador, in 1960. Would you have moved to the new city of Brasília if you had been given the chance? Write a letter to a friend explaining why you are planning to move to Brasília or why you are not moving there.

Writing Tip State your choice clearly. Then give three reasons to support your choice.

Prepare to Read

Objectives

In this section you will
1. Learn how geography has affected the way people live in the three regions of Peru.
2. Discover what life is like in the cities and towns of the Altiplano.

Taking Notes

As you read this section, look for the ways that people live in the three regions of Peru. Copy the table below and record your findings in it.

Region	Geography	How People Live
	• •	• •

Target Reading Skill

Identify Contrasts When you contrast two regions, you examine how they are different. In this section you will read about the three geographic regions of Peru and about the ways people have adapted to them. As you read, list the differences between the regions and the ways people live there.

Key Terms

- **Altiplano** (al tih PLAH noh) *n.* a high plateau in the Andes Mountains
- **sierra** (see EHR uh) *n.* the mountain region of Peru
- **oasis** (oh AY sis) *n.* a fertile area in a desert that has a source of water

When people on Tribuna, an island in Lake Titicaca, play soccer, they are very careful. That's because the island is made of straw. The ground is uneven, and when they walk on it they can feel the water shifting below. "It seems crazy to play soccer on water," says Luis Colo, who lives on Tribuna. "We don't jump on each other after a goal, or we'd probably fall through the field."

Tribuna is one of about 70 islands made by the Uros (oo ROHS). The Uros have adapted to the geography of Lake Titicaca. As you read in Chapter 3, they make their islands out of totora reeds. They join the floating roots together and then lay cut reeds on top. This process creates an island that is firm enough to support small communities of people with huts and livestock. When the Uros need more land, they simply build another island.

From the time of the Incas, the people of Peru—like people everywhere—have adapted to their geography. The Uros are only one example. You will read about other examples of how geography has affected culture in this section.

Reed boats moored by a totora-reed island

Peru

Peru is a country of geographic extremes. In the high mountains of the sierra, the air is almost too thin to breathe. The coast is largely desert except for scattered oases where rivers flow down from the mountains to the Pacific. Rain forest covers much of the eastern half of the country, or selva. As you study the map and charts below, think about how geography and climate affect the lives of Peruvians.

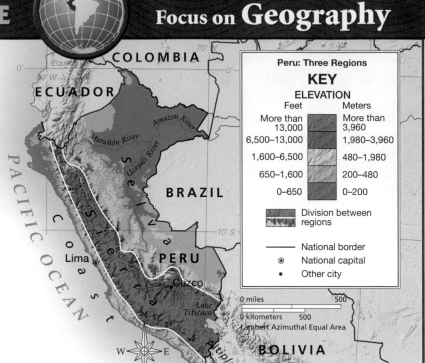

Peru: Three Regions

KEY

ELEVATION

Feet	Meters
More than 13,000	More than 3,960
6,500–13,000	1,980–3,960
1,600–6,500	480–1,980
650–1,600	200–480
0–650	0–200

Division between regions

National border

⊛ National capital

• Other city

0 miles 500
0 kilometers 500
Lambert Azimuthal Equal Area

Characteristics of Three Regions

Characteristic	Coastal Region	Sierra	Selva
Land area	11%	26%	63%
Dominant feature	Desert and oases	Mountains	Rain forest
Yearly precipitation	2 inches	Varies	75–125 inches
Main language	Spanish	Quechua	Varied indigenous languages
Major occupations	Professional; manufacturing and refining; agriculture	Farming and herding; tourism	Fishing; hunting and gathering

SOURCES: *Peru, Country Study, Department of the Army Handbook,* 1981; *Encyclopaedia Britannica; The World Today Series, Latin America 2002;* Library of Congress online

Peru's Population

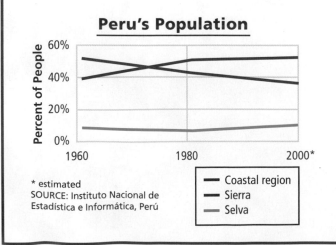

Percent of People
60%
40%
20%
0%
1960   1980   2000*

* estimated
SOURCE: Instituto Nacional de Estadística e Informática, Perú

— Coastal region
— Sierra
— Selva

Map and Chart Skills

1. **Identify** How do people earn a living in different parts of Peru?
2. **Analyze** What region of Peru has the most people? What region has lost population?
3. **Infer** What information in the map and charts indicates why these changes in population might have occurred?

Go **Online**
PHSchool.com

Use Web Code lfe-1612 for DK World Desk Reference Online.

The Regions and People of Peru

The Uros live on Lake Titicaca. Find Lake Titicaca on the map of Peru in the Country Profile. Lake Titicaca is in Peru's **Altiplano** (al tih PLAH noh), a high plateau in the Andes Mountains. The Altiplano is about 12,000 feet (3,658 meters) above sea level. It is located in southern Peru near the Bolivian border.

Peru's Three Geographic Regions The Andes Mountains, which run from northwest to southeast Peru, divide the country into three geographic regions. The mountain region, including the Andes and the Altiplano, is known as the **sierra.** Much of this region is so high that lower layers of the soil remain frozen all year. This kind of treeless plain, which supports only low-growing vegetation, is called tundra. Even so, people have lived in this region for centuries. The Incas built their empire in the Altiplano, with Cuzco as its capital. Today, some descendants of the Incas live much as their ancestors did. In addition to farming, these Native Americans herd sheep, cattle, llamas, and alpacas. Wool is one of the major products of the region.

The coastal region of Peru is very different from the sierra. This dry area is dotted with oases. An **oasis** is a fertile area in a desert that has a source of water. Before Europeans arrived, indigenous groups settled by these oases. Later, the Spanish also built cities along the coast. Today, this area is the economic center of Peru. In Lima (LEE muh), Peru's capital, historic Spanish buildings from the 1600s and 1700s stand next to modern skyscrapers. More than 6 million people—more than a quarter of Peru's population—live in Lima.

The third region of Peru is the large forested area that stretches from the lower slopes of the mountains to the lowlands of northeast Peru. Here, the weather is hot and humid all year. This isolated region is called the selva. It has few roads connecting it to the sierra and the coast. Little modern development has occurred here. Some Native American groups live in this rain forest much as their ancestors did.

A modern skyscraper stands beside a Spanish-style home in Lima.

A Peruvian Oasis
This small fertile area is surrounded by desert. **Draw Inferences** *Why do you think people settled by oases in this area of Peru?*

Explore how people make a living in Peru.

Peru's People Native Americans make up almost half of Peru's population. Most Native Americans living in Peru are Quechua. Another third of Peru's people are mestizo. The remaining Peruvians are of European, African, and Asian descent. Even though Native Americans are such a large part of the population of Peru, until recently many of them have remained isolated from the modern world.

✔ **Reading Check** Which two groups make up the majority of Peruvians?

Life in the Altiplano

Many Quechuas, Uros, and other Native Americans living on the Altiplano follow traditions that are hundreds of years old. Their communities, however, are slowly changing. Thousands of Native Americans have left for jobs in the city. And life is changing even for those who stay in their villages.

Old and New The past is constantly present in the Altiplano. The ruins of Incan cities, such as Machu Picchu, are found in the countryside. Even in modern cities, the old mixes with the new. Most city dwellers in the Altiplano have electricity. The streets are paved, and there are telephones. But there are also remnants of the past. In Cuzco, for example, parts of the old Incan wall that once surrounded the city are still standing. Modern houses are made of adobe and have red tile roofs, but their foundations are the remains of Incan stonework. There are also buildings constructed by the Spanish colonists.

Lost City of the Incas
The ruins of Machu Picchu were "discovered" in 1911 when a local guide led American scholars to the site. It has stone buildings, walkways, and staircases, as well as agricultural terraces that were once watered by an aqueduct. **Conclude** *How did the Incan builders adapt their city to the mountain site?*

A Day in a Quechua Village Village life is very different from city life. In the isolated towns of the Altiplano, there are no telephones. Few buses drive through the villages. Most people are Quechua or Aymara.

Like their Incan ancestors, many Quechua rely on raising animals for their wool. The Incas tamed wild llamas and alpacas, and then they raised them to use as pack animals and as a source of wool. Today, many Quechua families keep sheep instead. Sheep are not native to the region but were brought to the Americas by European settlers.

Modesto Mamani (moh DES toh MUH mahn ee) is a 13-year-old Quechua boy. He wakes before dawn to the freezing mountain air and eats breakfast as soon as the sun comes up. Breakfast is always the same: a few rolls, coffee with sugar, and whole wheat kernels that can be eaten like popcorn. His only other meal may be lunch. It is usually potato and barley soup with *chunos*—freeze-dried potato skins.

On some days, Modesto spends much of his time working in the field with his father and brothers. On other days, he looks after the sheep or goes with his mother to the market. Even with school and chores, Modesto finds time to play soccer on the tundra in back of his house.

Like many other children who live in Altiplano villages, Modesto's life mixes the modern and the traditional. He wants to study to become an engineer so he can bring technology to the Altiplano. Meanwhile, much of his time revolves around the sheep his family raises. Not only does Modesto tend the sheep, he also uses their wool to knit sweaters.

School, Work, and Play
Modesto attends school—with his soccer ball! (left), and shows off one of his family's sheep (right). **Infer** *Why do you think people raise sheep in the region seen in the photo?*

Identify Contrasts
Target Skill What are two ways that life in a Quechua village differs from life in Cuzco?

Modern Suspension Bridge
Tourists stand on a modern suspension bridge that is based on a design developed by the Incas. **Analyze** *How does this type of bridge suit its environment?*

Geography and Culture You have seen how the Uros adapted to their environment by living on islands they create themselves, much as their ancestors did. But they are also modern people who play soccer. In another part of the Altiplano, Quechua families raise sheep, animals that are suited to the tundra. But their children learn about technology in school.

Long ago, the Incas solved a problem of their mountain environment: how to cross the deep gorges between mountain peaks. They invented suspension bridges. Modern versions of these bridges are still used in the Andes today. They are one more example of how geography and the past influence the present in Peru.

✓ **Reading Check** Explain how one group of Peruvians has adapted to their environment.

Section 2 Assessment

Key Terms
Review the key terms at the beginning of this section. Use each term in a sentence that explains its meaning.

Target Reading Skills
How are the three geographic regions of Peru different?

Comprehension and Critical Thinking
1. (a) Describe What are the three regions of Peru, and what are they like?

(b) Identify Cause and Effect Why is the coastal plain the economic center of Peru?
2. (a) Describe How does Cuzco represent both old and new?
(b) Compare How is life for the Quechua similar to and different from life for the Uros?
(c) Predict Do you think the Uros and Quechua will preserve their traditional ways of life in this century? Explain.

Writing Activity
Write a letter that Modesto might send to a friend in Cuzco, inviting the friend to visit him in his village. Have Modesto describe what his friend might see and do on his visit.

For: An activity on Peru
Visit: PHSchool.com
Web Code: lfd-1602

Chile
Land of Contrasts

Prepare to Read

Objectives

In this section you will
1. Find out how the geography of Chile creates regions where people live very differently.
2. Learn how Chile's people live and what products they produce.
3. Find out how Chile restored democracy.

Taking Notes

As you read this section, look for the main ideas and details and how they relate to each other. Use the format below to create an outline of the section.

> I. The geography of Chile
>   A. The longest, narrowest country
>   1. Only 100 miles wide
>   2.

🎯 Target Reading Skill

Compare and Contrast One way to understand regions is to compare and contrast them, or identify similarities and differences. When you compare, you look at similarities between things. When you contrast, you look at differences. As you read this section, compare and contrast the geographic regions and lifestyles of Chile.

Key Terms

- **Ferdinand Magellan** (FUR duh nand muh JEL un) *n.* Portuguese explorer sailing for Spain, whose expedition first circumnavigated the globe
- **circumnavigate** (sur kum NAV ih gayt) *v.* to sail or fly all the way around something, such as Earth
- **glacier** (GLAY shur) *n.* a large, slow-moving mass of ice and snow
- **Augusto Pinochet Ugarte** (ah GOO stoh pea noh SHAY oo gahr TAY) *n.* military dictator of Chile from 1973 to 1988

When Ferdinand Magellan first saw the Pacific Ocean in 1520, tears ran down his cheeks. **Ferdinand Magellan was a Portuguese explorer sailing for Spain.** He was searching for a way around or through the Americas. Ever since Christopher Columbus had failed to find a westward sea route all the way to Asia, explorers had been looking for one. But the continents of North and South America were in the way.

Magellan sailed from Spain in 1519 and worked his way south along the coast of South America. Bad weather forced him to spend the winter on the stormy southern coast. His crew threatened to rebel, but Magellan kept exploring. Finally, he found a way through the islands at the "bottom" of South America. His ships sailed through this narrow, dangerous passage to the Pacific Ocean. Magellan wept when he realized his great accomplishment. He knew that now he could sail to Asia—and all the way around the world.

The passage that Magellan discovered is in present-day Chile. It allowed European sailors to explore the western coast of South America.

Magellan's ship nears the strait that bears his name.

Chile

Chile produces more copper than any other country in the world. To avoid relying too much on one resource, however, the government of Chile has encouraged agriculture and new industry. The United States is Chile's largest trade partner. About 18 percent of Chile's exports are sold to the United States. Today, Chile's economy is seen as strong and stable. Study the map and charts. Think about how Chile's location and resources have affected its economy.

Chile: Products and Resources

KEY

- Copper
- Petroleum
- Manufacturing
- Fruits
- Fish
- — National border
- ⊛ National capital
- • Other city

0 miles 800
0 kilometers 800
Lambert Azimuthal Equal Area

Average Annual Income per Citizen

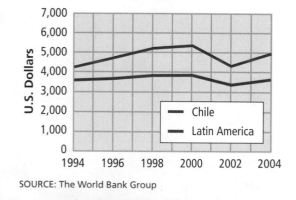

SOURCE: The World Bank Group

Chile's Exports

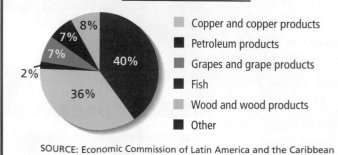

- Copper and copper products — 40%
- Petroleum products
- Grapes and grape products
- Fish
- Wood and wood products
- Other

8%, 7%, 7%, 2%, 36%

SOURCE: Economic Commission of Latin America and the Caribbean

Map and Chart Skills

1. **Locate** Where are Chile's mineral resources found?
2. **Identify** Which economic resources are found in most parts of the country?
3. **Compare** How do Chile's agricultural and seafood exports compare to its copper exports?
4. **Analyze Information** What do you learn about Chile's economy from the line graph?
5. **Draw Conclusions** Do you think Chile has been successful in using its resources to create a diversified economy? Explain your answer.

Go Online
PHSchool.com
Use Web Code lfe-1613 for **DK World Desk Reference Online.**

The Geography of Chile

The passage that Magellan discovered is now named after him. Find the Strait of Magellan on the map of Chile in the Country Profile. It is a major sea lane to this day. Although it is dangerous to sail through, the Strait of Magellan is safer than going all the way around Cape Horn to the south. Many ships have been lost in the Strait's stormy waters. While Magellan was lucky to get through the Strait, he was not lucky enough to return to Spain. He died during the voyage. Of the five ships that started Magellan's expedition, only one returned all the way to Spain. But it was the first ship to **circumnavigate,** or go all the way around, the globe.

The Longest, Narrowest Country Look at the map titled Physical Latin America on page 4. Find the Andes Mountains. They run down the whole length of Chile like a giant spine. Chile is narrow and shaped like a string bean. On average, it is only about 100 miles (161 kilometers) wide, but it is extremely long. It runs 2,650 miles (4,265 kilometers) down the Pacific Coast all the way to the tip of South America. It is the longest, narrowest country in the world.

The Driest Place in the World Chile contains an amazing variety of landforms and climates. In the north is the Atacama Desert, the driest region in the world. Not many plants or animals can survive there. But the desert is rich in copper, so the region is dotted with mines. Chile exports more copper than any country in the world.

Compare and Contrast How is sailing through the Strait of Magellan different from sailing around Cape Horn? How is it similar?

A man examines salt formations in the Atacama Desert (above). Magellanic penguins (left) sometimes come ashore near the Strait of Magellan.

Varied Landscapes Chile's long central valley has rolling hills, high grasses, and dense forests. This is the region where most of the people live and where the capital of Chile, Santiago, is located. Both farming and mining are important here. In the southern part of central Chile is the beautiful Lakes Region, with forests, waterfalls, and mountains topped by glaciers. **A glacier** is a huge mass of slowly moving ice and snow. Many of the mountains of this region are volcanoes, and volcanic eruptions and earthquakes occur often in Chile.

The southern third of Chile is cold and wet and often stormy. Far to the south, the Strait of Magellan separates the mainland of Chile from the islands of Tierra del Fuego (tee EHR uh del FWAY goh), which are divided between Chile and Argentina. Tierra del Fuego is Spanish for "Land of Fire." When Magellan sailed past these islands, he saw smoke from the fires of the indigenous people who lived there. Because of the smoke, he called the large island Tierra del Fuego. This region is only about 600 miles (970 kilometers) from Antarctica. Icebergs dot the sea, and penguins come ashore.

✓ **Reading Check** **Describe the central region of Chile.**

Land of Contrasts
Icebergs float away from a glacier off Chile's southern coast (small photo). Below, a waterfall cascades in the central forest region. **Draw Conclusions** *What accounts for this difference in Chile's waterways?*

Chile's People and Products

The lifestyles of Chileans vary from region to region. In the far south, sheep herders in heavy wool sweaters brave the strong winds. Farther north in the central valley, farmers grow wheat, potatoes, sugar beets, corn, tomatoes, and many fruits. In the cities, people in business suits hurry in and out of tall skyscrapers. Few people live in the Atacama Desert of the far north. While mining continues today, there are also ghost towns, or abandoned mining settlements, in the Atacama.

The People of Chile Chile's early Spanish settlers married Native Americans already living there. Today, mestizos make up more than 90 percent of the population. Only about 10 percent of Chileans are Native Americans.

Tonino Fuentes (toh NEE noh FWEN tays) lives in the countryside near Santiago. His family is mestizo. They work on a farm owned by a wealthy man of Spanish descent. Tonino's father trains horses that will appear in rodeos. He is teaching Tonino to be a rodeo rider. But Tonino has other things he must do. Every morning at sunrise, he and his mother milk their two cows. Then Tonino does his homework. That's because his school is in the afternoon, from 2:00 P.M. until 6:00 P.M. In the evening, Tonino often plays soccer with his friends.

Chile's Cities Today, more than 80 percent of Chile's people live in cities. Many rural Chileans have come to Santiago. In this capital city, old Spanish buildings stand near gleaming skyscrapers. The city is in the valley of the central plain, so the altitude is low enough to allow mild weather. The sea makes the air humid. Palm trees grow in the public parks. The snowcapped Andes lie to the east.

Unfortunately, the beautiful sights of Santiago are sometimes blocked by a thick layer of smog. The city is surrounded by mountains on three sides. The mountains trap exhaust from vehicles and smoke from factories in the valley. This is especially true in the winter, when there is not much wind. Pollution has become so bad that it makes many small children and elderly people sick. On a bad day, people wear surgical masks in order to breathe, or they press scarves to their faces.

The Spanish designed many of Chile's cities around a central square. Their buildings could not withstand Chile's earthquakes, however. Few colonial structures remain in Valparaiso, an important port. Chile's second-largest city, Concepción, was moved several miles inland in 1754 to protect it from tsunamis.

Links to
Language Arts

The "Real" Robinson Crusoe Many people have read the adventure story *Robinson Crusoe,* but few have visited the island named for this fictional character. The 1719 novel by Daniel Defoe is about a man named Robinson Crusoe who is stranded on a tropical island. It is based on the true story of Alexander Selkirk. In 1704, Selkirk, a Scottish sailor, quarreled with his captain and asked to be put ashore on one of the Juan Fernández Islands. He lived alone there until he was discovered by an English ship in 1709. Today, these islands are part of Chile. The largest island is named Robinson Crusoe and the second-largest is called Alexander Selkirk. An N. C. Wyeth illustration of the novel is shown below.

Explore Chile's capital, Santiago.

Farming Fuels the Economy
Grapes are harvested (below) and then shipped around the world from ports like this one in Valparaiso (bottom photo). **Identify Effects** *How does farming create jobs for people other than farm workers?*

Chile's Agricultural Revolution When copper prices fell in the 1980s, Chile realized that it must diversify its economy. One way was to sell more crops. By the late 1980s, agriculture had become a billion-dollar industry, providing jobs for about 900,000 Chileans. Chile shipped wheat, potatoes, and other vegetables and fruits around the world.

The United States, Japan, and Europe are especially good markets for Chilean produce. From October through May, it is cold in the Northern Hemisphere but warm in the Southern Hemisphere. Chile provides fruits and vegetables to the United States during the months when American farmers cannot.

Another reason that Chilean produce is welcome in other countries is that Chile's fruits and vegetables are free of many common plant pests. Chile's farming regions are protected by the Andes Mountains, so some of the insect pests and animal diseases that plague other countries never reach Chile. The government wants to make sure that Chilean produce remains this way. Customs inspectors at Chile's airports search baggage carefully. They are checking that no plant or animal matter from foreign places is allowed into the country because it might bring disease to Chile's crops.

✓ **Reading Check** **Why is Chilean produce free of many plant pests?**

Restoring Democracy

Today, Chile has a democratic government. But a dark cloud from its past still hangs over the country. In 1973, the armed forces took control of the government. They were led by General **Augusto Pinochet Ugarte** (ah GOO stoh pea noh SHAY oo gahr TAY), who became a brutal dictator. The Chilean congress could not meet during his rule. Opposition political parties were banned. People who spoke out against the military regime were killed, imprisoned, or "disappeared."

Nevertheless, there were national days of protest. The Catholic Church spoke out against the human rights abuses of the government. In the 1988 elections—even though Pinochet's name was the only one on the ballot—the people of Chile rejected him by voting "no." Democratic government was restored. Pinochet, however, remained an army general.

In 1998, at the age of 82, Pinochet went to London, England, for medical treatment. The government of Spain issued a warrant for his arrest for crimes against humanity. This caused an international crisis. Eventually, Pinochet was declared unfit for trial, and he returned to Chile. Some Chileans wanted him prosecuted; others did not. There is still controversy over bringing to trial those responsible for the abuses of the Pinochet regime.

Anti-Pinochet demonstrators gathered in London when the former dictator was there for medical treatment.

✓ **Reading Check** How did Pinochet's rule end?

Section 3 Assessment

Key Terms
Review the key terms at the beginning of this section. Use each term in a sentence that explains its meaning.

Target Reading Skills
What are two ways that Tonino's life in the countryside is different from life in Santiago?

Comprehension and Critical Thinking
1. (a) Identify Describe Chile's geographic regions.

(b) Identify Cause and Effect How does Chile's geography contribute to its variety of climates and vegetation?

2. (a) Name What kinds of crops are grown in Chile?

(b) Identify Causes Why is Chilean produce so popular in foreign countries?

3. (a) Recall Describe life in Chile when Pinochet was in power.

(b) Evaluate Information Do you think Pinochet should be brought to trial? Explain.

Writing Activity
How do you think Magellan's crew must have felt during their exploration of Tierra del Fuego? Write a journal entry that one of the crew might have written about the experience.

Go Online
PHSchool.com

For: An activity on Chile
Visit: PHSchool.com
Web Code: lfd-1603

Synthesizing Information

When Madelyn returned from Chile, she entertained the class with a wonderful presentation—a map of the route she had taken, a slide show of the Andes Mountains, and a videotape she had made of life in a small village. She had even managed to ask the villagers a couple of questions in Spanish.

When she finished, the class applauded. Her teacher beamed.

"Madelyn, the amount of information you have gathered is stunning," Mr. Rishell said. "Now perhaps you could synthesize all this material for us."

"Sure!" Madelyn replied. Then she paused. "Um . . . how do you synthesize something?"

When you synthesize information, you find the main ideas of several different sources and use them to draw a conclusion. This skill is particularly useful when you are doing research for a report.

Learn the Skill

To synthesize information, follow these steps.

1 **Identify the main idea of each of your sources.** Main ideas are broad, major ideas that are supported by details.

2 **Identify details that support each main idea.** Look in each source for supporting details. Jot them down or create a chart.

3 **Look for connections between pieces of information.** These connections may be similarities, differences, causes, effects, or examples.

4 **Draw conclusions based on the connections you found.** Be sure to use all of your sources.

Peru	
Main Ideas	**Supporting Details**
1. Peru has three distinct geographic regions:	• Coastal Region—Desert and oases
	• Sierra—Mountains
	• Selva—Rain forest
2. Peruvians speak different languages:	•
	•
	•

Practice the Skill

Use the steps on page 186 to synthesize information about Peru. Use these sources: the text under the heading The Regions and People of Peru and the Country Profile of Peru on page 174. Make a table like the one started above.

1 Study the information about Peru in the text as well as in the map and charts in the Country Profile. Add at least two main ideas to the first column of the table.

2 Now write details that support each main idea. You may find details that support one idea in several different sources.

3 Do the main ideas show contrasts or similarities within Peru's geographic regions? Jot down connections.

4 Your main ideas should help you write a one- or two-sentence conclusion that answers a question such as, "What have I learned about the regions of Peru?"

Apply the Skill

Use the steps you have just practiced to synthesize information about Brazil. Select information from text, maps, photographs, captions, and other sources beginning on page 166. Do not try to summarize everything you read about Brazil, but choose a major topic, such as city life.

Brasília, Brazil

Prepare to Read

Objectives

In this section you will
1. Find out how Venezuela was made wealthy by oil.
2. Learn how the ups and downs of oil prices affected the economy and people of Venezuela.
3. Understand how Venezuela is changing.

Taking Notes

As you read this section, look for ways that oil prices affect Venezuela. Copy the cause-and-effect chain below and record your findings in it. Add boxes as needed.

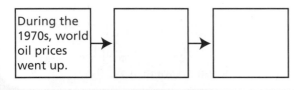

During the 1970s, world oil prices went up. → →

Target Reading Skill

Make Comparisons
Comparing two or more situations enables you to see how they are alike. As you read this section, compare life in Venezuela before and after the oil boom. Consider the economy, the government, and the lives of ordinary people.

Key Terms

- **Caracas** (kuh RAH kus) *n.* the capital of Venezuela
- **boom** (boom) *n.* a period of business growth and prosperity
- **privatization** (pry vuh tih ZAY shun) *n.* the government's sale of land or industries it owns to private businesses or individuals
- **coup** (koo) *n.* the overthrow of a ruler or government by an organized group, which then takes power

Caracas, Venezuela

Welcome to **Caracas** (kuh RAH kus), the capital and largest city of Venezuela. The view from a high-rise apartment building can be breathtaking. At night, thousands of lights dot the surrounding hills. Steep mountains rise in the distance. Now look down at street level. During the day, well-dressed people walk to their jobs in modern office buildings. Others may be going to a museum or to one of the city's public gardens. Later, they may stroll by on their way to dinner or the theater or a concert.

Outside, the air is balmy. It is also clean. Caracas is in a valley that runs from east to west. Winds blow through it. They sweep the exhaust of the city's many cars, buses, and taxis out of Caracas. The subway system also helps by transporting many people who would otherwise have to drive.

Of course, not everyone in Caracas is wealthy and well dressed. The city—and the whole nation of Venezuela—went through a period of rapid growth and prosperity. However, much of the country's population lives in poverty. The contrast between rich and poor has led to political tensions in Venezuela.

A Land Made Wealthy by Oil

Except for the Persian Gulf region, Venezuela has the largest oil reserves in the world. The map of Venezuela in the Country Profile on page 190 shows where Venezuela's vast supplies of oil are located. Venezuela's oil has earned millions of dollars on the world market. In the 1970s, many Venezuelans migrated from the countryside to work for the oil companies. They helped maintain the giant oil rigs in Lake Maracaibo (mar uh KY boh). They also worked in oil refineries.

Both the government and private corporations own oil companies in Venezuela. They have grown rich pumping, processing, and selling oil. In the early 1980s, Venezuela was the richest country in Latin America. Much of the money went to Caracas, the economic center of Venezuela. At that time, there seemed to be no end to the money that could be made in the oil industry.

Ups and Downs of Oil Prices During the 1970s, the price of oil went up. An oil **boom** began. A **boom** is a period of business growth and prosperity. The government spent huge sums of money and hired people to run government agencies and build roads and subways. Many people moved from the countryside to the cities to take these jobs. But from the mid-1980s through the 1990s, oil exporting countries produced more oil than the world needed. The price of oil fell, and many Venezuelans lost their jobs.

This economic downturn continued through the early twenty-first century. In 2002 and 2003, thousands of Venezuelan oil workers went on strike. Oil production and exports came to a standstill. The crisis kept about 200 million barrels of oil and gasoline from the world market. Soon after, oil prices began to rise. By 2004, oil prices were at their highest point in 20 years. They continued to soar into 2006.

Graph Skills

Oil pumped in Venezuela is important not only to that country but also to the United States. **Describe** According to the graph, what is the overall pattern of American imports of Venezuelan oil? **Predict** What do you think might happen to both countries if oil production were interrupted?

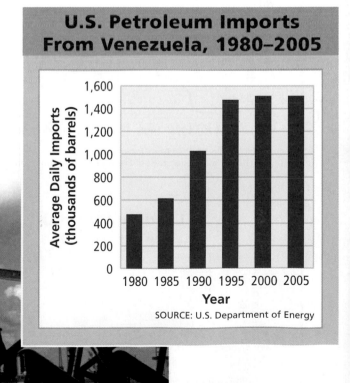

U.S. Petroleum Imports From Venezuela, 1980–2005

Average Daily Imports (thousands of barrels) vs. Year

SOURCE: U.S. Department of Energy

Venezuela

Venezuela's economy is dominated by oil. Much of this oil lies under Lake Maracaibo, but there are also large deposits in the northeastern part of the country and near the Orinoco River. Venezuela also has large amounts of coal, iron ore, and minerals. In addition, Venezuela has large areas of rain forest that have less economic value. As you examine the map and graphs, notice where Venezuela's resources are located. Think about how resources and their location can shape a nation's economy and culture.

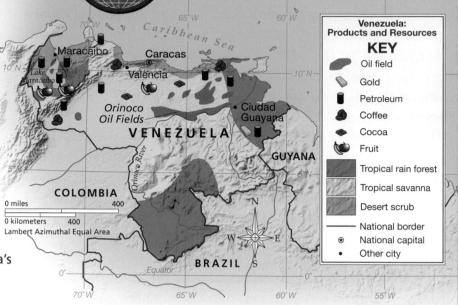

Venezuela: Products and Resources

KEY

- Oil field
- Gold
- Petroleum
- Coffee
- Cocoa
- Fruit
- Tropical rain forest
- Tropical savanna
- Desert scrub
- —— National border
- ⊛ National capital
- • Other city

0 miles 400
0 kilometers 400
Lambert Azimuthal Equal Area

World Crude Oil Prices, 1970–2005

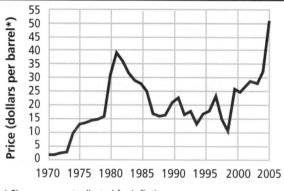

Price (dollars per barrel*)

1970 1975 1980 1985 1990 1995 2000 2005

* Figures are not adjusted for inflation.
SOURCE: U.S. Department of Energy, Energy Information Administration

Leading World Oil Exporters, 2004

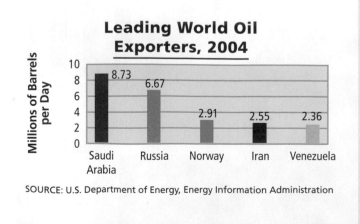

Millions of Barrels per Day

Saudi Arabia	8.73
Russia	6.67
Norway	2.91
Iran	2.55
Venezuela	2.36

SOURCE: U.S. Department of Energy, Energy Information Administration

Venezuela: Earnings from Exports, 2005

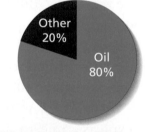

Other 20%
Oil 80%

SOURCE: *CIA World Factbook*

Map and Chart Skills

1. **Describe** What is the pattern of the world price of oil from 1990 to 2005?

2. **Synthesize Information** How do two of the graphs show the importance of oil to Venezuela?

3. **Predict** In what ways could changes in the world price of oil affect Venezuela?

4. **Draw Conclusions** More than 80 percent of Venezuela's people live in cities. Use the information on the map and graphs to explain why Venezuela's cities are located in the north of the country.

Go Online PHSchool.com
Use Web Code lfe-1614 for **DK World Desk Reference Online.**

The New Poverty Despite growing prosperity from high oil prices, poverty remains a major problem in Venezuela. People who came from conditions of poverty in the countryside often moved to areas in the cities that lacked basic services, such as roads, hospitals, and permanent housing. Although the poverty rate began to decline in the early 2000s, it remained well above 30 percent in 2006.

✓ **Reading Check** **Why did many people lose their jobs in the 1980s and 1990s?**

The Economy and the People

During the oil boom, Venezuela changed from a traditional culture based on agriculture to a modern urban country. Now more than 80 percent of the population lives in cities.

Venezuelans and the Oil Economy This change can be seen in the story of Juan Varderi's family. Juan's grandfather raised sheep on a ranch east of Lake Maracaibo. He made a fairly good living selling wool and meat to people in Caracas. But Juan's father left the countryside and went to work on an oil rig that was owned by the government. By the time Juan was born, the family was living in Caracas in a small apartment. His father was making enough money for the family to have a television.

Juan loved living in the city, playing baseball in the street, and watching American television programs. "In the early 1980s, we thought we could live just like rich Americans seemed to live. We didn't understand it was only taking place on TV," Juan says. "We didn't know what was going to happen to us in just a few years."

Make Comparisons Many people moved to the cities to change their situation. How was their situation in the countryside similar to their situation after they moved to the cities?

Play Ball!
Boys enjoying a baseball game in Caracas **Infer** *Why do you think these boys are playing in this empty lot rather than on a baseball field?*

When Juan turned 15, oil prices suddenly fell. Juan's father was one of the many who lost their jobs. And like many other Venezuelan families, Juan's family was in danger of losing their apartment. Things looked bleak for those who had depended on the oil industry for their living.

Government Businesses Go Public In the late 1980s and the 1990s, the government sold some of its businesses to private corporations. **Privatization** (pry vuh tih ZAY shun) occurs when the government sells its industries to individuals or private companies. Under this policy, the government hoped the private companies would make big profits and hire more workers. The companies were able to hire many workers, but employees received less pay than they did when they worked for the government. This is what happened to Juan's father.

The Role of Weather The economic crisis grew in 1999 when Venezuela was hit by massive floods and mudslides. In some areas, unstable shacks were swept away or buried in mud, and many people were killed or made homeless. The destruction was so great that reconstruction and resettling of the homeless went on for years.

✓ **Reading Check** **How did salaries compare before and after privatization?**

Disaster!
In 1999, flooding and landslides caused devastation around Caracas (left), and destroyed much of the town of Macuto (right). **Draw Conclusions** *Explain how a major disaster like this would probably affect a country's economy.*

A Change in Government

In 1998, Hugo Chavez was elected president of Venezuela on a platform to help the poor. Many of his new programs caused deep political divisions between the rich and poor, and Chavez survived many challenges to his presidency. In April 2002, he was forced out of office for two days during a failed **coup** attempt. A **coup** (koo) is the overthrow of a ruler or government by an organized group, which then takes power. In 2002 and 2003, Chavez dealt with protests to his administration and the strike that halted oil production. In August 2004, a referendum, or vote, was called to remove him from office. The referendum failed when 59 percent of voters supported Chavez.

Learn about Simón Bolívar, the liberator of Venezuela.

Supporters and Opponents Many of Chavez's supporters defended the programs that were designed to help people living in poverty. Under the programs, oil revenues began to be used to provide health care, clean water, low cost food, electricity, and other basic services to the country's poor. The government also built new schools and created literacy programs.

Chavez's critics did not agree with many of his government policies, though. They denounced the government's increased military spending and interference in business. People in the international community condemned Chavez's strict control over the media. Many of Chavez's policies damaged the relationship between Venezuela and the United States.

Some Venezuelans support Hugo Chavez (left), while others oppose his government (right).

Recent improvements Chavez faces another presidential election in December 2006. The slow upturn in the economy may help Chavez's chances in the election. Since 2003, the number of people living in poverty has gradually declined. The unemployment rate decreased from 17% in 2004 to 14% in 2005.

Because of the recent spike in oil prices, Venezuela earned $36 billion from its oil industry in 2005-triple the amount received in 1998. Today oil accounts for 80% of Venezuelan exports. Oil prices will probably continue to control Venezuela's economy for some time. Whatever the country's future is, one thing is certain. The oil boom brought Venezuela into the modern world.

✓ **Reading Check** What are some recent signs that Venezuela's economy is improving?

Section 4 Assessment

Key Terms
Review the key terms at the beginning of this section. Use each term in a sentence that explains its meaning.

Target Reading Skills
How were the effects of the fall of oil prices in the 1980s similar to the effects of the torrential rainstorms of 1999?

Comprehension and Critical Thinking
1. (a) Describe How did the government of Venezuela react to the oil boom?

(b) Draw Conclusions Why did the drop in oil prices affect Venezuela so much?

2. (a) Recall What brought many people from the countryside to the cities in the 1970s?

(b) Identify Effects How did the oil boom and then privatization affect oil workers?

3. (a) Sequence How did Hugo Chavez gain power?

(b) Infer Why do you think that most Venezuelans supported Chavez in the 2004 referendum?

Writing Activity
Juan Varderi learned about American families from television programs. Write the first scene of a television script about a Venezuelan family. First choose a time and place for your program, such as the 1970s in Caracas or today in the countryside. Then think about how a family would live in that setting.

> **Writing Tip** List the setting and characters first. Then use the correct form to write dialogue and stage directions.

Review and Assessment

◆ Chapter Summary

Section 1: Brazil

- The geography of Brazil includes rain forests, plateaus, and savannas.
- Rain forests are important to Brazil and affect the whole world, but they face many dangers.
- Most Brazilians live in cities along the coast, but some live on farms and in the rain forest.

Section 2: Peru

- Most Peruvians live in the modern cities of the coastal plain.
- Many Native Americans still lead traditional lives in the mountain and forest regions.
- Old and new ways of life exist side by side in the Altiplano, the high plateau in the Andes Mountains.

Section 3: Chile

- The regions of Chile have distinct types of climate and geography, and people live very differently in each region.
- Although most of Chile's people live in cities, agriculture is very important to Chile's economy.
- Chileans voted out a dictator and replaced his brutal regime with a democratic government.

Section 4: Venezuela

- Oil production made Venezuela rich.
- A decrease in oil prices caused problems for Venezuela's economy and for ordinary people.
- Venezuela's president, Hugo Chavez, has worked against poverty and supported many controversial policies.

Brazil

◆ Key Terms

Define each of the following terms.

1. Altiplano
2. sierra
3. oasis
4. boom
5. savanna
6. coup
7. canopy
8. Brasília
9. circumnavigate
10. privatization
11. Caracas
12. glacier
13. Rio de Janeiro
14. Amazon rain forest

Review and Assessment (continued)

◆ Comprehension and Critical Thinking

15. (a) Describe What are the characteristics of a rain forest?
(b) Apply Information Why is the Amazon rain forest important even to countries far from Brazil?

16. (a) Identify Where do most of Brazil's people live?
(b) Identify Causes Why did the Brazilian government want people to move to the interior of the country?
(c) Analyze Why do you think Brazil's population is distributed the way it is?

17. (a) Identify Describe the three geographical regions of Peru.
(b) Predict How do you think the coming of modern conveniences such as electricity will change life for the indigenous people of Peru? Explain.

18. (a) Summarize Describe Magellan's discovery of the strait that bears his name.
(b) Identify Effects How does Chile's geography contribute to both its pollution problem and its agricultural boom?
(c) Infer How might the fact that Chile is so long and narrow affect Chilean society?

19. (a) Describe How did Venezuela grow rich from oil?
(b) Contrast In what ways have Chile's and Venezuela's economic histories been different?

◆ Skills Practice

Synthesizing Information In the Skills for Life activity in this chapter, you learned how to synthesize information from many sources. You also learned how to use what you found out to draw a conclusion about a particular topic.

Review the steps you followed to learn the skill. Then use those steps to synthesize information about Venezuela's economy from different sources within Section 4. Finally, draw a conclusion that pulls together what you learned.

◆ Writing Activity: Science

Suppose you are a science reporter for a local television station in Santiago, Chile. Santiago has been experiencing a week of very bad smog. Write a report explaining why the smog is so bad this week and suggesting how people might protect themselves from the pollution. Make sure your report can be read in two to three minutes.

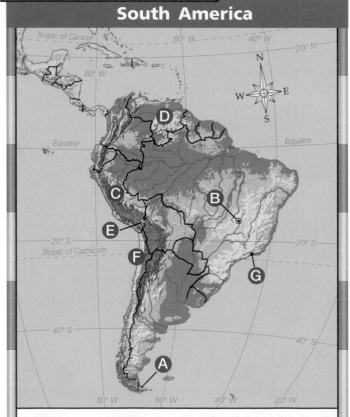

MAP MASTER™
Skills Activity

South America

Place Location For each place listed below, write the letter from the map that shows its location.

1. Peru
2. Brasília
3. Chile
4. Lake Titicaca
5. Tierra del Fuego
6. Venezuela
7. Rio de Janeiro

Go Online
PHSchool.com Use Web Code lfp-1301 for an **interactive map**.

Standardized Test Prep

Test-Taking Tips

Some questions on standardized tests ask you to analyze a reading selection to find the main ideas. Read the passage below. Then follow the tips to answer the sample question.

> Brazil is a major world coffee grower. Brazil's farms and plantations also grow soybeans, wheat, rice, corn, sugar cane, cacao, oranges, and lemons. The country's factories make many goods. Cars, iron, steel, shoes, textiles, and electrical equipment are all important industries.

This paragraph concerns which basic economic question?

   A What goods does Brazil produce?
   B What services does Brazil produce?
   C How are goods and services produced in Brazil?
   D Who will buy these goods and services?

TIP Read the whole passage to understand the main idea. Notice that it lists two kinds of goods from Brazil, those that grow and those made in factories.

Think It Through Notice that three of the answers contain the word *produce* or *produced*. You know that the main idea of the paragraph is that Brazil produces two kinds of goods—crops grown on farms and goods made in factories. The passage does not describe how the goods are produced (answer C) or who buys them (answer D). There is nothing in the paragraph about services (answer B). Therefore the answer is A.

TIP Look for key words in the passage and in the answer choices to help you answer the question. *Grow* and *make* both mean "produce."

Practice Questions

Choose the letter of the best answer.

1. Chilean produce has a large market in the United States from October through May because

   A Americans eat more produce over the winter.
   B less produce is grown in the United States during the winter than in the summer.
   C Chileans do not consume as much of their own produce during those months.
   D it is easiest to transport goods during those months.

2. What caused Venezuela's oil industry to decline in the mid-1980s?

   A The oil fields began to dry up.
   B People weren't driving cars as much.
   C The country began to focus on steel production.
   D World oil prices fell.

Read the passage below and answer the question that follows.

Peru has three distinct geographic regions: the cold, mountainous sierra; the dry coastal plain; and the warm, forested selva. The ways people live in these regions are very different. For example, many people on the coastal plain live in cities, while most people in the sierra live in small villages.

3. Which statement best expresses the main idea of the passage?

   A Peru's geography is varied.
   B Peru's sierra is mountainous and cold.
   C Peru's geography affects the lives of its people.
   D There are no cities in Peru's sierra region.

Go Online
PHSchool.com
Use Web Code lfa-1601
for a **Chapter 6 self-test.**

Projects

Create your own projects to learn more about Latin America. At the beginning of this book, you were introduced to the **Guiding Questions** for studying the chapters and special features. But you can also find answers to these questions by doing projects on your own or with a group. Use the questions to find topics you want to explore further. Then try the projects described on this page or create your own.

1 **Geography** What are the main physical features of Latin America?

2 **History** How has Latin America been shaped by its history?

3 **Culture** What factors have affected cultures in Latin America?

4 **Government** What types of government have existed in Latin America?

5 **Economics** How has geography influenced the ways in which Latin Americans make a living?

Project

RESEARCH LATIN AMERICAN MUSIC

A Latin American Concert
As you study Latin America, find out about the music of each region. Research the kinds of instruments people play and what they are made of. Learn how history and geography influenced the development of different kinds of music. Did you know, for example, that people in the Andes make a kind of rattle out of the hooves of llamas? That reggae developed as political protest? Find some examples of recorded Latin American music in the library, play them for your class, and report on what you learned about the music.

Project

CREATE A CLASS BULLETIN BOARD

Latin America in the News
As you read about Latin America, keep a class bulletin board display called Latin America in the News. Look in magazines and newspapers for articles about Latin American culture and current events. Print out articles from reliable online news sources. Choose a time, such as once a week, for the class to review and discuss the articles. You might have several students present the information to the class as a radio or television news report.

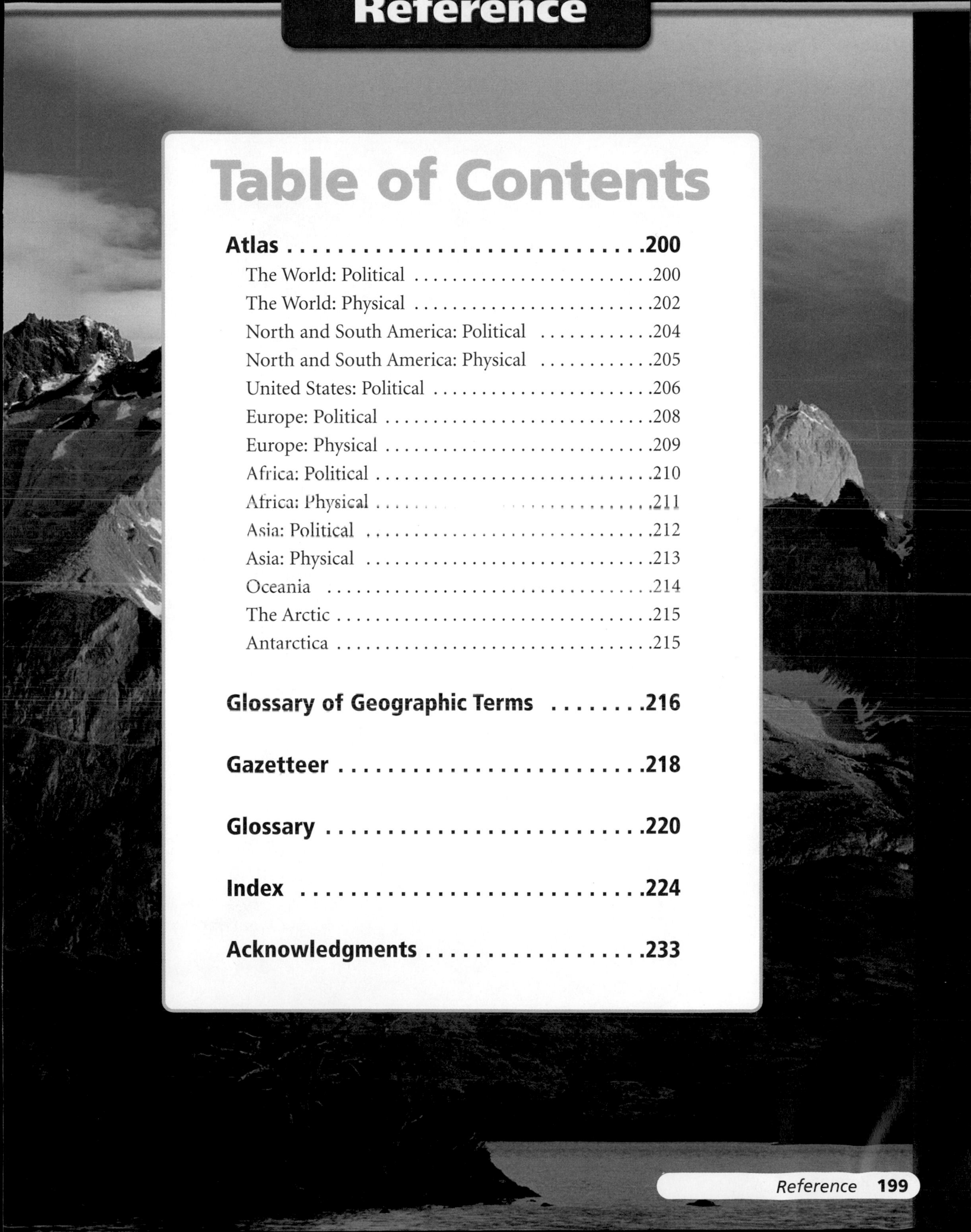

Reference

Table of Contents

The World: Political

ARCTIC OCEAN

RUSSIA

ALASKA
(U.S.)

GREENLAND
(Denmark)

Reykjavík

C A N A D A

NORTH
AMERICA

Ottawa

UNITED STATES

Washington, D.C.

AZORES
(Portugal)

ATLANTIC
OCEAN

MEXICO

Tropic of Cancer

HAWAII (U.S.)

CAPE
VERDE

20° N

Mexico City

Praia

CENTRAL AMERICA
AND THE CARIBBEAN
For detail, see map
North and South
America: Political

Caracas

MARSHALL
ISLANDS
Majuro

K I R I B A T I

NAURU

Tarawa

PALMYRA ATOLL (U.S.)

Equator

GALÁPAGOS ISLANDS
(Ecuador)

VENEZUELA

Georgetown

Bogotá

Paramaribo

COLOMBIA

GUYANA
SURINAME

FRENCH GUIANA
(France)

Quito

ECUADOR

SOUTH
AMERICA

B R A Z I L

TUVALU

SOLOMON
ISLANDS

Honiara

Funafuti

P A C I F I C
O C E A N

PERU

Lima

VANUATU

SAMOA

Port-Vila

FIJI

Apia

AMERICAN
SAMOA
(U.S.)

COOK
ISLANDS
(New Zealand)

FRENCH POLYNESIA
(France)

La Paz

BOLIVIA

Brasília

Suva

NIUE (New Zealand)

Sucre

Nuku'alofa

TONGA

Tropic of Capricorn

PITCAIRN
ISLANDS
(U.K.)

PARAGUAY

Asunción

NEW
CALEDONIA
(France)

CHILE

URUGUAY

NEW
ZEALAND

Santiago

Montevideo

Buenos Aires

40° S

Wellington

A R G E N T I N A

FALKLAND ISLANDS
(U.K.)

SOUTH GEORGIA &
SOUTH SANDWICH ISLANDS
(U.K.)

60° S

S O U T H E R N   O C E A N

Antarctic Circle

ANTARCTICA

0 miles   2,000

0 kilometers   2,000

Robinson

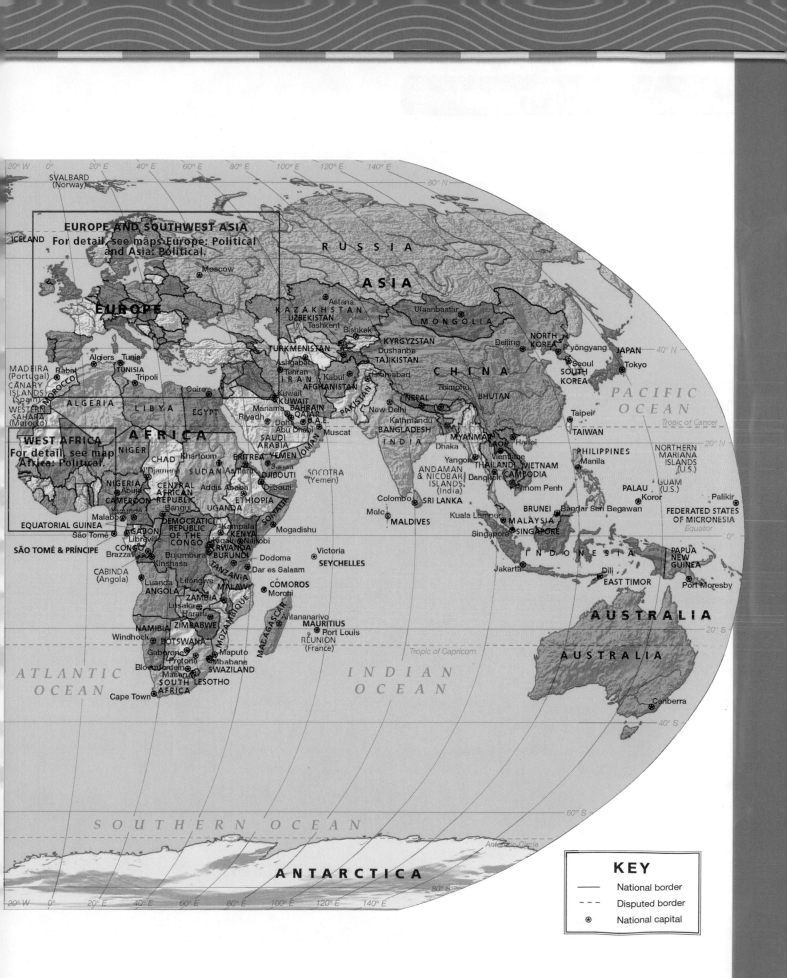

EUROPE AND SOUTHWEST ASIA
For detail, see maps Europe: Political
and Asia: Political.

ICELAND

SVALBARD
(Norway)

RUSSIA

ASIA

EUROPE

Moscow

Astana

KAZAKHSTAN

UZBEKISTAN
Tashkent   Bishkek

Ulaanbaatar

MONGOLIA

Beijing

NORTH
KOREA

Pyŏngyang   JAPAN

TURKMENISTAN   Dushanbe   KYRGYZSTAN
TAJIKISTAN

Seoul   Tokyo
SOUTH
KOREA

Algiers   Tunis

Ashgabat

Tehran   Kabul

Islamabad

CHINA

MADEIRA
(Portugal)
CANARY
ISLANDS
(Spain)

Rabat

TUNISIA
Tripoli

IRAN   AFGHANISTAN

Thimphu

BHUTAN

PACIFIC
OCEAN

MOROCCO

Cairo

Kuwait

NEPAL

Tropic of Cancer

WESTERN
SAHARA
(Morocco)

ALGERIA

LIBYA   EGYPT

KUWAIT
Manama   BAHRAIN
Doha   QATAR
Riyadh   U.A.E.
Abu Dhabi   Muscat

New Delhi
Kathmandu

BANGLADESH

MYANMAR

Taipei

TAIWAN

WEST AFRICA
For detail, see map
Africa: Political.

AFRICA

NIGER   CHAD

SAUDI
ARABIA

OMAN

INDIA

Dhaka

Hanoi

20° N

Khartoum
N'Djamena

ERITREA   YEMEN
Asmara   Sanaa

Yangon   Vientiane

LAOS

VIETNAM

PHILIPPINES

NORTHERN
MARIANA
ISLANDS
(U.S.)

SUDAN

DJIBOUTI
Djibouti

SOCOTRA
(Yemen)

ANDAMAN
& NICOBAR
ISLANDS
(India)

THAILAND
Bangkok

CAMBODIA
Phnom Penh

Manila

PALAU

GUAM
(U.S.)

Palikir

NIGERIA
Abuja
CAMEROON

CENTRAL
AFRICAN
REPUBLIC

Addis Ababa

UGANDA

ETHIOPIA

Colombo

SRI LANKA

BRUNEI
Bandar Seri Begawan

FEDERATED STATES
OF MICRONESIA

EQUATORIAL GUINEA

Malabo

Bangui

SÃO TOMÉ & PRÍNCIPE

São Tomé
Libreville

GABON

DEMOCRATIC
REPUBLIC
OF THE
CONGO

Kampala
Kigali   Nairobi
RWANDA

Mogadishu

Malé

Kuala Lumpur

MALDIVES   Singapore

MALAYSIA
SINGAPORE

Equator

INDONESIA

PAPUA
NEW
GUINEA

CABINDA
(Angola)

CONGO
Brazzaville
Kinshasa

Luanda

ANGOLA

BURUNDI
Bujumbura

TANZANIA

KENYA

Dodoma

Dar es Salaam

Victoria

SEYCHELLES

Jakarta

Dili

EAST TIMOR

Port Moresby

Lilongwe

MALAWI

COMOROS
Moroni

AUSTRALIA

ZAMBIA

MOZAMBIQUE

MADAGASCAR

Antananarivo

MAURITIUS

Lusaka   Harare

AUSTRALIA

NAMIBIA   ZIMBABWE

Windhoek   BOTSWANA

Gaborone   Maputo
Pretoria   Mbabane
SWAZILAND

Port Louis
RÉUNION
(France)

Tropic of Capricorn

20° S

INDIAN
OCEAN

ATLANTIC
OCEAN

Bloemfontein
SOUTH   LESOTHO
AFRICA   Maseru
Cape Town

Canberra

40° S

SOUTHERN   OCEAN

80° S

Antarctic Circle

ANTARCTICA

KEY

—————   National border

- - - - -   Disputed border

⊛   National capital

The World: Physical

ARCTIC OCEAN

Beaufort Sea

Greenland

Baffin Island

Yukon R.

Bering Sea

Mackenzie R.

Hudson Bay

Labrador Sea

Aleutian Islands

ROCKY MOUNTAINS

NORTH AMERICA

CANADIAN SHIELD

GREAT PLAINS

Great Lakes

St. Lawrence R.

Missouri R.

Mississippi R.

APPALACHIAN MTS.

Colorado R.

ATLANTIC OCEAN

Rio Grande

Gulf of Mexico

Tropic of Cancer

Hawaiian Islands

West Indies

Caribbean Sea

MICRONESIA

Galápagos Islands

Orinoco R.

GUIANA HIGHLANDS

Equator

AMAZON BASIN

Amazon R.

SOUTH AMERICA

P O L Y N E S I A

ANDES

PACIFIC OCEAN

BRAZILIAN HIGHLANDS

MELANESIA

N
W   E
S

Tropic of Capricorn

Tasman Sea

North Island

PAMPAS

Rio de la Plata

PATAGONIA

South Island

Cape Horn

Drake Passage

SOUTHERN OCEAN

Antarctic Circle

ANTARCTIC PENINSULA

Ross Sea

Weddell Sea

ANTARCTICA

0 miles   2,000
0 kilometers   2,000
Robinson

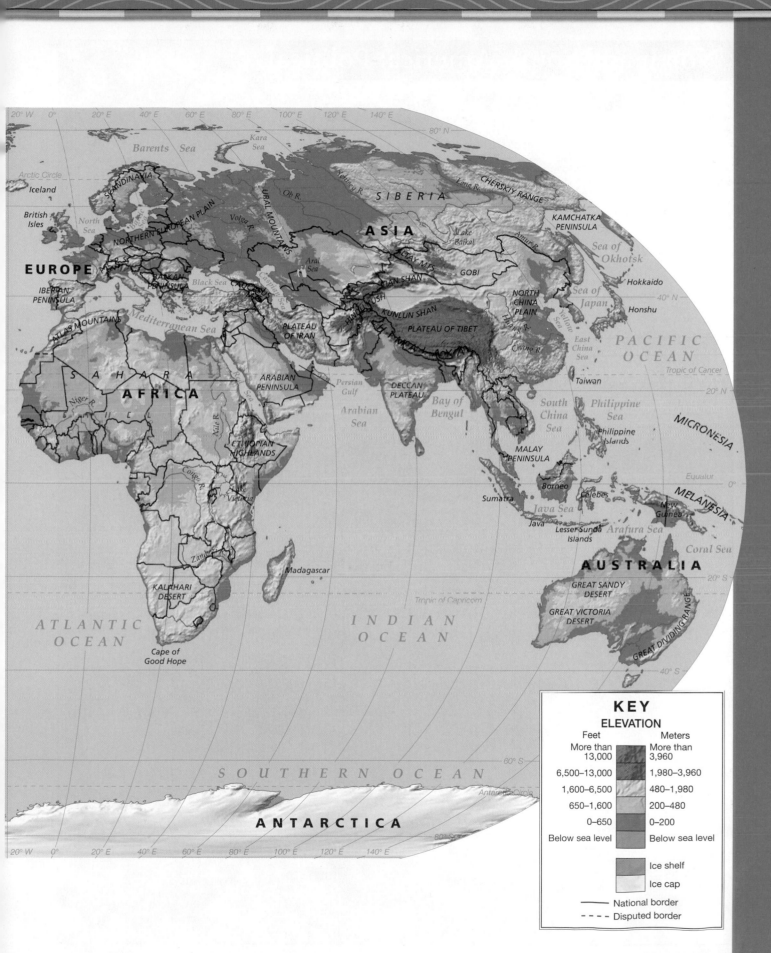

20° W | 0° | 20° E | 40° E | 60° E | 80° E | 100° E | 120° E | 140° E | 80° N

Barents Sea

Kara Sea

Arctic Circle

Iceland

British Isles

North Sea

SCANDINAVIA

Ob R.

Volga R.

URAL MOUNTAINS

Yenisey R.

Lena R.

S I B E R I A

CHERSKIY RANGE

KAMCHATKA PENINSULA

NORTHERN EUROPEAN PLAIN

A S I A

Lake Baikal

Amur R.

Sea of Okhotsk

EUROPE

BALKAN PENINSULA

Black Sea

CAUCASUS MTS.

Aral Sea

Caspian Sea

ALTAY MTS.

TIAN SHAN

GOBI

NORTH CHINA PLAIN

Hokkaido

Sea of Japan

40° N

IBERIAN PENINSULA

HINDU KUSH

KUNLUN SHAN

PLATEAU OF TIBET

Huang R.

Honshu

Yellow Sea

ATLAS MOUNTAINS

Mediterranean Sea

PLATEAU OF IRAN

HIMALAYA

Chang R.

East China Sea

PACIFIC OCEAN

S A H A R A

Red Sea

ARABIAN PENINSULA

Persian Gulf

DECCAN PLATEAU

Tropic of Cancer

A F R I C A

Niger R.

S A H E L

Nile R.

Arabian Sea

Bay of Bengal

Taiwan

20° N

ETHIOPIAN HIGHLANDS

South China Sea

Philippine Sea

MICRONESIA

Philippine Islands

Congo R.

Lake Victoria

MALAY PENINSULA

Equator

0°

Sumatra

Borneo

Celebes

Java Sea

MELANESIA

New Guinea

Zambezi R.

Madagascar

Java

Lesser Sunda Islands

Arafura Sea

Coral Sea

KALAHARI DESERT

AUSTRALIA

20° S

GREAT SANDY DESERT

ATLANTIC OCEAN

GREAT VICTORIA DESERT

Tropic of Capricorn

I N D I A N O C E A N

GREAT DIVIDING RANGE

Cape of Good Hope

40° S

S O U T H E R N   O C E A N

60° S

Antarctic Circle

A N T A R C T I C A

80° S

20° W | 0° | 20° E | 40° E | 60° E | 80° E | 100° E | 120° E | 140° E

KEY

ELEVATION

Feet		Meters
More than 13,000		More than 3,960
6,500–13,000		1,980–3,960
1,600–6,500		480–1,980
650–1,600		200–480
0–650		0–200
Below sea level		Below sea level

Ice shelf

Ice cap

——— National border

- - - - Disputed border

North and South America: Political

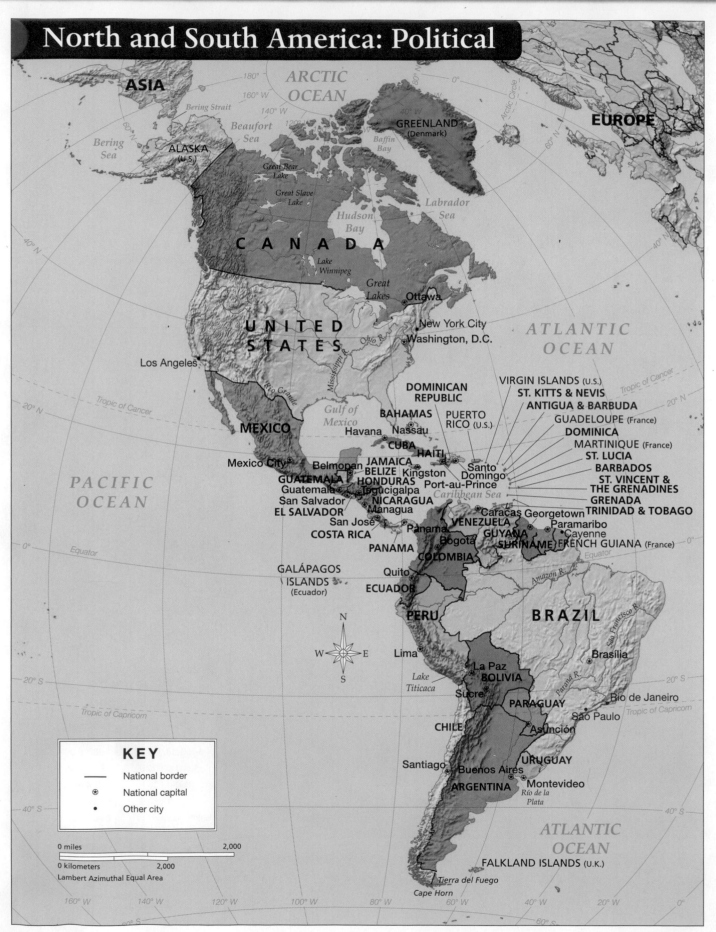

ASIA

ARCTIC OCEAN

EUROPE

Bering Strait

Beaufort Sea

GREENLAND (Denmark)

Bering Sea

ALASKA (U.S.)

Baffin Bay

Great Bear Lake

Great Slave Lake

Labrador Sea

Hudson Bay

C A N A D A

Lake Winnipeg

Great Lakes

Ottawa

U N I T E D S T A T E S

Ohio R.

New York City

Washington, D.C.

ATLANTIC OCEAN

Los Angeles

Rio Grande

Mississippi R.

Tropic of Cancer

DOMINICAN REPUBLIC

VIRGIN ISLANDS (U.S.)

ST. KITTS & NEVIS

ANTIGUA & BARBUDA

Gulf of Mexico

BAHAMAS

PUERTO RICO (U.S.)

GUADELOUPE (France)

MEXICO

Havana Nassau

DOMINICA

CUBA

MARTINIQUE (France)

Mexico City

HAITI

ST. LUCIA

JAMAICA

Belmopan

BELIZE Kingston

Santo Domingo

BARBADOS

GUATEMALA

Guatemala

HONDURAS

Port-au-Prince

ST. VINCENT & THE GRENADINES

Caribbean Sea

Tegucigalpa

GRENADA

San Salvador

NICARAGUA

TRINIDAD & TOBAGO

EL SALVADOR

Managua

San José

Caracas Georgetown

Panama

VENEZUELA

Paramaribo

COSTA RICA

GUYANA

Cayenne

PANAMA

Bogotá

SURINAME

FRENCH GUIANA (France)

COLOMBIA

Equator

PACIFIC OCEAN

GALÁPAGOS ISLANDS (Ecuador)

Quito

Amazon R.

ECUADOR

PERU

B R A Z I L

São Francisco R.

N

W   E

S

Lima

Brasília

La Paz

Lake Titicaca

BOLIVIA

Sucre

Paraná R.

PARAGUAY

Rio de Janeiro

Tropic of Capricorn

São Paulo

CHILE

Asunción

URUGUAY

Santiago Buenos Aires

Montevideo

ARGENTINA

Río de la Plata

ATLANTIC OCEAN

FALKLAND ISLANDS (U.K.)

Tierra del Fuego

Cape Horn

KEY

—— National border

⊛ National capital

• Other city

0 miles   2,000

0 kilometers   2,000

Lambert Azimuthal Equal Area

North and South America: Physical

ASIA

ARCTIC OCEAN

EUROPE

Bering Strait

Bering Sea

Beaufort Sea

Greenland

Mt. McKinley 20,320 ft (6,194 m)

Aleutian Islands

Alaska Range

Gulf of Alaska

Mackenzie R.

Great Bear Lake

Great Slave Lake

Baffin Bay

Davis Strait

Baffin Island

Labrador Sea

Arctic Circle

Hudson Bay

CANADIAN SHIELD

Newfoundland

ROCKY MOUNTAINS

GREAT PLAINS

Lake Winnipeg

Great Lakes

Missouri R.

Appalachian Mts.

Ohio R.

Mississippi R.

California R.

ATLANTIC OCEAN

Tropic of Cancer

Baja California

Sierra Madre Occidental

Sierra Madre Oriental

Río Grande

Gulf of Mexico

Tropic of Cancer

Gulf of California

Yucatán Peninsula

Cuba

Greater Antilles

Hispaniola

Lesser Antilles

PACIFIC OCEAN

Caribbean Sea

Isthmus of Panama

Galápagos Islands

Orinoco R.

Guiana Highlands

Equator

AMAZON BASIN

Amazon R.

ANDES

São Francisco R.

Brazilian Highlands

Lake Titicaca

Gran Chaco

Paraguay R.

Paraná R.

Tropic of Capricorn

Tropic of Capricorn

Aconcagua 22,834 ft (6,960 m)

Pampas

Río de la Plata

Patagonia

ATLANTIC OCEAN

Falkland Islands

Tierra del Fuego

Cape Horn

KEY

ELEVATION

Feet		Meters
More than 13,000		More than 3,960
6,500–13,000		1,980–3,960
1,600–6,500		480–1,980
650–1,600		200–480
0–650		0–200

Ice cap

National border

0 miles 2,000

0 kilometers 2,000

Lambert Azimuthal Equal Area

N
W E
S

United States: Political

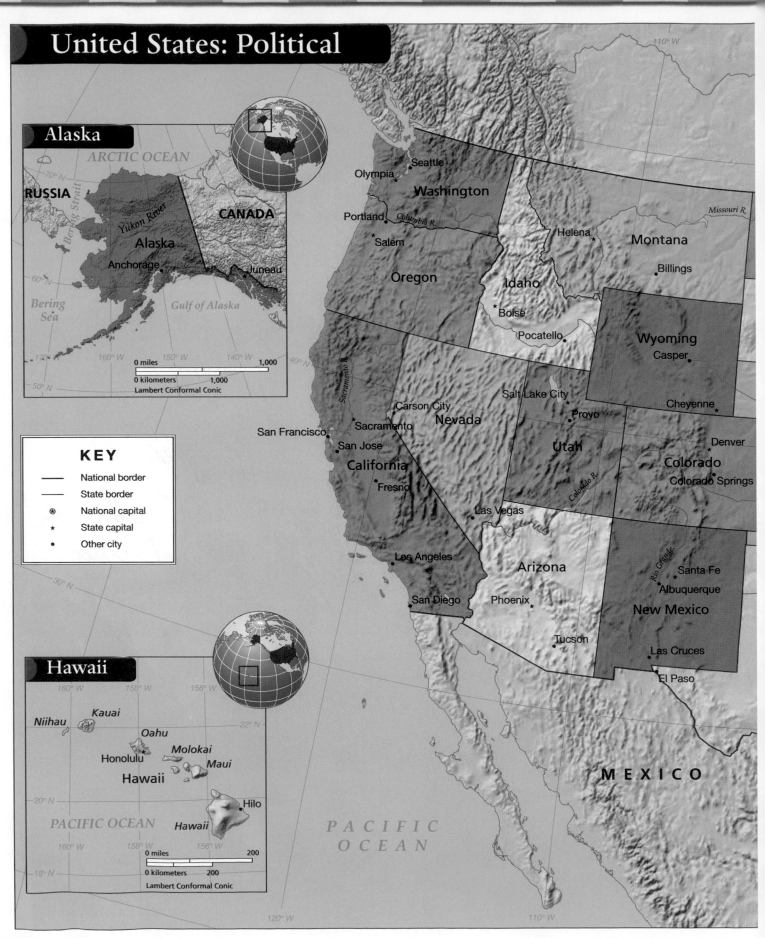

Alaska

ARCTIC OCEAN

RUSSIA

CANADA

Yukon River

Alaska

Anchorage

Juneau

Bering Strait

Bering Sea

Gulf of Alaska

70° N

60° N

50° N

170° W   160° W   150° W   140° W

0 miles   1,000
0 kilometers   1,000

Lambert Conformal Conic

KEY

— National border
— State border
⊗ National capital
★ State capital
• Other city

Hawaii

Niihau

Kauai

Oahu

Honolulu

Molokai

Maui

Hawaii

Hilo

Hawaii

PACIFIC OCEAN

160° W   158° W   156° W

22° N

20° N

18° N

0 miles   200
0 kilometers   200

Lambert Conformal Conic

(Main map labels)

Seattle

Olympia

Washington

Portland

Columbia R.

Salem

Oregon

Helena

Montana

Billings

Idaho

Boise

Pocatello

Wyoming

Casper

Cheyenne

Salt Lake City

Carson City

Provo

Nevada

Denver

Sacramento

Utah

Colorado

San Francisco

San Jose

Colorado Springs

California

Colorado R.

Fresno

Las Vegas

Los Angeles

Arizona

Rio Grande

Santa Fe

Albuquerque

San Diego

Phoenix

New Mexico

Tucson

Las Cruces

El Paso

Sacramento R.

Missouri R.

MEXICO

PACIFIC OCEAN

110° W
120° W
110° W

40° N
30° N

CANADA

North Dakota
Bismarck
Fargo

Minnesota

South Dakota
Pierre
Sioux Falls

Lake Superior

St. Paul
Minneapolis

Wisconsin

Mississippi R.

Milwaukee
Madison

Lake Michigan

Michigan

Grand Rapids
Lansing

Lake Huron

Detroit

Lake Erie

Lake Ontario

Albany

Buffalo

New York

Maine
Augusta

Vermont
Montpelier
Portland

New Hampshire
Concord

Boston
Massachusetts
Providence
Hartford
Rhode Island
Connecticut

New York City

Iowa
Des Moines

Nebraska
Omaha

Lincoln

Missouri R.

Chicago
Cedar Rapids

Illinois

Springfield

Fort Wayne

Indiana

Indianapolis

Ohio

Columbus

Cincinnati

Ohio R.

Pennsylvania

Cleveland   Harrisburg

Pittsburgh

New Jersey
Trenton
Philadelphia

Delaware
Baltimore   Dover
Washington, D.C.   Annapolis
Maryland

Kansas
Topeka

Wichita

Arkansas R.

Kansas City
Jefferson City

St. Louis

Missouri

Louisville

Frankfort

Kentucky

Charleston

West
Virginia   District of Columbia

Richmond

Virginia

Norfolk

Oklahoma
Tulsa

Oklahoma City

Arkansas
Fort Smith
Little Rock

Red R.

Memphis

Mississippi R.

Tennessee
Nashville   Knoxville

Tennessee R.

North Carolina
Raleigh
Charlotte

South Carolina
Columbia

Charleston

ATLANTIC
OCEAN

Texas

Dallas
Fort Worth

Austin

San Antonio

Houston

Shreveport
Louisiana

Baton Rouge

Mississippi

Jackson

Gulfport
New Orleans

Alabama
Birmingham

Montgomery

Mobile

Atlanta

Columbus

Georgia

Tallahassee

Savannah

Jacksonville

Florida

Orlando

Tampa

Miami

Gulf of Mexico

N
W   E
S

0 miles   250
0 kilometers   250
Lambert Azimuthal Equal Area

Europe: Political

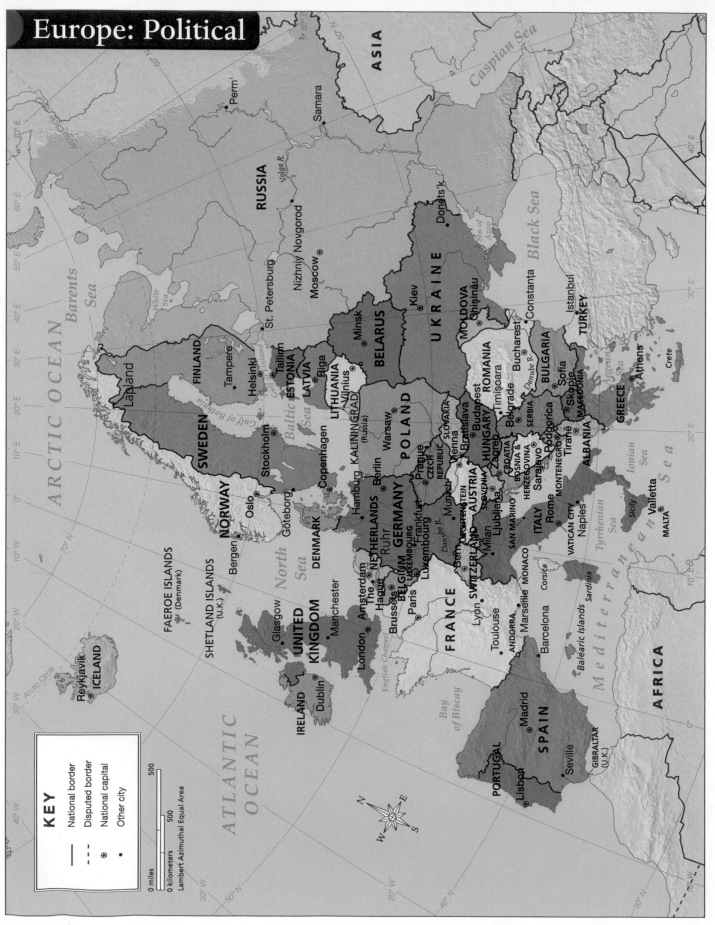

ASIA

Caspian Sea

Perm'

Samara

RUSSIA

Volga R.

Nizhniy Novgorod

Moscow

St. Petersburg

Donets'k

Sea of Azov

Black Sea

Barents Sea

White Sea

Kiev

UKRAINE

MOLDOVA
Chişinău

Constanţa

Istanbul

TURKEY

FINLAND

Tampere

Helsinki

Tallinn

ESTONIA

LATVIA

Riga

LITHUANIA

Vilnius

Minsk

BELARUS

Warsaw

POLAND

ROMANIA

Bucharest

Danube R.

BULGARIA

Sofia

Skopje

MACEDONIA

GREECE

Athens

Aegean Sea

Crete

Lapland

SWEDEN

Stockholm

Göteborg

Gulf of Bothnia

Baltic Sea

Copenhagen

KALININGRAD
(Russia)

Hamburg

Berlin

Prague

CZECH
REPUBLIC

SLOVAKIA

Bratislava

Vienna

Budapest

HUNGARY

Timişoara

Belgrade

SERBIA

Zagreb

CROATIA

BOSNIA &
HERZEGOVINA

Sarajevo

MONTENEGRO

Podgorica

Tiranë

ALBANIA

Ionian Sea

ARCTIC OCEAN

NORWAY

Oslo

Bergen

DENMARK

North Sea

NETHERLANDS

Amsterdam

The Hague

BELGIUM

Brussels

LUXEMBOURG

Luxembourg

Paris

GERMANY

Ruhr

Frankfurt

Munich

LIECHTENSTEIN

Bern

SWITZERLAND

AUSTRIA

SLOVENIA

Ljubljana

Milan

Zagreb

SAN MARINO

ITALY

Rome

VATICAN CITY

Naples

Tyrrhenian Sea

Sicily

Valletta

MALTA

Mediterranean Sea

FAEROE ISLANDS
(Denmark)

SHETLAND ISLANDS
(U.K.)

Glasgow

UNITED
KINGDOM

Manchester

London

Dublin

IRELAND

English Channel

FRANCE

Lyon

Toulouse

Marseille

MONACO

Corsica

Sardinia

Danube R.

Reykjavík

ICELAND

Arctic Circle

ATLANTIC
OCEAN

Bay
of Biscay

ANDORRA

Barcelona

Baléaric Islands

Madrid

SPAIN

Seville

GIBRALTAR
(U.K.)

PORTUGAL

Lisbon

AFRICA

KEY

National border

Disputed border

National capital

Other city

⊛   •

0 miles   500

0 kilometers   500

Lambert Azimuthal Equal Area

N
E
S
W

Europe: Physical

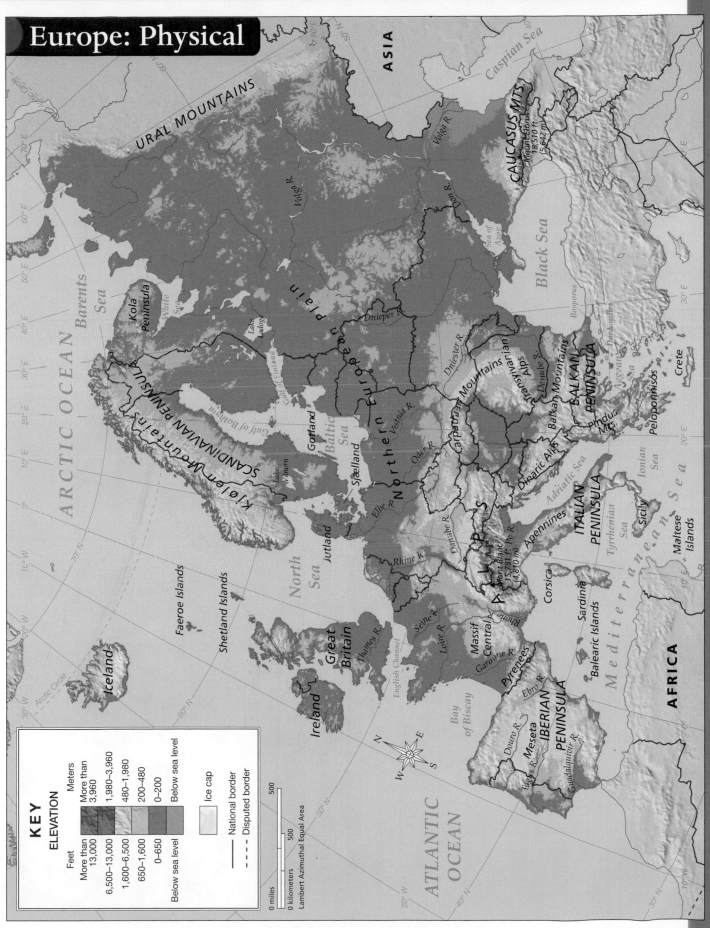

ASIA

URAL MOUNTAINS

Caspian Sea

CAUCASUS MTS.
Mount Elbrus
18,510 ft
(5,642 m)

Volga R.

Don R.

Sea of Azov

Black Sea

Barents Sea

Kola Peninsula

White Sea

Lake Ladoga

Dnieper R.

Dniester R.

Carpathian Mountains

Transylvanian Alps

Danube R.

BALKAN PENINSULA

Bosporus

Dardanelles

ARCTIC OCEAN

Gulf of Finland

European Plain

Northern

Vistula R.

Oder R.

Balkan Mountains

Dinaric Alps

Pindus Mts.

Aegean Sea

Crete

SCANDINAVIAN PENINSULA

Kjølen Mountains

Gulf of Bothnia

Lake Vänern

Gotland

Baltic Sea

Sjælland

Elbe R.

Rhine R.

Danube R.

A L P S

Po R.

Apennines

Adriatic Sea

ITALIAN PENINSULA

Ionian Sea

Tyrrhenian Sea

Sicily

Mediterranean Sea

Maltese Islands

Iceland

Faeroe Islands

Shetland Islands

North Sea

Jutland

Great Britain

Ireland

English Channel

Thames R.

Seine R.

Loire R.

Massif Central

Garonne R.

Bay of Biscay

Pyrenees

Ebro R.

Mont Blanc
15,781 ft
(4,810 m)

Rhône R.

Corsica

Sardinia

Balearic Islands

Arctic Circle

IBERIAN PENINSULA

Douro R.

Meseta

Tagus R.

Guadalquivir R.

AFRICA

ATLANTIC OCEAN

N E S W

KEY

ELEVATION

Feet	Meters
More than 13,000	More than 3,960
6,500–13,000	1,980–3,960
1,600–6,500	480–1,980
650–1,600	200–480
0–650	0–200
Below sea level	Below sea level

Ice cap

—— National border

- - - Disputed border

0 miles 500
0 kilometers 500

Lambert Azimuthal Equal Area

Africa: Political

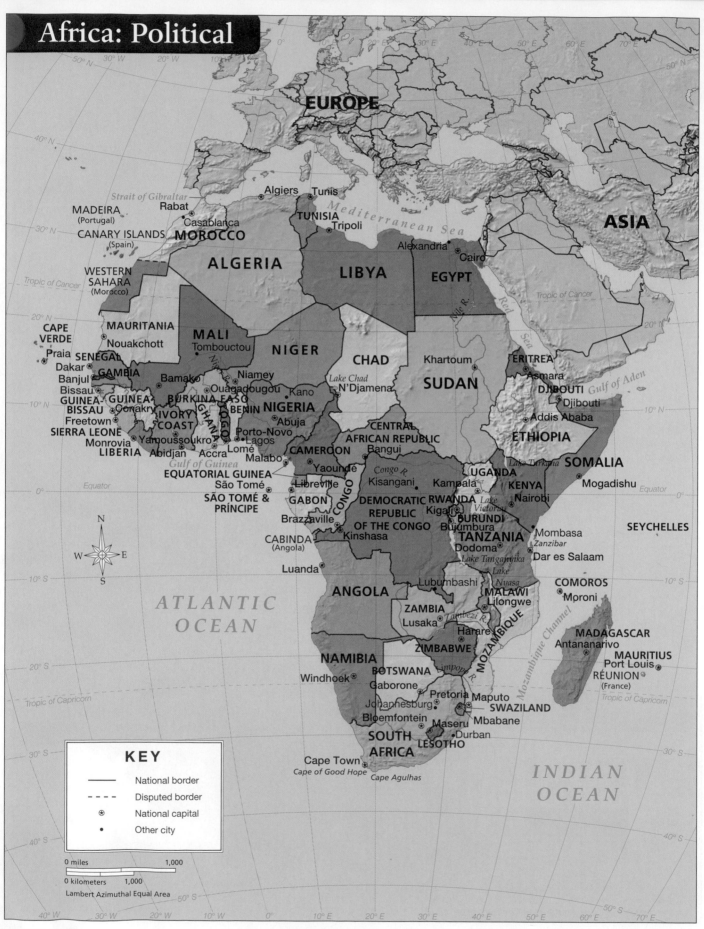

EUROPE

ASIA

Strait of Gibraltar

MADEIRA
(Portugal)
CANARY ISLANDS
(Spain)

Algiers · Tunis
Rabat
TUNISIA
Casablanca
MOROCCO
Tripoli

Mediterranean Sea

Alexandria · Cairo

WESTERN
SAHARA
(Morocco)

Tropic of Cancer

ALGERIA

LIBYA

EGYPT

Nile R.

Tropic of Cancer

Red Sea

CAPE
VERDE
· Praia
Dakar
Banjul
Bissau
GUINEA-
BISSAU
Freetown
SIERRA LEONE
Monrovia
LIBERIA

MAURITANIA
Nouakchott
SENEGAL
GAMBIA
Bamako
GUINEA
Conakry
IVORY
COAST
Yamoussoukro
Abidjan

MALI
Tombouctou

Niger R.

Niamey
Ouagadougou
BURKINA FASO
GHANA
BENIN
TOGO
Accra Lomé

Kano
NIGERIA
Abuja
Porto-Novo
Lagos
CAMEROON

NIGER

CHAD
N'Djamena
Lake Chad

Khartoum

SUDAN

ERITREA
Asmara
DJIBOUTI
Djibouti

Gulf of Aden

CENTRAL
AFRICAN REPUBLIC
Bangui

Addis Ababa

ETHIOPIA

SOMALIA
Mogadishu

EQUATORIAL GUINEA
São Tomé
SÃO TOMÉ &
PRÍNCIPE
GABON
Libreville

Yaounde
Congo R.
Kisangani

CONGO
Brazzaville

CABINDA
(Angola)

DEMOCRATIC
REPUBLIC
OF THE CONGO
Kinshasa

RWANDA
Kigali
BURUNDI
Bujumbura

UGANDA
Kampala
Lake
Victoria

KENYA
Nairobi

Lake Turkana

Equator

SEYCHELLES

TANZANIA
Dodoma

Mombasa
Zanzibar
Dar es Salaam

Lake Tanganyika

Luanda

ATLANTIC
OCEAN

ANGOLA

Lubumbashi

Lake
Nyasa

MALAWI
Lilongwe

COMOROS
Moroni

ZAMBIA
Lusaka

Zambezi R.

MOZAMBIQUE

Mozambique Channel

MADAGASCAR
Antananarivo

MAURITIUS
Port Louis
RÉUNION
(France)

NAMIBIA
Windhoek

BOTSWANA
Gaborone

Harare
ZIMBABWE

Limpopo R.

Tropic of Capricorn

INDIAN
OCEAN

Pretoria Maputo
Johannesburg
Bloemfontein
Maseru
SOUTH
AFRICA
LESOTHO
Durban

SWAZILAND
Mbabane

Cape Town
Cape of Good Hope
Cape Agulhas

N
W E
S

KEY

——— National border

– – – Disputed border

⊛ National capital

· Other city

0 miles 1,000

0 kilometers 1,000

Lambert Azimuthal Equal Area

Africa: Physical

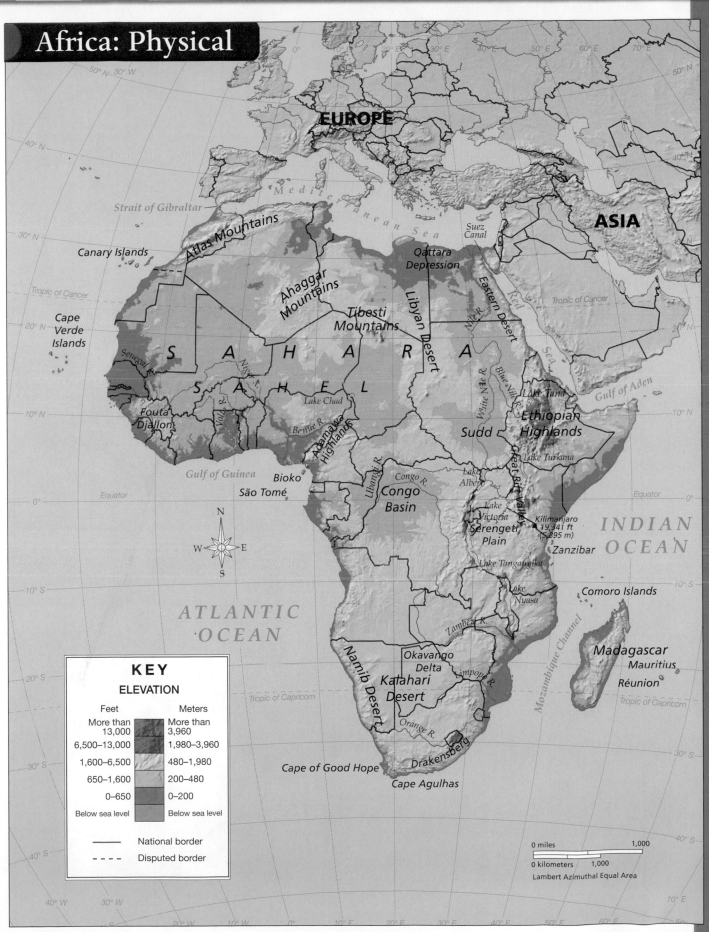

EUROPE

ASIA

Strait of Gibraltar

Mediterranean Sea

Suez Canal

Canary Islands

Atlas Mountains

Qattara Depression

Tropic of Cancer

Cape Verde Islands

SAHARA

Ahaggar Mountains

Tibesti Mountains

Libyan Desert

Eastern Desert

Nile R.

Red Sea

Tropic of Cancer

Senegal R.

SAHEL

Niger R.

Lake Chad

White Nile R.

Blue Nile R.

Lake Tana

Gulf of Aden

Fouta Djallon

Volta R.

Benue R.

Adamawa Highlands

Ethiopian Highlands

Sudd

Lake Turkana

Gulf of Guinea

Bioko

São Tomé

Ubangi R.

Congo R.

Congo Basin

Lake Albert

Great Rift Valley

Equator

Lake Victoria

Serengeti Plain

Kilimanjaro 19,341 ft (5,895 m)

Zanzibar

Equator

INDIAN OCEAN

Lake Tanganyika

ATLANTIC OCEAN

Lake Nyasa

Comoro Islands

Zambezi R.

Mozambique Channel

Madagascar

Namib Desert

Okavango Delta

Kalahari Desert

Limpopo R.

Mauritius

Réunion

Tropic of Capricorn

Tropic of Capricorn

Orange R.

Cape of Good Hope

Drakensberg

Cape Agulhas

N W E S

KEY
ELEVATION

Feet		Meters
More than 13,000		More than 3,960
6,500–13,000		1,980–3,960
1,600–6,500		480–1,980
650–1,600		200–480
0–650		0–200
Below sea level		Below sea level

——— National border

- - - Disputed border

0 miles 1,000

0 kilometers 1,000

Lambert Azimuthal Equal Area

Asia: Political

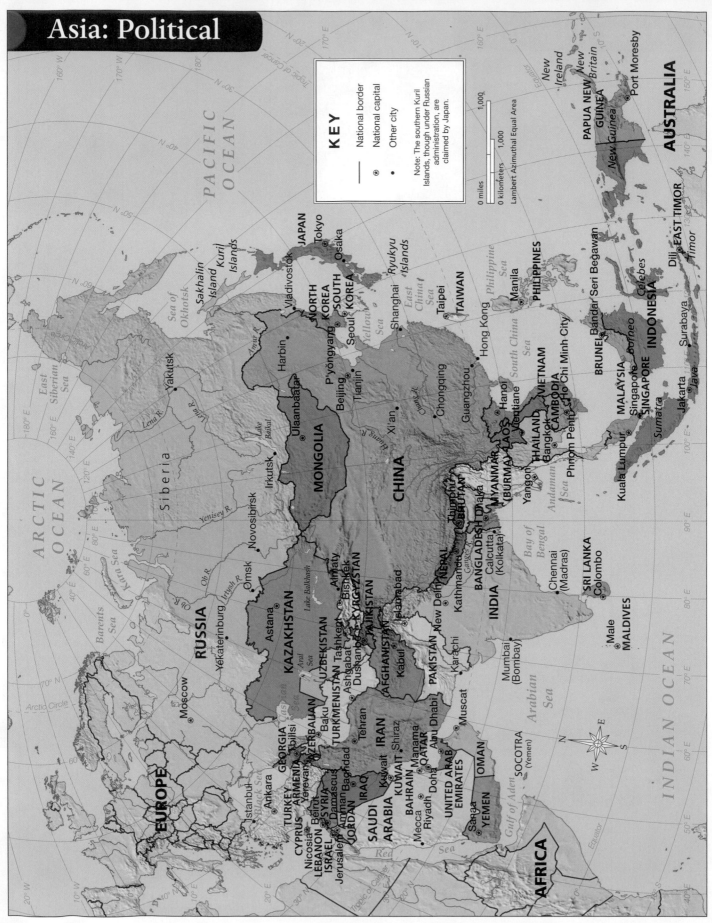

KEY

— National border
⊛ National capital
• Other city

Note: The southern Kuril Islands, though under Russian administration, are claimed by Japan.

0 miles 1,000
0 kilometers 1,000
Lambert Azimuthal Equal Area

PACIFIC OCEAN

ARCTIC OCEAN

East Siberian Sea

Sea of Okhotsk

Sakhalin Island

Kuril Islands

JAPAN
Tokyo
Vladivostok
Osaka

Ryukyu Islands

NORTH KOREA
P'yŏngyang
SOUTH KOREA
Seoul

Shanghai
East China Sea

TAIWAN
Taipei

Hong Kong

Philippine Sea

PHILIPPINES
Manila

Harbin
Ulaanbaatar
MONGOLIA

Beijing
Tianjin

CHINA

Xi'an
Chongqing
Guangzhou

Chang R.
Huang R.

VIETNAM
Hanoi
Vientiane
LAOS
THAILAND
Bangkok
CAMBODIA
Phnom Penh
Ho Chi Minh City

MYANMAR (BURMA)
Yangon

South China Sea

BRUNEI
Bandar Seri Begawan
Borneo
MALAYSIA
Kuala Lumpur
SINGAPORE
Singapore
INDONESIA
Sumatra
Jakarta
Java
Surabaya
Celebes

EAST TIMOR
Dili
Timor

PAPUA NEW GUINEA
New Guinea
New Britain
New Ireland
Port Moresby

AUSTRALIA

Siberia

Yakutsk

Irkutsk
Lake Baikal

Amur R.
Lena R.
Vilyui R.

Novosibirsk
Omsk

Yenisey R.
Ob R.
Irtysh R.

RUSSIA

Yekaterinburg

Moscow

Astana

KAZAKHSTAN

Aral Sea
Lake Balkhash

Almaty
Bishkek
KYRGYZSTAN
Tashkent
UZBEKISTAN
TAJIKISTAN
Dushanbe
TURKMENISTAN
Ashgabat

AFGHANISTAN
Kabul
Islamabad
PAKISTAN
Karachi

NEPAL
New Delhi
Kathmandu
BHUTAN
Thimphu
BANGLADESH
Dhaka
Calcutta (Kolkata)

INDIA

Mumbai (Bombay)

Chennai (Madras)

Bay of Bengal

SRI LANKA
Colombo

Male
MALDIVES

Andaman Sea

Arabian Sea

INDIAN OCEAN

Caspian Sea

GEORGIA
Tbilisi
ARMENIA
Yerevan
AZERBAIJAN
Baku

Tehran
IRAN
Shiraz

TURKEY
Ankara
Istanbul
Black Sea
CYPRUS
Nicosia
LEBANON
Beirut
SYRIA
Damascus
ISRAEL
Jerusalem
Amman
JORDAN
Baghdad
IRAQ
Kuwait
KUWAIT
BAHRAIN
Manama
QATAR
Doha
Riyadh
Abu Dhabi
UNITED ARAB EMIRATES

SAUDI ARABIA

Mecca

Muscat
OMAN

YEMEN
Sana
Aden

SOCOTRA (Yemen)

Gulf of Aden

Red Sea

EUROPE

AFRICA

Barents Sea
Kara Sea

Arctic Circle

Tropic of Cancer

Equator

Tropic of Capricorn

Asia: Physical

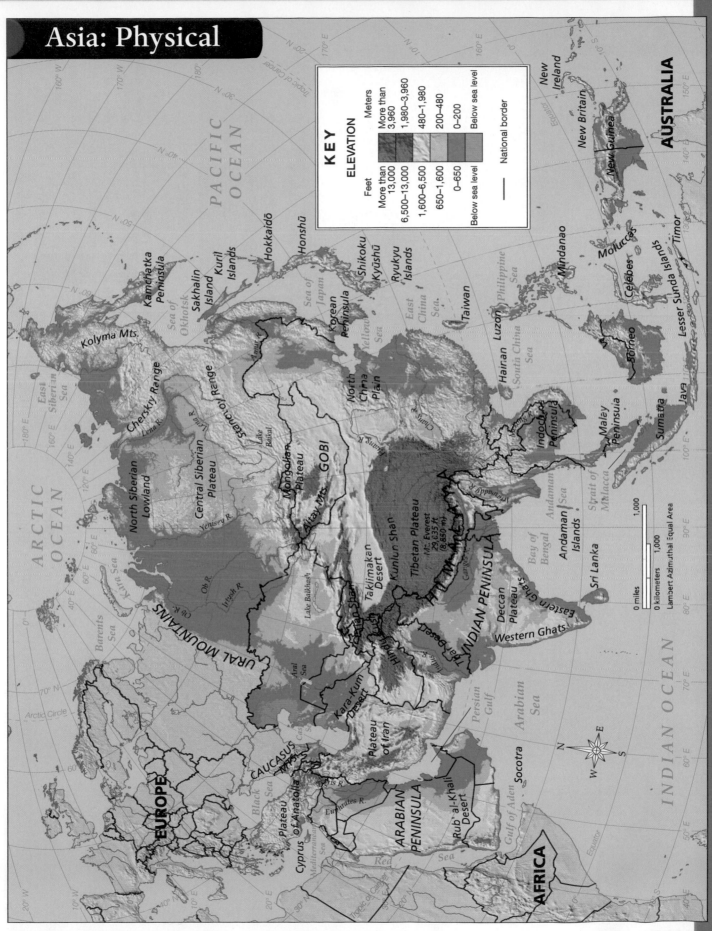

KEY

ELEVATION

Feet	Meters
More than 13,000	More than 3,960
6,500–13,000	1,980–3,960
1,600–6,500	480–1,980
650–1,600	200–480
0–650	0–200
Below sea level	Below sea level

—— National border

ARCTIC OCEAN

PACIFIC OCEAN

INDIAN OCEAN

EUROPE

AFRICA

AUSTRALIA

Barents Sea

Kara Sea

East Siberian Sea

Arctic Circle

Kolyma Mts.

Sea of Okhotsk

Kamchatka Peninsula

Sakhalin Island

Kuril Islands

Hokkaidō

Honshū

Sea of Japan

Shikoku

Kyūshū

Ryukyu Islands

Korean Peninsula

Yellow Sea

East China Sea

Taiwan

Philippine Sea

Luzon

Mindanao

New Ireland

New Britain

New Guinea

Moluccas

Celebes

Borneo

Lesser Sunda Islands

Timor

Java

Sumatra

Malay Peninsula

Strait of Malacca

South China Sea

Hainan

Cherskiy Range

Lena R.

Stanovoy Range

Amur R.

North Siberian Lowland

Central Siberian Plateau

Yenisey R.

Lake Baikal

Mongolian Plateau

Altay Mts.

GOBI

North China Plain

Chang R.

Huang R.

Mekong R.

Indochina Peninsula

Irrawaddy R.

Andaman Sea

Andaman Islands

Bay of Bengal

Sri Lanka

Eastern Ghats

Western Ghats

Deccan Plateau

INDIAN PENINSULA

Ganges R.

Indus R.

Thar Desert

HIMALAYAS

Mt. Everest 29,035 ft (8,850 m)

Tibetan Plateau

Kunlun Shan

Taklimakan Desert

Tian Shan

Hindu Kush

Ural R.

Lake Balkhash

Aral Sea

Ob R.

Irtysh R.

URAL MOUNTAINS

Kara-Kum Desert

Caspian Sea

Plateau of Iran

CAUCASUS MTS.

Plateau of Anatolia

Cyprus

Mediterranean Sea

Black Sea

Tigris R.

Euphrates R.

ARABIAN PENINSULA

Rub' al-Khali Desert

Persian Gulf

Arabian Sea

Gulf of Aden

Socotra

Red Sea

Tropic of Cancer

Tropic of Cancer

Equator

Equator

0 miles 1,000

0 kilometers 1,000

Lambert Azimuthal Equal Area

Oceania

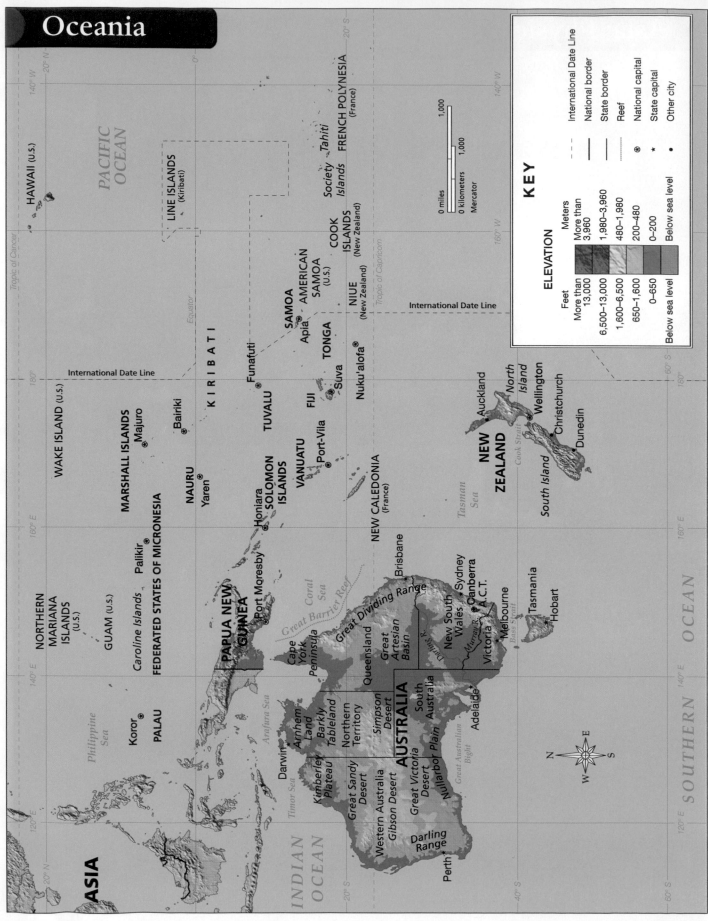

KEY

ELEVATION

Feet	Meters
More than 13,000	More than 3,960
6,500–13,000	1,980–3,960
1,600–6,500	480–1,980
650–1,600	200–480
0–650	0–200
Below sea level	Below sea level

- – – – International Date Line
- ——— National border
- State border
- ········ Reef
- ⊛ National capital
- ★ State capital
- • Other city

Mercator

0 miles 1,000
0 kilometers 1,000

Map labels

ASIA

PACIFIC OCEAN

HAWAII (U.S.)

Tropic of Cancer

LINE ISLANDS (Kiribati)

NORTHERN MARIANA ISLANDS (U.S.)

GUAM (U.S.)

WAKE ISLAND (U.S.)

MARSHALL ISLANDS
Majuro ⊛

Caroline Islands Palikir ⊛
FEDERATED STATES OF MICRONESIA

Koror ⊛
PALAU

Philippine Sea

International Date Line

K I R I B A T I

Bairiki ⊛

NAURU
Yaren ⊛

Equator

FRENCH POLYNESIA (France)

Society Islands Tahiti

COOK ISLANDS (New Zealand)

AMERICAN SAMOA (U.S.)

SAMOA
Apia ⊛

NIUE (New Zealand)

TONGA
Nuku'alofa ⊛

Funafuti ⊛
TUVALU

FIJI
Suva ⊛

VANUATU
Port-Vila ⊛

Tropic of Capricorn

International Date Line

SOLOMON ISLANDS
Honiara ⊛

PAPUA NEW GUINEA
Port Moresby ⊛

NEW CALEDONIA (France)

Cape York Peninsula

Great Barrier Reef

Coral Sea

Great Dividing Range

Brisbane

Queensland

Great Artesian Basin

Darwin

Arnhem Land

Barkly Tableland

Kimberley Plateau

Northern Territory

Simpson Desert

Great Sandy Desert

Western Australia

Gibson Desert

Great Victoria Desert

South Australia

Nullarbor Plain

Adelaide ★

Great Australian Bight

AUSTRALIA

New South Wales

Sydney •
Canberra ⊛
A.C.T.

Victoria

Melbourne ★

Murray R.
Darling R.

Bass Strait

Tasmania

Hobart ★

Darling Range

Perth ★

INDIAN OCEAN

Timor Sea

Arafura Sea

Tasman Sea

NEW ZEALAND

North Island

Auckland •

Wellington ⊛

Cook Strait

South Island

Christchurch •

Dunedin •

SOUTHERN OCEAN

N E W S

20° N
20° S
40° S
60° S
20° N

120° E 140° E 160° E 180° 160° W 140° W

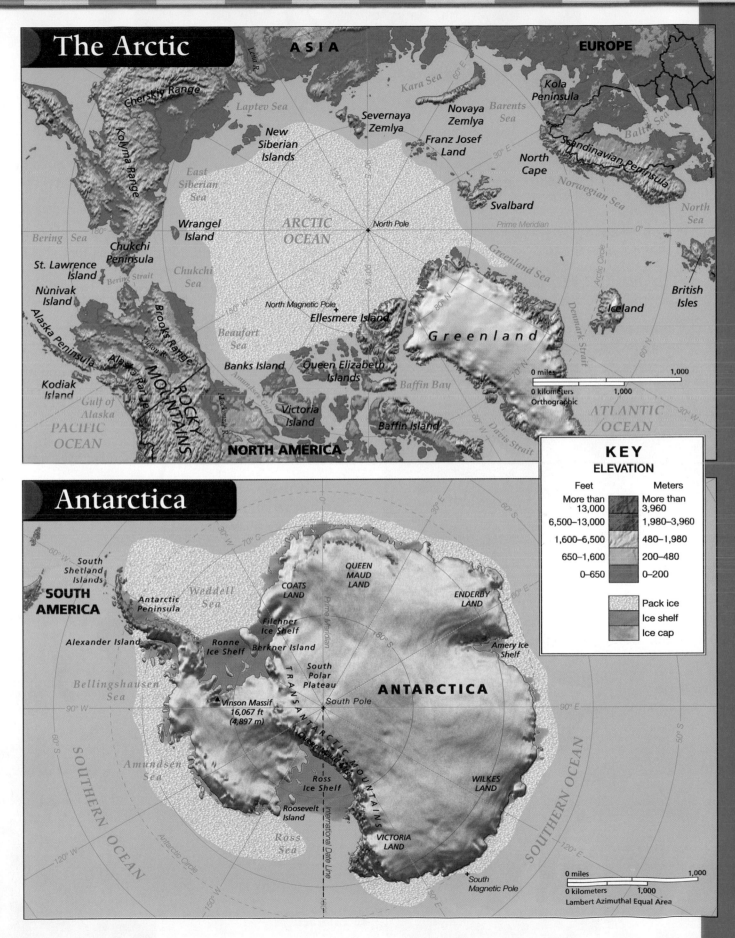

The Arctic

ASIA   EUROPE

Lena R.

Cherskiy Range

Kolyma Range

Laptev Sea

Kara Sea

60° E

Severnaya Zemlya

Novaya Zemlya

Barents Sea

Kola Peninsula

New Siberian Islands

Franz Josef Land

30° E

North Cape

Scandinavian Peninsula

Baltic Sea

East Siberian Sea

90° E

North Sea

Wrangel Island

ARCTIC OCEAN

North Pole

Svalbard

Norwegian Sea

Bering Sea

180°

Prime Meridian

0°

Chukchi Peninsula

Chukchi Sea

Greenland Sea

Arctic Circle

St. Lawrence Island

150° E

North Magnetic Pole

80° N

Greenland

Denmark Strait

60° N

Iceland

British Isles

Nunivak Island

Beaufort Sea

Ellesmere Island

70° N

Brooks Range

Yukon R.

Alaska Peninsula

Alaska Range

ROCKY MOUNTAINS

Banks Island

Amundsen Gulf

Queen Elizabeth Islands

Baffin Bay

30° W

ATLANTIC OCEAN

Kodiak Island

Mackenzie R.

Victoria Island

Baffin Island

Davis Strait

Gulf of Alaska

PACIFIC OCEAN

NORTH AMERICA

0 miles   1,000
0 kilometers   1,000
Orthographic

Antarctica

60° W

South Shetland Islands

30° E

70° W

60° E

SOUTH AMERICA

Antarctic Peninsula

Weddell Sea

COATS LAND

QUEEN MAUD LAND

ENDERBY LAND

60° E

Alexander Island

Filchner Ice Shelf

Ronne Ice Shelf

Berkner Island

Prime Meridian

Amery Ice Shelf

Bellingshausen Sea

TRANSANTARCTIC MOUNTAINS

South Polar Plateau

80° S

ANTARCTICA

90° E

90° W

Vinson Massif 16,067 ft (4,897 m)

South Pole

Amundsen Sea

Ross Ice Shelf

WILKES LAND

Roosevelt Island

International Date Line

SOUTHERN OCEAN

120° W

Ross Sea

VICTORIA LAND

120° E

SOUTHERN OCEAN

Antarctic Circle

150° W

South Magnetic Pole

50° S

0 miles   1,000
0 kilometers   1,000
Lambert Azimuthal Equal Area

KEY
ELEVATION

Feet		Meters
More than 13,000		More than 3,960
6,500–13,000		1,980–3,960
1,600–6,500		480–1,980
650–1,600		200–480
0–650		0–200

Pack ice

Ice shelf

Ice cap

Glossary of Geographic Terms

basin
an area that is lower than surrounding land areas; some basins are filled with water

bay
a body of water that is partly surrounded by land and that is connected to a larger body of water

butte
a small, high, flat-topped landform with cliff-like sides

▲ **butte**

canyon
a deep, narrow valley with steep sides; often with a stream flowing through it

cataract
a large waterfall or steep rapids

delta
a plain at the mouth of a river, often triangular in shape, formed where sediment is deposited by flowing water

flood plain
a broad plain on either side of a river, formed where sediment settles during floods

glacier
a huge, slow-moving mass of snow and ice

hill
an area that rises above surrounding land and has a rounded top; lower and usually less steep than a mountain

island
an area of land completely surrounded by water

isthmus
a narrow strip of land that connects two larger areas of land

mesa
a high, flat-topped landform with cliff-like sides; larger than a butte

mountain
a landform that rises steeply at least 2,000 feet (610 meters) above surrounding land; usually wide at the bottom and rising to a narrow peak or ridge

▶ **glacier**

◀ **cataract**

◀ delta

mountain pass
a gap between mountains

peninsula
an area of land almost completely surrounded by water but connected to the mainland

plain
a large area of flat or gently rolling land

plateau
a large, flat area that rises above the surrounding land; at least one side has a steep slope

river mouth
the point where a river enters a lake or sea

strait
a narrow stretch of water that connects two larger bodies of water

tributary
a river or stream that flows into a larger river

valley
a low stretch of land between mountains or hills; land that is drained by a river

volcano
an opening in Earth's surface through which molten rock, ashes, and gases escape from the interior

▶ **volcano**

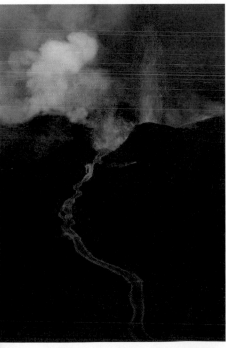

Glossary of Geographic Terms **217**

Gazetteer

A

Amazon rain forest (0° S, 49° W) a large tropical rain forest in the drainage basin of the Amazon River in northern South America, p. 166

Amazon River (0° S, 49° W) the longest river in South America, flowing across Brazil into the Atlantic Ocean, p. 14

Andes Mountains (20° S, 67° W) a mountain system extending along the western coast of South America, p. 13

Argentina (34° S, 64° W) a country in South America, p. 160

Atacama Desert (25° S, 69° W) a desert in Chile, South America, p. 17

B

Bolivia (17° S, 65° W) a country in South America, p. 161

Brasília (15°47' S, 47°55' W) the capital city of Brazil, p. 167

Brazil (10° S, 55° W) the largest country in South America, p. 166

C

Canal Zone (9° N, 80° W) a 10-mile wide strip of land along the Panama Canal, stretching from the Atlantic Ocean to the Pacific Ocean, once governed by the United States, p. 120

Caracas (10°30' N, 66°56' W) the capital city of Venezuela, p.188

Caribbean Sea (15° N, 73° W) a sea bounded by the West Indies, Central America, and South America; part of the Atlantic Ocean, p. 12

Central America (11° N, 80° W) the part of Latin America south of Mexico and north of South America; it includes the seven republics of Guatemala, Honduras, El Salvador, Nicaragua, Costa Rica, Panama, and Belize, p. 12

Chile (30° S, 71° W) a country in South America, p. 179

Colombia (4° N, 72° W) a country in South America, p. 162

Cuba (21° N, 80° W) an island country, the largest of the Caribbean islands, p. 134

Cuzco (13°31' S, 71°59' W) a city in Peru; capital of the Incan empire, p. 46

E

El Salvador (13° N, 88° W) a country in Central America, p. 99

G

Guatemala (15° N, 90° W) a country in Central America, p. 109

H

Haiti (19° N, 72° W) a country in the Caribbean Sea, on the island of Hispaniola, p. 142

Hispaniola (19° N, 71° W) an island in the Caribbean Sea, divided between Haiti in the west and the Dominican Republic in the east, p. 84

I

Isthmus of Panama (9° N, 79° W) the narrow strip of land in Panama that separates the Atlantic Ocean and the Pacific Ocean, p. 116

J

Jamaica (18° N, 77° W) an island country in the Caribbean Sea, p. 131

L

Lake Titicaca (16° S, 69° W) the world's highest lake on which vessels can travel, located in the Andes Mountains in South America, p. 87

Lima (12°03' S, 77°03' W) the capital city of Peru, p. 175

M

Mexico (23° N, 102° W) a country in North America, south of the United States, p. 102

Mexico City (19°24' N, 99°09' W) the capital of and largest city in Mexico; one of the largest urban areas in the world, p. 105

Miami (25°46' N, 80°11' W) a city in south-eastern Florida, p. 138

Middle America (11° N, 80° W) another term for Mexico and Central America, p. 11

N

New York City (40°43' N, 74°01' W) a city in southeastern New York State, p. 150

P

Panama (9° N, 80° W) a country in Central America, p. 116

Panama Canal (9° N, 79° W) an important shipping canal across the Isthmus of Panama, linking the Caribbean Sea (and the Atlantic Ocean) to the Pacific Ocean, p. 117

Paraguay (23° S, 58° W) a country in South America, p. 163

Peru (10° S, 76° W) a country in South America, p. 173

Port-au-Prince (18°32' N, 72°20' W) the capital city and chief port of Haiti, p. 143

Puerto Rico (18° N, 64° W) an island commonwealth of the United States in the Caribbean Sea, p. 148

R

Rio de Janeiro (22°55' S, 43°30' W) a major city in Brazil, p. 167

S

San Juan (18°28' N, 66°07' W) the capital and largest city in Puerto Rico, p. 152

Santiago (33°27' S, 70°40' W) the capital city of Chile, p. 183

São Paulo (23°32' S, 46°37' W) the largest city in Brazil, p. 77

South America (15° S, 60° W) the world's fourth-largest continent, bounded by the Caribbean Sea, the Atlantic Ocean, and the Pacific Ocean, and linked to North America by the Isthmus of Panama, p. 13

Strait of Magellan (54° S, 71° W) a waterway separating mainland South America from the islands of Tierra del Fuego, at the southernmost tip of South America, p. 179

T

Tenochtitlán (19°24' N, 99°09' W) the capital of the Aztec empire, located where modern Mexico City now stands, p. 42

Tierra del Fuego (54° S, 67° W) an archipelago, or chain of islands, at the southernmost tip of South America, separated from the mainland by the Strait of Magellan, p. 180

Trinidad and Tobago (11° N, 61° W) a republic of the West Indies, on the two islands called Trinidad and Tobago, p. 133

V

Valley of Mexico (19° N, 99° W) the area in central Mexico where Mexico City is located and where most of the population lives, p. 42

Venezuela (8° N, 66° W) a country in South America, p. 188

W

West Indies (19° N, 70° W) the islands of the Caribbean, p. 82

Glossary

A

ally (AL eye) *n.* a country joined with another for a special purpose, p. 136

Altiplano (al tih PLAH noh) *n.* a high plateau in the Andes Mountains, p. 175

Amazon rain forest (AM uh zahn rayn FAWR ist) *n.* a large tropical rain forest occupying the Amazon Basin in northern South America, p. 166

Amazon River (AM uh zahn RIV ur) *n.* a long river in northern South America, p. 14

Andes Mountains (AN deez MOWN tunz) *n.* a mountain system extending along the western coast of South America, p. 13

aqueduct (AK wuh dukt) *n.* a pipe or channel used to carry water from a distant source, p. 48

Aristide, Jean-Bertrand (ah rees TEED, zhan behr TRAHN) *n.* former president of Haiti, p. 142

B

Bolívar, Simón (boh LEE vahr, see MOHN) *n.* a leader in the fight to free South America from Spanish rule, p. 59

boom (boom) *n.* a period of business growth and prosperity, p. 189

Brasília (bruh ZIL yuh) *n.* capital of Brazil, built in the 1950s to encourage people to move to the interior of the country, p. 167

C

campesino (kahm peh SEE noh) *n.* a poor Latin American farmer or farm worker, p. 74

Canal Zone (kuh NAL zohn) *n.* a 10-mile wide strip of land along the Panama Canal, once governed by the United States, p. 120

canopy (KAN uh pea) *n.* the dense mass of leaves and branches forming the top layer of a rain forest, p. 166

Caracas (kuh RAH kus) *n.* the capital of Venezuela, p. 188

Carnival (KAHR nuh vul) *n.* a lively annual celebration just before Lent in Latin America; similar to Mardi Gras in the United States, p. 85

cash crop (kash krahp) *n.* a crop grown mostly for sale rather than for a farmer's own needs, p. 91

Castro, Fidel (KAS troh, fih DEL), *n.* the leader of Cuba's government, p. 134

caudillo (kaw DEE yoh) *n.* a military officer who rules a country very strictly, p. 61

census (SEN sus) *n.* an official count of all the people in an area, p. 47

circumnavigate (sur kum NAV ih gayt) *v.* to sail or fly all the way around something, such as Earth, p. 181

citizen (SIT uh zun) *n.* a person with certain rights and responsibilities under a particular government, p. 149

Columbus, Christopher (kuh LUM bus, KRIS tuh fur) *n.* Italian explorer sponsored by Spain, who landed in the West Indies in 1492, p. 51

commonwealth (KAHM un welth) *n.* a self-governing political unit with strong ties to a particular country, p. 149

communism (KAHM yoo niz um) *n.* an economic system in which the government owns all large businesses and most of a country's land, p. 135

Carnival in Trinidad

conquistador (kahn KEES tuh dawr) *n.* one of a group of conquerors who claimed and ruled land in the Americas for the Spanish government in the 1500s, p. 52

constitution (KAHN stuh TOO shun) *n.* a statement of a country's basic laws and values, p. 148

Cortés, Hernán (kohr TEZ, hur NAHN) *n.* conquistador who conquered the Aztecs, p. 52

coup (koo) *n.* short for coup d'état (koo day TAH), a French term meaning the overthrow of a ruler or government by an organized group which then takes power, p. 193

Creole (KREE ohl) *n.* a person of mixed European and African descent; in Haiti, a language that mixes French and African languages, p. 146

criollo (kree OH yoh) *n.* a person with Spanish parents who was born in the Spanish colonies in Latin America, p. 58

Cuzco (KOOS koh) *n.* the capital of the Incan empire; a city in modern Peru, p. 46

D

dictator (DIK tay tur) *n.* a ruler of a country with complete power, p. 65

diversify (duh VUR suh fy) *v.* to add variety, p. 30

diversity (duh VUR suh tee) *n.* variety, p. 74

E

economy (ih KAHN uh mee) *n.* the ways that goods and services are produced and made available to people, p. 21

ecotourism (ek oh TOOR iz um) *n.* travel to unspoiled areas in order to observe wildlife and learn about the environment, p. 122

elevation (el uh VAY shun) *n.* the height of land above sea level, p. 18

El Niño (el NEEN yoh) *n.* a warming of the ocean water along the western coast of South America; this current influences global weather patterns, p. 15

emigrate (EM ih grayt) *v.* to leave one country to settle in another, p. 79

encomienda (en koh mee EN dah) *n.* the right of Spanish colonists to demand taxes or labor from Native Americans, granted by the Spanish government, p. 56

ethnic group (ETH nik groop) *n.* a group of people who share the same ancestry, language, religion, or cultural traditions, p. 83

exile (EK syl) *n.* a person who leaves or is forced to leave his or her homeland for another country, often for political reasons, p. 137

export (eks PAWRT) *v.* to send products from one country to be sold in another country; (EKS pawrt) *n.* a product that is sold in another country, p. 65

F

foreign debt (FAWR in det) *n.* money owed by one country to another country or foreign financial institution, p. 66

G

gaucho (GOW choh) *n.* a cowboy of the pampas of South America, p. 89

glacier (GLAY shur) *n.* a large slow-moving mass of ice and snow, p. 182

H

hacienda (hah see EN dah) *n.* a large farm or plantation, often growing cash crops for export, p. 55

hieroglyphics (hy ur oh GLIF iks) *n.* a system of writing using signs and symbols, used by the Maya and other peoples, p. 41

hydroelectricity (hy droh ee lek TRIS ih tee) *n.* electrical power produced from rushing water, p. 26

I

illiterate (ih LIT ur ut) *n.* unable to read or write, p. 136

immigrant (IM uh grunt) *n.* a person who comes into a foreign country to make a new home, p. 79

import (im PAWRT) *v.* to bring products into one country from another; (IM pawrt) *n.* a product brought from another country to sell, p. 65

indigenous people (in DIJ uh nus PEA pul) *n.* people who are descended from the people who first lived in a region, p. 74

isthmus (IS mus) *n.* a narrow strip of land that has water on both sides and joins two larger bodies of land, p. 12

L

ladino (luh DEE noh) *n.* a mestizo, or person of mixed Spanish and Native American ancestry in Guatemala, p. 110

land reform (land ree FAWRM) *n.* the effort to distribute land more equally and fairly, p. 110

lock (lahk) *n.* a section of waterway in which ships are raised or lowered by adjusting the water level, p. 119

L'Ouverture, Toussaint (loo vehr TOOR, too SAN) *n.* a former slave who led the people of Haiti in their fight for independence, p. 57

M

Magellan, Ferdinand (muh JEL un, FUR duh nand) *n.* a Portuguese explorer sailing for Spain whose expedition was the first to circumnavigate the globe, p. 179

maize (mayz) *n.* corn, p. 41

maquiladora (mah kee luh DOHR ah) *n.* a factory that assembles imported parts to make products for export, often located in Mexico near the United States border, p. 77

mestizo (meh STEE zoh) *n.* in Latin America, a person of mixed Spanish and Native American ancestry, p. 55

Mexico City (MEKS ih koh SIT ee) *n.* the capital and largest city of Mexico, p. 105

Middle America (MID ul uh MEHR ih kuh) *n.* Mexico and Central America, p. 11

migrant worker (MY grunt WUR kur) *n.* a laborer who travels from one area to another, picking crops that are in season, p. 102

Moctezuma (mahk tih ZOO muh) *n.* ruler of the Aztec empire at the time the Spanish arrived there, p. 50

N

natural resources (NACH ur ul REE sawrs uz) *n.* things found in nature that people use to meet their needs, p. 24

O

oasis (oh AY sis) *n.* a fertile area in a desert that has a source of water, p. 175

one-resource economy (wun REE sawrs ih KAHN uh mee) *n.* a country's dependence largely on one resource or crop for income, p. 28

P

pampas (PAM puz) *n.* flat grasslands in South America; a region similar to the Great Plains in the United States, p. 13

Panama Canal (PAN uh mah kuh NAL) *n.* a shipping canal across the Isthmus of Panama, linking the Caribbean Sea (and the Atlantic Ocean) to the Pacific Ocean, p. 117

Pinochet Ugarte, Augusto (pea noh SHAY oo gahr TAY, ah GOO stoh) *n.* military dictator of Chile from 1973 to 1988, p. 185

Pizarro, Francesco (pea SAHR oh, frahn SEES koh) *n.* conquistador who conquered the Incas, p. 53

plateau (pla TOH) *n.* a large raised area of mostly level land, p. 12

plaza (PLAH zuh) *n.* a public square at the center of a village, a town, or a city, p. 103

political movement (puh LIT ih kul MOOV munt) *n.* a large group of people who work together for political change, p. 112

privatization (pry vuh tih ZAY shun) *n.* a government's sale of land or industries it owns to individuals or private companies, p. 192

Q

quipu (KEE poo) *n.* knotted strings on which the Incas recorded information, p. 47

R

rain forest (rayn FAWR ist) *n.* a dense evergreen forest that has abundant rainfall throughout the year, p. 13

refugee (ref yoo JEE) *n.* a person who leaves his or her homeland for personal safety or to escape persecution, p. 143

regime (ruh ZHEEM) *n.* a particular administration or government, p. 67

revolution (rev uh LOO shun) *n.* the overthrow of an existing government, with another government taking its place, p. 58

Rio de Janeiro (REE oh day zhuh NEHR oh) *n.* a large city in Brazil, p. 167

rural (ROOR ul) *adj.* having to do with the countryside, p. 77

S

San Martín, José de (sahn mahr TEEN, hoh SAY deh) *n.* a leader in the fight to free South America from Spanish rule, p. 60

savanna (suh VAN uh) *n.* a flat, grassy region, or open plain with scattered trees and thorny bushes, p. 167

sierra (see EHR uh) *n.* a range of mountains, such as the one that runs from northwest to southeast Peru, p. 175

squatter (SKWAHT ur) *n.* a person who settles on someone else's land without permission, p. 105

strike (stryk) *n.* a refusal to work until certain demands of workers are met, p. 113

subsistence farming (sub SIS tuns FAHR ming) *n.* growing only enough food to meet the needs of the farmer's family, p. 91

T

Tenochtitlán (teh nawch tee TLAHN) *n.* the capital of the Aztec empire, located where Mexico City now stands, p. 42

Topa Inca (TOH puh ING kuh) *n.* emperor of the Incas, who expanded their empire, p. 46

treaty (TREE tee) *n.* an agreement in writing made between two or more countries, p. 52

tributary (TRIB yoo tehr ee) *n.* a river or stream that flows into a larger river, p. 14

tundra (TUN druh) *n.* a treeless plain that supports only low-growing vegetation because the lower levels of the soil remain frozen all year; in mountains, the area above the tree line, p. 175

U

urban (UR bun) *adj.* having to do with cities, p. 77

W

West Indies (west IN deez) *n.* the Caribbean islands, p. 82

Rain forest in Brazil

Index

The *m*, *g*, or *p* following some page numbers refers to maps (*m*), charts, tables, graphs, timelines or diagrams (*g*), or pictures (*p*).

political movement, 223
political systems, 112–113, 112p
pollution, 107, 107p, 169, 183. See also
  environment
poncho, 49
Popocatépetl Volcano, 4, 4p
population
  of Argentina, 160
  of Bolivia, 161
  of Brazil, 161, 167, 170m
  of Caribbean Islands, 128–133
  of Central America, 77, 98–101
  of Chile, 161
  of cities, 77g, 78
  of Colombia, 162
  of Ecuador, 162
  of Guatemala, 125g
  of Guyana, 163
  in Mexico, 77, 100, 102, 106
  of Paraguay, 163
  of Peru, 163, 174g, 176
  of Puerto Rico, 151m
  of South America, 160–165
  of Suriname, 164
  of Uruguay, 164
  of Venezuela, 95g, 165
Port-au-Prince, 131, 143, 147, 219
Port-of-Spain, 133
Portugal,
  Brazil and, 3m, 3p, 52, 61, 161
  colonization by, 54–56, 179
  settlers from, 12
  poverty, 64, 99, 161, 172
  in Haiti, 131, 146–147
  in South America, 92, 92p
  in Venezuela, 191
Pre-Columbian art, 75
Préval, René, 142, 145
privatization, 192, 223
Projects, 198
Puerto Rico, 12, 127m, 131, 204m, 219
  commonwealth of, 149
  culture of, 152, 152p
  government of, 148, 151, 151g, 151m
  independence question, 154, 154p
  languages of, 149
  music of, 152p
  population of, 151m
  Spain and, 60
  statehood question, 153, 153p
  timeline of, 157
  United States and, 148–150, 149g,
    149p, 151, 151g, 153–154, 153p,
    154p

Q

Quechua, 49, 89, 176, 177, 177p, 178
Quetzalcoatl, 53, 53p
Quiché Maya, 109
quipus, 45p, 47, 223

R

rain forest, 13, 122, 122p, 132, 223,
  223p
  in Brazil, 7, 7m, 7p, 166, 166p, 167,
    167p
  importance of the, 168–169, 168g,
    169p
  indigenous people in the, 170
  medicine from the, 168, 169
  of Peru, 174
  threats to the, 169
ranchos, 92
reading skills
  analyze author's purpose, RW1
  asking questions, 24
  clarifying meaning, 38
  comparing and contrasting, 158, 166,
    179
  distinguish between facts and opin-
    ions, RW1
  evaluate credibility, RW1
  identify contrasts, 173
  identify evidence, RW1
  identifying implied main ideas, 148
  identifying main ideas, 126, 134
  identifying supporting details, 142
  informational texts, RW1
  make comparisons, 188
  paraphrasing, 50, 54
  predicting, 15
  previewing, 10, 15, 24
  reading ahead, 45, 64
  recognizing multiple causes, 82
  rereading, 64
  setting a purpose, 10
  summarizing, 57
  understanding effects, 87
  using cause and effect, 72, 74
  using context, 96, 102, 109, 116
  using the reading process, 8
Redonda, 128
reforms, 67
refugees, 143, 223
reggae music, 86, 198
regime, 67, 223
religion
  of Argentina, 160
  Aztec, 42
  of Bolivia, 161
  of Brazil, 161

in Caribbean Islands, 84, 128–133
in Central America, 76, 76p, 98–101
of Chile, 161
of Colombia, 162
of Ecuador, 162
of Guyana, 163
Incan, 48
of Mayas, 41, 41p
in Mexico, 76, 76p, 95g, 100
of Native Americans, 76
of Paraguay, 163
of Peru, 163
in South America, 160–165
of Suriname, 164
of Uruguay, 164
in Venezuela, 165
See also individual religions
revolution, 57–58, 223
Rio de Janeiro, 3m, 3p, 64p, 167, 172,
  172p, 219, 223
Río de la Plata, 14
Rivera, Diego, 75p, 76, 100p
River Platte, 164
Robinson Crusoe (Defoe), 183
Roosevelt, Theodore, 66, 119
Roseau, 130
rural, 223

S

Saint-Domingue, 57
Saint George's, 130
Saint John's, 128, 128p
St. Kitts and Nevis, 132
St. Lucia, 127m, 132
St. Vincent and the Grenadines,
  127m, 132
Samuels, Dorothy, 84
San Geronimo Fortress, 152p
San José, Costa Rica, 77, 99
San Juan, 131, 152, 152p, 219
San Martín, José de, 60, 223
San Salvador, 99, 129
Santiago, Chile, 161, 182, 183, 219
Santo Domingo, 130
São Paulo, Brazil, 7, 7m, 89, 89p, 219
savanna, 167, 223
science, 17, 17p, 32, 48, 124, 167. See
  also technology
Selkirk, Alexander. See Robinson
  Crusoe
selva, 174g, 175
shipping, 117, 117p, 121, 121p
sierra, 174, 175, 223

Acknowledgments

Cover Design

Pronk&Associates

Staff Credits

The people who made up *World Studies* team—representing design services, editorial, editorial services, educational technology, marketing, market research, photo research and art development, production services, project office, publishing processes, and rights & permissions—are listed below. Bold type denotes core team members.

Greg Abrom, Ernie Albanese, Rob Aleman, Susan Andariese, **Rachel Avenia-Prol,** Leann Davis Alspaugh, Penny Baker, Barbara Bertell, **Peter Brooks,** Rui Camarinha, John Carle, **Lisa Del Gatto,** Paul Delsignore, Kathy Dempsey, Anne Drowns, Deborah Dukeshire, Marlies Dwyer, **Frederick Fellows,** Paula C. Foye, Lara Fox, Julia Gecha, **Mary Hanisco,** Salena Hastings, Lance Hatch, Kerri Hoar, **Beth Hyslip,** Katharine Ingram, Nancy Jones, John Kingston, Deborah Levheim, Constance J. McCarty, **Kathleen Mercandetti,** Art Mkrtchyan, Ken Myett, **Mark O'Malley,** Jen Paley, Ray Parenteau, **Gabriela Pérez Fiato,** Linda Punskovsky, Kirsten Richert, **Lynn Robbins,** Nancy Rogier, Bruce Rolff, Robin Samper, Mildred Schulte, Siri Schwartzman, **Malti Sharma,** Lisa Smith-Ruvalcaba, Roberta Warshaw, Sarah Yezzi.

Additional Credits

Jonathan Ambar, Tom Benfatti, Lisa D. Ferrari, Paul Foster, Florrie Gadson, Phil Gagler, Ella Hanna, Jeffrey LaFountain, Karen Mancinelli, Michael McLaughlin, Lesley Pierson, Debi Taffet.

DK The DK Designs team who contributed to *World Studies* were as follows: Hilary Bird, Samantha Borland, Marian Broderick, Richard Czapnik, Nigel Duffield, Heather Dunleavy, Cynthia Frazer, James A. Hall, Lucy Heaver, Rose Horridge, Paul Jackson, Heather Jones, Ian Midson, Marie Ortu, Marie Osborn, Leyla Ostovar, Ralph Pitchford, Ilana Sallick, Pamela Shiels, Andrew Szudek, Amber Tokeley.

Maps

DK Maps and globes were created by **DK Cartography.** The team consisted of Tony Chambers, Damien Demaj, Julia Lunn, Ed Merritt, David Roberts, Ann Stephenson, Gail Townsley, Iorwerth Watkins.

Illustrations

Kenneth Batelman: 55, 141 t; Morgan Cain & Associates: 107; Jen Paley: 10, 15, 24, 28, 40, 45, 46-47, 50, 57, 64, 66, 74, 77, 80, 81, 82, 87, 95, 102, 104, 109, 111, 116, 118, 125, 131 b., 131 t., 134, 137, 140, 141 m, 142, 144, 148, 149, 151, 157, 161, 166, 168, 170, 173, 174, 179, 180, 186, 187, 188, 189, 190.

Photos

Cover Photos

tl, W. Bertsch/Bruce Coleman Inc.; **tm,** Gianni Dagli Orti/Corbis/Magma; **tr,** Heatons/Firstlight.ca; **b,** Michael J P Scott/Getty Images, Inc.

Title Page

Michael J P Scott/Getty Images, Inc.

Table of Contents

iv–v, Bruna Stude/Omni-Photo Communications, Inc.; **v,** David Hiser/PictureQuest; **vi,** Stuart Westmorland/Corbis; **vii,** Michel Zab/Dorling Kindersley; **xi,** National Geographic Image Collection

Learning With Technology

xiii, Discovery Channel School

Reading and Writing Handbook

RW, Michael Newman/PhotoEdit; **RW1,** Walter Hodges/Getty Images, Inc.; **RW2,** Digital Vision/Getty Images, Inc.; **RW3,** Will Hart/PhotoEdit; **RW5,** Jose Luis Pelaez, Inc./Corbis

MapMaster Skills Handbook

M, James Hall/DK Images; **M1,** Mertin Harvey/Gallo Images/Corbis; **M2–3 m,** NASA; **M2–3,** (globes) Planetary Visions: **M5 br,** Barnabas Kindersley/DK Images; **M6 tr,** Mike Dunning/DK Images; **M10 b,** Bernard and Catherine Desjeux/Corbis; **M11,** Hutchinson Library; **M12 b,** Pa Photos; **M13 r,** Panos Pictures; **M14 l,** Macduff Everton/Corbis; **M14 t,** MSCF/NASA; **M15 b,** Ariadne Van Zandbergen/Lonely Planet Images; **M16 l,** Bill Stormont/Corbis; **M16 b,** Pablo Corral/Corbis; **M17 t,** Stone Les/Sygma/Corbis; **M17 b,** W. Perry Conway/Corbis

Guiding Questions

1 t, Michel Zab/Dorling Kindersley; **1 b,** Travel Pix/Getty Images, Inc.

Regional Overview

2 l, Linda Whitwam/Dorling Kindersley; **3 tr,** Art Directors & TRIP; **4 tr,** Charles and Josette Lenars/Corbis; **5 t,** Getty Images; **5 b,** Hubert Stadler/Corbis; **6 b,** Galen Rowell/Corbis; **6 l,** Nik Wheeler/Corbis; **6 r,** Carol Halebian Photography; **7 t,** Owen Franken/Corbis: **7 b,** T. Bognar/Art Directors & TRIP

Chapter One

8–9, Darell Gulin/Getty Images, Inc.; **10,** Jimmy Dorantes/LatinFocus.com; **11,** Discovery Channel School; **12,** Jeff Hunter/Getty Images, Inc.; **13,** Corbis; **14,** Herve Collart/Corbis; **15,** R. B. Husar/NASA/SPL/Photo Researchers, Inc., **17,** Prenas Nicaragua/Corbis Sygma; **18 t,** Bobby Model/Getty Images, Inc.; **18 b,** Ed Simpson/Getty Images, Inc.; **19,** Jonathan Blair/Corbis; **21,** Miguel Reyes/LatinFocus.com; **22,** Richard Haynes; **23,** Warren Morgan/Corbis; **24,** Fenno Jacobs/SuperStock, Inc.; **26 t,** Richard Bickel/Corbis; **26 l,** Jacques Jangoux/Peter Arnold, Inc.; **27 l,** Jonathan Smith; Cordaiy Photo/Corbis; **27 r,** Carlos Goldin/DDB Stock Photo; **28,** Sean Sprague/Stock Boston; **29,** AP/Wide World Photos/Jaime Puebla; **30,** Pablo Corral Vega/Corbis; **31 t,** Corbis; **31 m,** Miguel Reyes/LatinFocus.com; **31 b,** Jacques Jangoux/Peter Arnold, Inc.; **34,** Bryan Knox/Corbis; **35,** EyeWire Collection/Getty Images, Inc.; **36,** David Zimmerman/Corbis; **37,** Courtesy of Alma Flor Ada

Chapter Two

38–39, Macduff Everton/Corbis; **40-41 b,** Allen Prier/Panoramic Images; **41 t,** Private Collection/Bridgeman Art Library; **42,** Chip and Rosa Maria de la Cueva Peterson; **43 m,** DK Images, **43 t,** Mary Evans Picture Library; **43 b,** South American Pictures; **44,** David Hiser/PictureQuest; **45,** Werner Forman/Art Resource, New York; **46 t,** Chris Sharp/DDB Stock Photo; **46 b,** Bowers Museum of Cultural Art/Corbis; **47 t,** Charles & Josette Lenars/Corbis; **47 m,** Lee Boltin/Boltin Picture Library; **47 b,** Dorling Kindersley; **48,** Katie Attenborough/Bridgeman Art Library; **49,** Larry Luxner/Luxner News; **50,** Bridgeman Art Library; **51 t,** Sebastian Munster/The New York Public Library/Art Resource, New York; **51 b,** The Granger Collection, New York; **52,** Gianni Dagli Orti/Corbis; **53,** Biblioteca Nacional Madrid, Spain/Bridgeman Art Library; **53 inset l,** Dave King/Dorling Kindersley; **53 inset m,** Michel Zab/Dorling Kindersley; **53 inset r,** Michel Zab/Dorling Kindersley; **53 inset b,** Dorling Kindersley; **55,** Discovery Channel School; **56,** The Granger Collection, New York; **57,** North Wind Picture Archives; **58,** Robert Frerck/Odyssey Productions; **60,** Rudi von Briel/PhotoEdit; **61,** AFP/Corbis; **62 t,** Werner Forman/Art Resource, New York; **62 b,** Bettmann/Corbis; **63,** Richard Haynes; **64,** Bibliothèque Nationale, Paris, France/Bridgeman Art Library; **65,** Underwood & Underwood/Corbis; **66,** Brand X Pictures/Getty Images, Inc.; **67,** AP/Wide World Photos/Natacha Pisarenko; **68,** D. Donne Bryant/DDB Stock Photo; **69,** Lee Boltin/Boltin Picture Library

Chapter Three

72–73, Steve Simonsen/Lonely Planet Images; **74,** Sheryl Bjorkgren/LatinFocus.com; **75 t,** CNAC/MNAM/Dist. Reunion des Musees Nationaux/Art Resource, New York; **75 b,** Philadelphia Museum of Art/Corbis; **76,** AP/Wide World Photos/Victor M. Camacho; **77,** Tibor Bognar/Corbis; **78,** Lonely Planet Images; **79,** Joe Caveretta/LatinFocus.com; **82,** Michael Graham-Stewart/Bridgeman Art Library; **83,** Robert Fried Photography; **84 t,** MC Pherson Colin/Corbis Sygma; **84 b,** Doug Armand/Getty Images, Inc.;

85 t, Discovery Channel School; 85 b, Craig Duncan/DDB Stock Photo; 86, Bob Krist/Corbis; 87, Alex Irvin Photography; 88, A. Ramey/Woodfin Camp & Associates; 89, D. Donne Bryant/DDB Stock Photo; 89 inset, Larry Luxner/Luxner News; 90, Pelletier Micheline/Corbis Sygma; 91 t, Owen Franken/Corbis; 91 b, Bo Zaunders/Corbis; 92, Michael Brennan/Corbis; 93 t, Joe Caveretta/LatinFocus.com; 93 m, Robert Fried Photography; 93 b, Owen Franken/Corbis

Chapter Four

96–97, Sandy Ostroff/Index Stock Imagery, Inc.; 98 t, Discovery Channel School; 98 b, Frans Lanting/Minden Pictures; 100 t, National Geographic Image Collection; 100 b, Ben Blackwell/San Francisco Museum of Modern Art; 102, Jimmy Dorantes/LatinFocus.com; 103, Bob Krist/Corbis; 105 l, Mark Edwards/Peter Arnold, Inc.; 105 r, National Geographic Image Collection; 106 t, Discovery Channel School; 106 b, Keith Dannemiller/Corbis; 108, Cuartoscuro/Corbis Sygma; 109 t, Keith Gunnar/Bruce Coleman Inc.; 109 b, Michel Zab/Dorling Kindersley; 110, Suzanne Murphy-Larronde; 111, Discovery Channel School; 112, AP/Wide World Photos/Jaime Puebla; 113, Stone/Allstock/Getty Images Inc.; 114, GoodShoot/SuperStock, Inc.; 115 t, AP/Wide World Photos/Rodrigo Abd; 115 b, Wesley Bocxe/Photo Researchers, Inc.; 116, Jimmy Dorantes/LatinFocus.com; 117, Alex Farnsworth/The Image Works; 119 t, Discovery Channel School; 119 m, Panama Canal Museum; 119 b, Getty Images, Inc./Hulton Archive Photos; 120 t, C. W. Brown/Photo Researchers, Inc.; 120 b, J. Raga/Masterfile Corporation; 121 t, Corbis; 121 b, DK Images; 122, Danny Lehmann/Corbis; 123 t, Keith Dannemiller/Corbis; 123 m, Michel Zab/Dorling Kindersley; 123 b, Alex Farnsworth/The Image Works

Chapter Five

126–127, Philip Coblentz/Digital Vision/Getty Images, Inc.; 128 t, Discovery Channel School; 128 b, Bob Krist/Corbis; 130, Reinhard Eisele/Corbis; 131 t, Jimmy Dorantes/LatinFocus.com; 131 b, Jimmy Dorantes/LatinFocus.com; 133, Konrad Wothe/Minden Pictures; 134, Najlah Feanny/Corbis; 135 t, Bettmann/Corbis; 135 b, Discovery Channel School; 136 l, AP/Wide World Photos; 136 r, 2002 Getty Images Inc.; 137, Discovery Channel School; 138 t, Peter Muhly/AFP/Corbis; 138 b, Robert Holmes/Corbis; 139, Angelo Cavalli/SuperStock Inc.; 140, Paul Thompson/Eye Ubiquitous/Corbis; 141, Jan Butchofsky-Houser/Corbis; 142, AP Wide World Photos; 143 t, Carol Halebian Photography; 143 b, Discovery Channel School; 145, Bettmann/Corbis; 146 t, Wesley Bocxe/Photo Researchers, Inc.; 146 b, Philip Gould/Corbis; 147, Owen Franken/Corbis; 148, Robert Fried Photography; 149, Rudy Von Briel/PhotoEdit; 150 t, Benno Friedman; 150 b, Tom Bean/Corbis; 151, Discovery Channel School; 152 t, Stephanie Maze/Corbis; 152 b, Robert Frerck/Odyssey Productions Inc.; 153, AP/Wide World Photos; 154, Stephanie Maze/Corbis; 155, Angelo Cavalli/SuperStock Inc.

Chapter Six

158–159, Barbara Haynor/Index Stock Imagery, Inc.; 160 t, Discovery Channel School; 160 b, Paul A. Souders/Corbis; 162, Art Wolfe/Getty Images, Inc.; 164, Carlos Goldin/Focus/DDB Stock Photo; 165, Ulrike Welsch/PhotoEdit; 166, Wayne Lynch/

DRK Photo; 167, Fabio Colombini/Animals Animals/Earth Scenes; 168 t, Discovery Channel School; 168 m, David Frazier/Image Works; 168 b, Larry Luxner/Luxner News; 169, Domingo Rodrigues/UNEP/Peter Arnold, Inc.; 170 l, AFP/Vanderlei Almeida/Corbis; 170 r, Joel W. Rogers/Corbis; 171 t, Greg Fiume/Corbis; 171 b, Cynthia Brito/DDB Stock Photo; 172, PhotoDisc/Getty Images, Inc.; 173, Roman Soumar/Corbis; 175 t, Inga Spence/DDB Stock Photo; 175 b, Alejandro Balaguer/Getty Images, Inc.; 176 t, Discovery Channel School; 176 b, Philippe Colombi/Getty Images, Inc.; 177 l, David Mangurian/Intern-American Development Bank; 177 r, David Mangurian/Intern-American Development Bank; 178, Stuart Westmorland/Corbis; 179, Gebbie & Co./Library of Congress; 181 l, Joseph Van Os/Getty Images, Inc.; 181 r, Charles O'Rear/Corbis; 182 t, Zezmer Amos/Omni-Photo Communications, Inc.; 182 b, Ludovic Maisant/Corbis; 183, The Wilmington Library; 184 t, Discovery Channel School; 184 m, Jaime Villaseca/Getty Images, Inc.; 184 b, HIRB/Index Stock Imagery, Inc.; 185, AP/Wide World Photos/Alistair Grant; 186 lt, Hubert Stadler/Corbis; 186 lb, Hubert Stadler/Corbis; 186 rt, Jeremy Horner/Corbis; 186 rb, Frank Perkins/Index Stock Imagery, Inc.; 187, Yann Arthus-Bertrand/Corbis; 188, Larry Lee/Corbis; 189, AP/Wide World Photos/Jose Caruci; 191, Pablo Corral V/Corbis; 192, Kike Arnal/Corbis; 193 t, Discovery Channel School; 193 b, AFP/Corbis; 194 l, Reuters NewMedia Inc./Corbis; 194 r, AFP/Corbis; 195, Greg Fiume/Corbis

Projects

198 t, Travel Pix/Getty Images, Inc.; 198 m, C Squared Studios/Getty Images, Inc.; 198 b, Steve Cole/Getty Images, Inc.

Reference

199, Francesc Muntada/Corbis

Glossary of Geographic Terms

216 t, A & L Sinibaldi/Getty Images, Inc.; 216 b, John Beatty/Getty Images, Inc.; 216-217 b, Spencer Swanger/Tom Stack & Associates; 217 t, Hans Strand/Getty Images, Inc.; 217 m, Paul Chesley/Getty Images, Inc.

Glossary

220, Doug Armand/Getty Images, Inc.; 221, R.B.Husar/NASA/SPL/Photo Researchers, Inc.; 222, Bridgeman Art Library; 223, Fabio Colombini/Animals Animals/Earth Scenes

Text
Chapter One

Page 34, Exerpt from "The Surveyor," from *Where the Flame Trees Bloom* by Alma Flor Ada. Copyright © 1994 by Alma Flor Ada.

Note: Every effort has been made to locate the copyright owner of material used in this textbook. Omissions brought to our attention will be corrected in subsequent editions.